STUDIES IN

AFRICAN AMERICAN HISTORY AND CULTURE

edited by

GRAHAM RUSSELL HODGES
COLGATE UNIVERSITY

A GARLAND SERIES

JACK TAR
vs.
JOHN BULL

THE ROLE OF NEW YORK'S SEAMEN IN PRECIPITATING THE REVOLUTION

JESSE LEMISCH

DEPARTMENT OF HISTORY
John Jay College of Criminal Justice
of the City University of New York

GARLAND PUBLISHING, INC.
NEW YORK & LONDON / 1997

Library of Congress Cataloging-in-Publication Data

Lemisch, Jesse, 1936–
    Jack Tar vs. John Bull : the role of New York's seamen in
precipitating the Revolution / Jesse Lemisch.
        p.   cm. — (Studies in African American history and
culture)
    Originally presented as the author's thesis (Ph. D.)—Yale
University, 1962.
    Includes bibliographical references and index.
    ISBN 0-8153-2788-9 (alk. paper)
    1. New York (N.Y.)—History—Revolution, 1775–1783.
2. Merchant mariners—New York (State)—New York—History—
18th century. 3. Impressment—New York (State)—New York—
History—18th century. I. Title. II. Title: Jack Tar versus John
Bull. III. Series.
E263.N6L46 1997
973.3'4471—dc21   97-10449

Printed on acid-free, 250-year-life paper
Manufactured in the United States of America

For my mother,
Beatrice C. Lemisch
1908–1985

Contents

Foreword

Moscow's Hotel Rossiya, off Red Square, March, 1991: Again and again Jesse Lemisch and I explained our mission to the sometimes suspicious, sometimes uncomprehending clerks: we were searching for a group of Siberian miners who had come to Russia's capital city to wage a hunger strike. Each one shook his or her head and answered, "they are not in this section of the hotel." We realized, of course, that we might have been getting the run-around. Not one of these clerks would have *wanted* these hunger strikers in his or her section. But in a hotel of 5,000 rooms, and in a country with a history of bureaucratic incompetence, we could not be certain. There we were, searching for "history from the bottom up" in the making, in a country where early in the century those on the bottom had made some earth-shaking history.

We would not find the miners that day, but we had managed to make other connections and to learn a great deal about the popular ferment that gripped Russia after the fall of Communism and the dismantling of the Soviet Union. We had already visited Boris Kagarlitsky, the dissident left-wing intellectual and organizer who had been imprisoned during the Brezhnev years for publishing a Eurocommunist journal called *Left Turn*, so that we might strengthen ties within the international peace movement. And we had attended a small demonstration—a "speak out"—at Manezh Square, where we had originally heard about the Siberian miners and their initiative. When I returned to the hotel the following day and continued to ask about the miners (Jesse had to depart for New York), I was at last saved by a hotel maid, who overheard me, pulled me aside, and furtively led me through a maze of corridors to a room in which sat six somewhat haggard but determined men. In the afternoon-long conversations that followed, I understood that a powerful history was at work; Russian miners had been among the first to form independent trade unions during the late 1980s, and were now taking the lead in defining the politics of a new era in Russian history. Their final words to me—"we shall overcome"—suggested an international consciousness of struggle and perhaps an American origin of their tactic, the hunger strike.[1]

I felt then, and I feel now, that there was a certain poetry in these adventures. My companion, Jesse Lemisch, was the historian who more than twenty years earlier had popularized the term "history from the bottom up." I had known Jesse for several years and was not surprised to witness his consistency in approaching past and present. He had long insisted, with Brecht, that kings had not built the Seven Gates of Thebes, had not hauled the craggy blocks of stone. Therefore when we went to Moscow to attend a conference on American history, he sought out not the likes of Gorbachev, Yeltsin, or other, lesser bosses, but rather a former political prisoner, demonstrators, and hunger strikers in order to discover the truths of a turbulent history rapidly unfolding before us.

* * * * * * *

Lemisch is, of course, widely and rightly known for his work in pioneering "history from the bottom up," which appeared in the late 1960s and early 1970s as a new kind of social history. He and others who helped to create this new form of "peoples' history" (Herbert G. Gutman, Staughton Lynd, Alfred F. Young) were part of a New Left, responding to and expressing the demands for a new history then being voiced by African-Americans, students, women, and workers, as they combined in various movements for peace, justice, and power. "History from the bottom up" thus arose as an explicit challenge to the elitist though insular traditions of historical writing within the American academy, and more specifically to the deadening "consensus" approach to the American past that had grown out of the repressive atmosphere of the Cold War. Lemisch helped to define and to write the new, more generous, more inclusive history, and he fought (and fought hard) for its place within the discipline and profession of history and the larger society, over and against the conservative assumptions and practices that were then dominant. This he did at considerable personal cost, as he was fired by the University of Chicago in 1966.

Lemisch nonetheless continued to wage the battle for the new history in speech and in print. His paper, "Present-Mindedness Revisited: Anti-Radicalism as a Goal of American Historical Writing Since World War II," was the centerpiece of one of the best attended and most contentious sessions in the recent history of the American Historical Association (Washington, D.C., December 1969); it was later published as *On Active Service in War and Peace: Politics and Ideology in the American Historical Profession* (Toronto: New

Hogtown Press, 1975). Its fate was to be despised by the right, ignored by the middle, and cherished by the left. Lemisch also carried on the struggle, with wicked wit, in his own specific field of study, when in 1976 he attacked the conservative "dean" of early American historians, Bernard Bailyn, who was, Lemisch announced in the *Radical History Review,* "Besieged in his Bunker."[2]

Lemisch also helped to internationalize American history and to make its study more sophisticated. One means was by adapting and popularizing the work of the British Marxist historians—Christopher Hill, Eric Hobsbawm, George Rudé, and especially E.P. Thompson, all of whom eschewed dogmatism, reductionism, determinism, and excessive abstraction in favor of a flexible, concrete humanism in the writing of politically-engaged history. But Lemisch also went beyond these distinguished scholars in several respects. If the British Marxist historians, along with the French historians Georges Lefebvre and Albert Soboul, had pioneered "history from below," which made historical actors of religious radicals, rioters, peasants, and artisans, Lemisch pushed the phrase and the history further and harder with "history from the bottom up," a more inclusive and comprehensive formulation that brought *all* subjects, especially slaves and women, more fully into the historian's field of vision. By insisting, in his research on sailors in the era of the American Revolution, upon the autonomous political hopes and demands of working people, he also went beyond the prevailing assumption among left historians that all popular movements before the great French Revolution were somehow "pre-political" or "sub-political." By insisting that sailors and other workers had ideas of their own, he made a point that many historians have yet to grasp—the history of the working class must be an intellectual as well as a social history.

A second way in which Lemisch has broadened and deepened the discussion of American history has been through international debate, particularly with Russian specialists in the history of the United States. Lemisch has since the 1970s kept up a steady dialogue with Soviet/Russian scholars such as N.N. Bolkhovitinov, Vladimir Sogrin, Valerii Tischkov, Gennadi Dubovitskii, and Sergei Zhuk. Since Lemisch's work is well known among Russian Americanists (who for many years followed trends in left historiography closely), it came as no surprise when he was scheduled to deliver a plenary address at a major conference in Moscow in 1991. He obliged with "American History Viewed Through a (No Longer) Red Lens: Will it be the Triumph of Capitalism, or Scholarship that Divorces Truth from Power?" Lemisch applauded Russian historians for their "startling new beginnings" in trying to write a new, less doctrinaire history of the

United States, but he also posed cautionary questions: "having bent with the Communist wind, will you now bend with the anti-Communist wind?" Or will you instead, he wondered hopefully, "write a proud new chapter in the history of the war between truth and power"?[3]

Lemisch's final question to the conference was but another way of saying what he has long maintained—"history from the bottom up" represents a democratization of the past and therefore the realization of one of America's most fundamental professed values. As he wrote in an SDS pamphlet in 1966, "History, the democrat believes, can happen from the bottom up, and the democrat as historian will write it from the bottom up."[4] Lemisch amplified this insight in what was in many respects his manifesto for a new history, "The American Revolution as Seen from the Bottom Up," which apppeared in 1967: "The American Revolution can best be re-examined from a point of view which assumes that all men [and women] are created equal, and rational, and that since they can think and reason they can make their own history. These assumptions are nothing more nor less than the democratic credo. All of our history needs re-examination from this perspective. The history of the powerless, the inarticulate, the poor has not yet begun to be written because they have been treated no more fairly by historians than they have been treated by their contemporaries."[5] The class perspective "from the bottom up," the insistence on the the history-making powers of those long excluded from the history books, the explicit link between past and present, these are the fundamental ideas for which Lemisch has stood and battled, with good humor and great determination, over many years.[6]

*   *   *   *   *   *   *

Jack Tar versus John Bull: The Role of New York's Seamen in Precipitating the Revolution was for many years something of an underground classic. I say "underground" not only because its author has associated himself with many an underground cause, but because the work (completed at Yale University in 1962, never published, and never easy to access) has nonetheless had a vibrant, influential, fugitive existence since its appearance thirty-five years ago. The original dissertation and the articles that grew out of it affected many, including Staughton Lynd, Alfred F. Young, and many others,[7] as acknowledged in Jon Wiener's account of the rise of "radical history" in the *Journal of American History* and Peter Novick's history of both historical "objectivity" and the historical profession as a whole, *That Noble Dream*.[8] Lemisch's influence has continued to be felt more recently, as, for example, at a conference on "Jack Tar in History" held in Halifax,

Nova Scotia in 1990, where Lemisch was (to his egalitarian discomfort) an intellectual and spiritual leader.[9]

Jack Tar versus John Bull reads well after all these years. Much of its lasting value arises from its extensive research and documentation; it boasts 583 endnotes in a text of modest length. Such painstaking scholarship was necessary to Lemisch's effort to establish new truths under the difficult circumstances of the Cold War, though of course he has always had great respect for historical evidence in its own right. *Jack Tar versus John Bull* is also judicious, often quite cautious, in its arguments, all of which are carried along in a graceful, well-written narrative. It seems to me that its thesis about conservatives, liberals, and radicals in the unfolding of the revolutionary era remains valid and valuable to this day.

Other strengths lie in the excellent all-around account of the political and material dimensions of the sailor's life (e.g., impressment and unemployment) which, crucially and characteristically, includes the sailor's creative response to such conditions, his self-activity. Lemisch's study also contains formulations that historians are just now beginning to take up as challenges. I have in mind here the brief but tantalizing observations about African-American sailors and the cooperation of sailors and slaves in American seaport mobs in the 1760s and 1770s, which has helped to move other scholars to address this important theme. And there on page 55 is an arresting idea, "the folk memory of tyranny," which should be of interest to the increasing number of historians who are working on the problem of historical memory.[10] *Jack Tar versus John Bull,* in short, continues to be relevant.

Jack Tar versus John Bull is, in the end, not only an influential piece of history; it is an historical document in its own right. It represents one of the important origins of "history from the bottom up," which was a profoundly new approach to both past and present. Perhaps it will continue to be influential, especially to the younger historians who will form the next New Left. It is an unusual pleasure to introduce a work and an author from which and from whom I and many others have learned so much. Long live the classic that has now, after so many years, emerged from the underground into the light of published day!

Marcus Rediker
Department of History
University of Pittsburgh

Notes

[1.] Marcus Rediker, "Recent Conversations in the U.S.S.R.," *The New People* (June, 1991). For an account of the conference that took us to Moscow, see Marcus Rediker, "The Old Guard, the New Guard, and the People at the Gates: New Approaches to the Study of American History in the U.S.S.R.," *William and Mary Quarterly* 3rd. ser. 48(1991), 580–597.

[2.] See Jesse Lemisch, "Bailyn Besieged in his Bunker," *Radical History Review* 3(1976), 72–83, and his review of Bailyn's *Ideological Origins of the American Revolution* (Cambridge, Mass.: Harvard University Press, 1968), "What Made Our Revolution?" *The New Republic* May 25, 1968, 25–28.

[3.] Jesse Lemisch, "American History Viewed Through a (No Longer) Red Lens: Will it be the Triumph of Capitalism, or Scholarship that Divorces Truth from Power?" paper delivered to the Third All-Union Symposium on American Historical Studies: "A New Way of Thinking and American Studies in the USSR," Academy of Sciences of the USSR, Moscow (1991). Published as "American History Seen Through a (No Longer) Red Lens: Present-Mindedness, *Konyunkturschina,* and the Divorce of Truth From Power," *Novaya i Novershaya Istoria [New and Contemporary History],* Moscow, (January–February, 1992).

[4.] Jesse Lemisch, "Towards a Democratic History," *A Radical Education Project Occasional Paper* (1967). See also the subsequent debate sparked by this pamphlet: Joan W. and Donald M. Scott, "Toward History: A Reply to Jesse Lemisch," and Lemisch's response, "New Left Elitism: A Rejoinder," both in *Radical America* 1(1967), 37–53.

[5.] Jesse Lemisch, "The American Revolution Seen from the Bottom Up," Barton J. Bernstein, ed., *Towards a New Past: Dissenting Essays in American History* (New York: Vintage, 1967), 29.

[6.] These were the ideas I found most compelling about Lemisch's work when I first encountered it in 1974, when, while working in a factory in Richmond, Virginia, I took a night class on the American Revolution at Virginia Commonwealth University and read the debate he and John Alexander waged with James H. Hutson on writing the history of the "inarticulate." See James H. Hutson, "An Investigation of the Inarticulate: Philadelphia's White Oaks," *William and Mary Quarterly* 3rd ser. 28(1971), 3–26; Jesse Lemisch and John K. Alexander, "The White Oaks, Jack Tar, and the Concept of the 'Inarticulate,'" *Ibid.,* 29(1972), 109–134; and "James H. Hutson's Rebuttal," in *Ibid.,* 29(1972), 136–142.

[7.] See Young's comments on Lemisch and his place in early American history in "American Historians Confront 'The Transforming Hand of Revolution,'" in Ronald Hoffman and Peter J. Albert, eds., *The Transforming Hand of*

Revolution: Reconsidering the American Revolution as a Social Movement (Charlottesville, Va.: University of Virginia Press, 1996), 433–438.

8. Jonathan M. Wiener, "Radical Historians and the Crisis in American History, 1959–1980," *Journal of American History* 76(1989), 399–434; Peter Novick, *That Noble Dream: The "Objectivity Question" and the American Historical Profession* (Cambridge: Cambridge University Press, 1988), ch. 13. Lemisch's most influential articles are "Jack Tar in the Streets: Merchant Seamen in the Politics of Revolutionary America," *William and Mary Quarterly* 3rd ser. 25(1968), 371-407 (recently selected as one of the best articles ever to be published in this distinguished journal); "Listening to the 'Inarticulate': William Widger's Dream and the Loyalties of American Revolutionary Seamen in British Prisons," *Journal of Social History* 3(1969–1970), 1–29; and "The American Revolution Seen from the Bottom Up." See also the reviews of *Towards a New Past* by Aileen S. Kraditor and David Donald and the exchange between Lemisch and Kraditor in the *American Historical Review,* 74(1968), 529–533, and 74(1969), 1766–1769.

9. The essays from the conference appeared in Colin Howell and Richard Twomey, eds., *Jack Tar in History: Essays on Maritime Life and Labour* (Fredericton, New Brunswick: Acadiensis Press, 1991). "Jack Tar versus John Bull" (even though I had serious difficulty getting my hands on it) helped to make possible my study of sailors and pirates in the eighteenth century, *Between the Devil and the Deep Blue Sea: Merchant Seamen, Pirates, and the Anglo-American Maritime World, 1700–1750* (Cambridge: Cambridge University Press, 1987).

10. Julius Scott, "The Common Wind: Currents of Afro-American Communication in the Era of the Haitian Revolution," Ph.D. dissertation Duke University, 1986; W. Jeffrey Bolster, "'To Feel Like a Man': Black Seamen in the Northern States, 1800–1860," *Journal of American History* 76(1990), 1173–1199; Marcus Rediker, "A Motley Crew of Rebels: Sailors, Slaves, and the Coming of the American Revolution," in Hoffman and Albert, eds., *The Transforming Hand of Revolution,* 155–198. Other historians who have drawn significantly on Lemisch's work in one way or another include Edward Countryman, Margaret Creighton, William Lamont, Peter Linebaugh, Gary B. Nash, Simon Newman, Richard Sheldon, Billy G. Smith, and Daniel Vickers. See also Margaret S. Creighton and Lisa Norling, eds., *Iron Men , Wooden Women: Gender and Seafaring in the Atlantic World, 1700–1920* (Baltimore: Johns Hopkins University Press, 1996), xi.

Preface

This study was born in the naive faith that the historian can find answers for whatever questions he choses to ask. Some years of limited acquaintance with the sources on the American Revolution led me to consider what American common seamen had to do with precipitating that Revolution. Many books gave passing mention to the seamen: here was a Stamp Act riot or a battle over impressment involving great numbers of seamen. But whenever such matters were mentioned, it seemed to me that the historian's vital task—to explain—was evaded. What explanation was offered for the participation of disproportionate numbers of seamen in violence in the city streets was generally couched in terms of irrationality, and this is no explanation at all: the historian has not really explained when he hints that seamen rioted because they are a roisterous and irresponsible lot, the willing victims of alcoholic fantasies. Nor is it really more adequate to explain the conduct of large groups of men in terms of manipulation. Again this denies that part of the liberal faith which thinks of man as a largely rational animal and thus assumes that his conduct can be rationally explained without making of him the puppet of alcohol or of his social superiors. This study, then, originated in the faith that the seamen's conduct could be explained and that the sources would yield such explanation.

The sources yielded answers most unwillingly. The seaman, generally illiterate, closed his lips to the historian and forced him to look elsewhere. My Bibliographical Note describes the methods used to pry the seaman's lips open. I took him to court, examined his will, and turned amateur genealogist. I quickly discovered that, with a few exceptions, there were to be no individual sources which would tell the whole story; my task was largely one of immersing myself in all the New York sources, squeezing out of them whatever bits of information each offered, and hoping that the cumulative result would be to produce solid answers.

I believe I have found enough answers to claim that I have explained the seamen's conduct. As the research progressed, I discovered additional evidence of seamen's participation in riots ashore: impressment riots, the Stamp Act riots, the Battle of Golden Hill, and other incidents. Soon I had the material for thorough descriptions of these events; meanwhile it began to become clear to me why the seamen were there. The bulk of the dissertation is devoted to describing these events and offering explanations for the seamen's actions. I found that seamen were early victims of British tyranny as impressed men; I found that seamen had a real interest in the choice of a strategy of opposition to the Stamp Act and to the other post-war legislation; I found that that legislation affected seamen as well as the rest of the population; I found that seamen had reason to be irritated by the actions both of the Navy and of the Army: finally, I have been able to say that these were rational men conducting themselves rationally in response to a long list of very real grievances.

As this study now stands, it is—if a graduate student may borrow a term from a great historian—"frankly fragmentary." Although the dissertation limits itself to New York, the completed work will deal with other colonies as well: considering the seaman's mobility, it is artificial to meet him in New York and ignore him elsewhere. Besides, I have evidence that he was equally active, in a political sense, in other places. Thus, especially in connection with impressment, the study will have greater depth when approached on the continental scale. The sections dealing with welfare measures for seamen will be given greater body when based not only on New York but on other major ports as well. Finally, the whole question of the seamen's Loyalism will be given greater attention than is done here: a consideration of the seaman's role in the Revolution itself was beyond the scope of this study, and thus I have only been able to offer evidence for the seaman's patriotism in what I take to be a convincing but nonetheless very general way.

Some words of definition are necessary. I have made extensive use of the terms "liberal," "radical," and "conservative." I do not believe that these terms are meaningless. When "reactionary" is added to the list, we have, without any idea of substantive measures, some very clear ideas about the pace with which various people want to see political change take place and about the extent of their dedication to the existing system. The conservative is largely content with the system and does not seek change. Liberals and radicals do seek changes, but there is a significant difference between them. The liberal is patient and is not willing to destroy the present system to achieve a better one. The radical wants change *now* and wants to replace the system with a new one.

Utilizing these not very original definitions, it becomes clear that the American Revolution cannot be thought of as conservative. Whatever the substance of the revolutionists' goals, it is clear that they had to seek political change to attain them. To note that they wanted to conserve certain values offers about as much justification for calling the whole process a conservative one as does the knowledge that, in the heat of battle, revolutionaries, like other men, attempt to conserve their lives. Thus I have thought of the Revolution as change and have therefore assumed that its leaders must have been either liberals or radicals. Although the temperament of many of the opponents of the Stamp Act—to take one important part of the British program—may have been what we call "conservative," I find it difficult to think of anyone opposed to the Stamp Act as a political conservative. Carl Becker saw two factions opposing the Stamp Act, and he, and many others, have called them "conservatives" and "radicals." The omission of the term, "liberal," led Becker to call the Sons of Liberty "ultra-radicals." I prefer to think of the two parties as "liberals" and "radicals." I believe that the significant political quarrels in the period from the Stamp Act to the Declaration of Independence were those between radicals and liberals, not between radicals and conservatives. I believe that the Revolution was not radical but not therefore conservative: it was liberal.

It is also essential to define Jack Tar. He is a merchant seaman. A *sailor* fights in the Royal Navy. A *mariner*, as used here, is the captain of a merchant vessel. These terms are used rigidly in this study, somewhat more rigidly than in the sources themselves, where there has been inconsistency in terminology. Thus if a source called a man a mariner or a sailor I have had to have evidence that he was in fact a merchant seaman before I would count him as one.[1]

Finally, it is my happy duty to thank the following people for their help: Frank James of the County Clerk's Office, Hall of Records, New York City: one of the few men in the City administration who knows and cares about historical records, he was a real help in guiding me through the maze of court records; the staff at the New-York Historical Society, where much of my research was done; Milton Klein; Catherine Crary; Robert Christen; Oliver Dickerson, who was good enough to correspond with me on the subject of Loyalism among seamen; and Edmund S. Morgan whose criticism was always perceptive and pungent and who allowed me to be the beneficiary of a noble tradition which, as I understand it, runs from Percy Holmes Boynton to Perry Miller[2] to

Edmund Morgan: I was given enough rope with which to hang myself and hope that the reader will conclude that I have not done so.

J.L.

Notes

[1] I.M.V., "Note," *Mariner's Mirror*, VII (November, 1921), 351 discusses these terms; I have not followed him precisely.

[2] Perry Miller, *Orthodoxy in Massachusetts*, 1630–1650 (2d ed.; Boston, 1959), p. xvii.

Jack Tar vs. John Bull

I. Who Was Jack Tar?

Here comes Jack Tar, his bowed legs carrying him up Broadway in a rolling stride[1] which immediately marks him as a man defending himself against non-existent dangers and perhaps ill-prepared for the solid and alien ground of New York City. In his dress he is, in the words of a superior, "very nasty and negligent";[2] his black stockings are ragged; his long, baggy trousers—blue or wine-colored, or striped—are tarred to make them waterproof; under his short pea jacket he wears a blue or a yellow vest, or possibly one of the spotted ermine kind sold by Philip Livingston; his large round hat, made of felt or beaver and perhaps with a yellow binding, slopes across his face, partially covering his wig.[3]

If we live in the eighteenth century our ideas about this man are well set. We know that his speech will be course and salty and that decent language will be wasted upon him, for he has been bred in "that very shambles of language," the merchant marine.[4] We think of him as a child, incapable of handling the simplest of his own affairs; and the laws treat him as a libertyless ward.[5] But although the seaman's heart is a child's, he has the passions of a man: he is lawless and bold, always ready for a fight, "concerned only," in the words of a member of one of New York's leading families, "for the present, and . . . incapable of thinking of, or inattentive to, future welfare. . . ."[6] He is always drunk.

A quick examination of the seaman's clothes, or of popular prejudices about him, tells us very little. Who, after all, was Jack Tar?

First of all, he was a very young man. The eighteenth century thought about child labor only long enough to conclude it a good thing.[7] Thomas Peake and Henry Pindar of New York and Alpheus Avery of Westchester, along with John Holland of Long Island, had already been at sea for an undetermined time at the age of seventeen— the latter possibly for four years. American-born seamen averaged between twenty-four and twenty-five years of age in New York, but

John Paul Jones went to sea at thirteen, and at the same age Walter Hopper saw his indentures sold by the captain of a Berwick vessel to the captain of a New York sloop for seven years.[8]

Some of these young men were educated on land by instructors offering courses in subjects useful at sea;[9] more of them received their education on shipboard as apprentices. Their indentures generally lasted seven years but could be for as few as four or as many as twelve years; their terms were similar to those of apprenticeship contracts in other trades. During the period of the indentures the master was supposed to supply the apprentice's physical needs—with meat, drink, clothes, lodging, and washing—and to teach him "the Art and Mistery of a Mariner" (when Captain Thomas Dun left apprentice Patrick Fling in New York, unfed, unclothed, unwashed, artless and mystified, Fling's mother brought suit and saw her son released from his apprenticeship). When his term was over, the young man, hopefully on his way to becoming master of his own vessel, was to be presented with a new suit of clothes, shirts, and such mariner's equipment as a quadrant, a forestaff, a compass, and a calendar.[10]

Why did the young man go to sea? Often he was driven by wanderlust: the desire for adventure, to see the world, to experience and survive "the Perils and uncertainty" of life at sea.[11] Boys growing up in the seaport towns could hardly escape an attack of sea-fever; in Boston young Benjamin Franklin was saved for a career in printing—and several other trades—only by the strong discipline of a father who refused to allow his son to succumb to his "strong Inclination for the Sea."[12] Others went and later returned as men to the city they had left as boys, many to ship out again, some to leave the sea behind, marry, and use their earnings to begin a trade or buy a farm.[13]

As to how many remained seamen and how many remained ashore, the youth of the average seaman indicates that a higher proportion remained ashore. But the whole question of the duration of the seaman's attachment to the sea cannot be simply answered. One must consider the ease with which the merchant seaman moved into and out of other maritime trades, the individual's movement between maritime and non-maritime jobs; and finally, one must examine a generational phenomenon: did the sons of seamen remain seamen?

In times of war the merchant seaman went to sea as a sailor in the Royal Navy. Life and duty were similar in both services, and the merchant seaman was generally familiar with the use of big guns, the cutlass, the musket, and the boarding pike. Thus, he was, as one historian says, "a man-o'-war's man ready-made," and the Admiralty depended on the merchant marine for a pool of ready manpower.[14]

In peace-time the discharged sailor who did not return to the merchant service might find himself in what some British officials called "the best seminary for seamen"—the fishery. The pursuit of whales and fish played a larger role in the life of New England communities than in New York, but New York's seamen did man a sizeable fishing fleet, including whalers.[15] This was a seasonal occupation, and the transition out of the merchant marine was regular and smooth.

Seamen ashore often worked in allied trades, and to some extent they took jobs unrelated to the sea. Sometimes they must have left the city completely and became part of the westward movement. Sometimes they could do no better than to become watchmen or, as in the case of one man whom the Common Council judged "Very poor," they became public whippers. Others, such as Adam Smith, Samuel Stevens, John Mason, and James McLaughlin can be followed as they are now seamen, now common laborers, now seamen again.[16]

Many did better. Wages were always high in the ports, and the demand for labor there and in the back country constantly mounted. It was the complaint of the British Navy that higher wages in the merchant service and ashore often snatched their men away.[17] The lure was less strong to merchant seamen, but fluctuations in the colonial economy often created imbalances between wages offered at sea and ashore, and the men responded with movements in the appropriate direction.

The sons of mariners seem to have moved fairly freely into other professions; one sees them being apprenticed to gentlemen, bakers, barbers, joiners, curriers, glaziers, hatmakers, butchers, sailmakers, and cordwainers, to name a few. Conversely the sons of merchants, boatmen, coopers, and others were apprenticed to mariners. No statistical measure is possible here, but it is clear that at least some professional mobility did exist between the generations.[18]

We will ignore a significant part of the answer to the question, "who was Jack Tar?" unless we note that he was frequently a recent immigrant. If an immigrant, he was usually young, but still slightly older than his American counterpart; the average New York seaman of foreign birth was just under twenty-eight years of age. This immigrant seaman came from many parts of the world, but predominantly from England or northern Ireland, each of these areas providing one-third of the total. The remaining third came from all over the world: Dutchman Hendrick Vessells, Germans and Prussians such as John Bummer and John Holshowen, Norwegian Tønnes Anderson, Danes such as Frederick Helmtein, Swedes such as Andrew Linquest, the Portuguese

Luis Ruderago, Italians such as Anthony Serone, and even Peter Defour from landlocked Switzerland.[19]
What, then, distinguishes Jack Tar from his fellows ashore? Apparently very little. Jack dresses differently and speaks somewhat more coarsely, but there are no rigid barriers between his trade and others. He maintains his connections ashore and seems often to have been only temporarily a seaman. As Albert Gallatin observed during a 1798 congressional debate over the construction of special hospitals for seamen:

> Institutions of the kind recommended in this bill might be used in other countries where there was a distinction between sailors and other citizens, but, in the United States, he had not been able to discover any material distinction between them and other classes of men.[20]

Jack Tar is simply a landman gone to sea, lured there by the pursuit of adventure, wanderlust, and good wages—all what a sociologist of the sea calls "positive" motives.[21]
If the sea was a place for the positively motivated, why did Josiah Franklin struggle against his son's desire to go to sea?[22]
"Call me Ishmael," begin the famous lines:

> some years ago . . . having little or no money in my purse, and nothing particular to interest me on shore, I thought I would sail about a little and see the watery part of the world. It is a way I have of driving off the spleen, and regulating the circulation. Whenever I find myself growing grim about the mouth; whenever it is a damp, drizzly November in my soul; whenever I find myself involuntarily pausing before coffin warehouses, and bringing up the rear of every funeral I meet; and especially whenever my hypos get such an upper hand of me, that it requires a strong moral principle to prevent me from deliberately stepping into the street, and methodically knocking people's hats off—then, I account it high time to get to sea as soon as I can. This is my substitute for pistol and ball. With a philosophical flourish Cato throws himself upon his sword; I quietly take to the ship.[23]

Ishmael is a man leaving the land for "negative" reasons rather than positively seeking the sea. No matter what we make of him, we cannot possibly make him into one of the "adventure-seeking boys" whom Samuel Eliot Morison has offered as the typical member of the Massachusetts merchant marine.[24] Others, perhaps, but not Ishmael.

Were there many Ishmaels? Were there many who left the land in flight and fear, outcasts, men with little hope of sharing the landman's constantly improving lot? "All masters of vessels are warned not to harbor, conceal, or employ him, as they will answer for it, as the law directs."[25] Weekly, daily, apprentices broke the chains of their indentures and took flight in what appeared to be the only direction promising real shelter: the sea. The more resourceful among them, Benjamin Franklin for instance, were able to return to normal society—albeit in a distant town.[26] Usually in their middle or late teens, but sometimes in their thirties, these young fugitives often found that their safety required that they remain at sea. Arriving there with diverse trades, some tried to pass for seamen and before too long discovered that they had indeed become seamen. Others started their flight a step lower on the mobility scale; they *were* seamen, apprenticed to one vessel, and ran away to another. Some had belonged to several vessels and had run away repeatedly only to rejoin the only profession which welcomed and sheltered fugitives.[27] For some of these men the sea had become a permanent home; for all of them it represented something more complex than a place for fulfilling childhood dreams of travel and adventure. How frequently was the sea a shelter rather than a dream? Frequently enough to necessitate laws against the employing of runaways at sea.

There were others who had isolated themselves from normal society by acts more extreme than the mere breaking of a contract. These reversed the order of Ishmael's flight, letting their hypos get the better of them and knocking people's hats off *before* they went to sea. Soldiers and sailors who had deserted, bail-jumpers, thieves, murderers[28]—here we approach closer to the true criminal element which we dare not exclude from its traditional place in the merchant marine.

The American merchant marine included a sizeable number of men whose motives were radically different from their companions and whose mobility was strictly limited: these were Negroes. Some were free men, including a number of Spaniards and Portuguese such as Theodo Twawoolshead, Peter Calumpoe, and John Diego. Some American Negroes had gained their freedom by serving on warships in the conflicts before 1763[29]; they were free to seek peacetime jobs in the merchant marine. But Negroes also served in the maritime trades as one of the burdens of their bondage. Some were ship-caulkers, longshoremen, and sail-makers,[30] but Negroes demonstrated as much capacity for handling vessels as white men, and their masters often hired them out or sold them to shipmasters. In the harbor slaves served as pilots,[31] and they usually manned the ferries.[32] They went to sea, and their experience there increased their value to their masters who could now advertise them as " . . . brought up from his Infancy to the Sea" or " . . . has been some Voyages to Sea."[33]

The presence of runaway slaves—fugitives of the most desperate and permanent sort—makes wanderlust appear an ironic parody of the motives which made at least some men seamen. Slaves headed for the sea might try to pass as freemen,[34] their attempt made plausible by the presence of free Negroes on ship. As with white runaways, newspaper advertisements would warn masters of vessels against harboring, concealing, or employing them lest they suffer the penalty of the law.[35] The need for such warnings and for such laws again indicates that the runaway slave was not a rare sight in the merchant marine.

There were many others who were not in the merchant service out of motives of wanderlust. Many a seaman began his career as a ship's boy, taken from a charity school or off the streets by the master of a vessel. Many landmen learned the seaman's skills after being forcibly impressed into the Royal Navy; some of these men were pressed directly from jails: thieves, rioters, smugglers, assaulters, pickpockets, counterfeiters, and murderers. Others, often derelicts, were lured into the merchant service by a little rum and a few dollars offered by a crimp.[36]

These men, the less mobile, the more permanently seamen, lacked the more nearly normal family life of those who were merely temporarily seamen, fated to settle down after a few years of adventure. These floaters drifted and slipped their moorings;[37] their wives ran off and left them, sometimes for other men.[38] While jealous anxiety drove some seamen to suicide,[39] others had no wives and no jealousy. Although no statistical conclusions are possible, to a surprising extent the beneficiaries in seamen's wills are not wives but rather friends, innkeepers, brothers, and sisters.[40] A seaman who has no one but an innkeeper to leave his worldly possessions to may be a fine fellow, but he is clearly not anchored to a stable family life.

The picture of Jack Tar which emerges from a close consideration is complex and at least double-faceted. On the one hand he is simply the American at sea. He is young and optimistic, and rightfully optimistic, for his prospects are good; at sea he may become master of his own vessel, or he may return to the land and share in the growth of the continent. He is stable in temperament and mobile in profession.

But the other Jack Tar is quite different. His temper is Ishmael's. He is a dissenter from the American mood. His goals differ from his fellows' ashore; he is the non-conformist, the rebel, the extreme individualist, the man without family ties. He has no steady employment but rather a series of separate jobs. When he is ashore he is unemployed; released from the discipline of shipboard life he is apt to be explosive and irresponsible rather than cautious and sober. He comes to the sea for negative reasons and may remain to become an "old salt."[41] He is, except for his personal possessions, propertyless, his income is unstable, and he does not build up any significant savings: he is a sea-going proletarian.[42]

Each of these men contributed to the over-all flavor of the merchant marine. The floaters, if only by dint of their longer tenure, necessarily contributed a greater part, although they were fewer in number. The more stable ones, visitors on the sea, had responded to a much-diluted version of the motives which drove the old salt, for they too had turned their backs on normal society, if only for a moment. They had been tourists in a country known to tradition and to reality as a haven for those who found it impossible to survive ashore.

Notes

[1.] Sometimes described as a "waddle": *New York Gazette: or Weekly Post-Boy*, September 3, 1759. Hereafter cited as *Post-Boy*.

[2.] [George Balfour?], "Memorandum," *Mariner's Mirror*, VIII (July, 1922), 248.

[3.] For the seaman's clothes see *Post-Boy*, December 10, 1759, October 14, December 16, 1762, November 3, 1763, March 6, June 26, 1766, October 1, 1767, January 29, 1770, July 6, 1772; Samuel Eliot Morison, *John Paul Jones: A Sailor's Biography* (Boston, 1959), p. 72 (hereafter cited as Morison, *John Paul Jones*); will of William Hughforth: *Abstracts of Wills on File in the Surrogate's Office, City of New York* (New-York Historical Society, *Collections*, 1892–1901 [New York, 1893–1902]), VI, 111 (hereafter cited as *Wills*). A pair of useful illustrations appears in *Mariner's Mirror*, IX (April, 1923), 128.

[4.] J. R. Hutchinson, *The Press-Gang, Afloat and Ashore* (New York, 1914), p. 29 (hereafter cited as Hutchinson, *Press-Gang*). For a landman's version of some seamen's dialogue see *Post-Boy*, December 10, 1767.

[5.] See below, pp. 59–61 for laws concerning the relations between seamen and tavern-keepers. The United States treated the seamen as a ward as late as 1915: see William L. Standard, *Merchant Seamen: A Short History of Their Struggles* (New York, 1947), pp. 29–30 (hereafter cited as Standard, *Merchant Seamen*); Elmo Paul Hohman, *Seamen Ashore: A Study of the*

United Seamen's Service and of Merchant Seamen in Port (New Haven, 1952), p. 214 (hereafter cited as Hohman, *Seamen Ashore*). The image of the seaman presented here is confirmed by the analysis of eighteenth-century literature in Harold Francis Watson, *The Sailor in English Fiction and Drama, 1550–1800* (New York, 1931), pp. 159–160.

6. Senator Livingston, April 10, 1798, in *Debates and Proceedings in the Congress of the United States*, Fifth Congress (Washington, 1851), p. 1388.

7. Edith Abbot, "A Study of the Early History of Child Labor in America," *American Journal of Sociology*, XIV (July, 1908), 23–24.

8. The average age is based on the ages of sixty-one American seamen of ascertainable age listed in *Muster Rolls of New York Provincial Troops: 1755–1764* (New-York Historical Society, *Collections*, 1891 [New York, 1892]) (hereafter cited as *Muster Rolls*). The exact figure is 24.3 years. Peake, Pindar, and Holland are all in *Muster Rolls*, as are all seamen appearing in this chapter without indication as to source. Other information about a seaman named John Holland is in John Holland v. John McCleve, Plea of Trespass, filed January 12, 1758, New York Supreme Court: Parchment 210-E-58, Office of County Clerk, Hall of Records, New York City. For Avery see American Loyalists: Transcripts of the Manuscript Books and Papers of the Commission of Enquiry into the Losses and Services of the American Loyalists held under Acts of Parliament of 23, 25, 26, 28 and 29 of George III (New York Public Library), XLIII, 500. Hereafter cited as Loyalist Transcripts. For Jones see Morison, *John Paul Jones*, p. 11. For Hopper see *The Burghers of New Amsterdam and the Freemen of New York, 1675–1866* (New-York Historical Society, *Collections*, 1885 [New York, 1886]), pp. 576–577. Hereafter cited as *Freemen*.

9. Carl Bridenbaugh, *Cities in Revolt: Urban Life in America, 1743–1776* (New York, 1955), p. 377. Hereafter cited as Bridenbaugh, *Cities in Revolt*.

10. Freemen, pp. 572, 576–578, 581–582, 592–593, 596, 600, 618, 620; *Indentures of Apprentices: October 21, 1718, to August 7, 1727* (New-York Historical Society, Collections, 1909 [New York, 1910]) pp. 143, 150, 153, 174, 184, 195 (hereafter cited as *Apprentices*). For Patrick Fling see Minutes of the General Quarter Sessions of the Peace for the City and County of New York, February 3, 4, 1773: Office of the Clerk of General Sessions, Criminal Courts Building, New York City.

11. Will of Isaac Preston, *Wills*, VII, 330.

12. Max Farrand, ed., *Benjamin Franklin's Memoirs: Parallel Text Edition: Comprising the texts of Franklin's Original Manuscript, the French translation by Louis Guillaume le Veillard, the French Translation Published by Buisson, and the version edited by William Temple Franklin, his Grandson* (Berkeley and Los Angeles, 1949), p. 20. Hereafter cited as Farrand, *Franklin's Memoirs*.

13. Samuel Eliot Morison, *The Maritime History of Massachusetts, 1783–1860* (Boston, 1921), pp. 105–106 (hereafter cited as Morison, *Maritime History*); Morison, *John Paul Jones*, pp. 22–23.

14. Hutchinson, *Press-Gang*, pp. 106–107.

15. *Post-Boy*, May 19, 1763, December 20, 1764; Michael Lewis, *British Ships and British Seamen* (London, 1940), p. 22.

16. *Post-Boy*, November 10, 1763; *Minutes of the Common Council of the City of New York, 1675–1776* (New York, 1905), V, 329. Hereafter cited as *Minutes of Common Council*. For Smith see below, pp. 71–72. For McLaughlin see The King v. Samuel Dobbins, Thomas McLaughlin, James McLaughlin, et al., Indictment for a Riot, filed October 19, 1774, New York Supreme Court: Pleadings K-316. For Mason see The King v. John Mason, Indictments for Assault and Battery, filed January 23, 24, 1772, New York Supreme Court: Pleadings K-387, K-395; Orders for Arrest of John Mason, May 1, 1773 and several other dates, New York Supreme Court: Parchments 186-D-2, 189-F-7, 185-C-6, 194-F-5, 189-F-5, 183-C-9, 189-G- 9, 184-K-4, 184-F-7, 184-K-9, 191-O-4, 190-D-6, 190-F-3, 190-E-8, 191-D-8.

17. William Pendleton to the Lords of Trade, March 6, 1711: Edmund Bailey O'Callaghan, ed., *Documents Relative to the Colonial History of the State of New York* (Albany, 1856–1887), V, 194. Hereafter cited as *N Y Col Docs*.

18. *Freemen*, pp. 577–578, 617, 620; *Apprentices*, pp. 122–123, 140–143, 150, 155, 166, 169, 181, 188, 189, 193, 195.

19. The average age—27.8—is based on the ages of 341 foreign-born seamen of ascertainable age listed in *Muster Rolls*. Of these 116 came from England or Wales, 127 from Northern Ireland, and scattered numbers, none exceeding 16, came from the other places listed in the text.

20. April 10, 1798, *Debates and Proceedings in the Congress of the United States*, Fifth Congress (Washington, 1851), p. 1392.

21. Hohman, *Seamen Ashore*, p. 217.

22. Farrand, *Franklin's Memoirs*, p. 20.

23. Herman Melville, *Moby Dick or the Whale* (New York, 1952), p. 1.

24. Morison, *Maritime History*, p. 106.

25. This is a composite of advertisements appearing in almost every issue of New York's newspapers. For some varying wordings see advertisements for Daniel Narraway, *Post-Boy*, May 17, 1764; Henry Basman, *ibid.*, May 24, 1764; John Foster, *ibid.*, June 27, 1765.

26. For Franklin's account of breaking his indentures and taking flight see Farrand, *Franklin's Memoirs*, pp. 50, 52.

27. This paragraph is based upon extensive study of advertisements for runaways and articles about them in the New York newspapers. The bare

outlines could be reproduced by referring to such items in the following issues of the *Post-Boy*: December 10, 1759, December 16, 1762, October 6, November 3, 1763, May 10, 24, July 19, September 6, 1764, April 4, 18, June 27, 1765, June 29, July 6, 1772.

28. *Ibid.*, September 3, 1759, October 14, 1762, July 21, 1763, March 29, September 20, 1764; *New-York Journal; or, The General Advertiser*; May 13, 1773. Hereafter cited as *Journal*.

29. Benjamin Quarles, *The Negro in the American Revolution* (Chapel Hill, 1961), p. 84. Hereafter cited as Quarles, *Negro in the Revolution*.

30. *Post-Boy*, July 7, November 17, 1763.

31. Loyalist Transcripts, XIX, 207 (see under Samuel Hallett).

32. George William Edwards, *New York as an Eighteenth Century Municipality, 1731- 1776* (New York, 1917), p. 178. Hereafter cited as Edwards, *New York as Eighteenth Century Municipality*.

33. *Post-Boy*, March 26, 1761, August 18, 1763.

34. *Journal*, October 13, 1774.

35. Again see almost any issue of any New York newspaper, e.g. *Post-Boy*, February 18, 1760, September 22, 1763, June 21, 1764, April 11, 1765.

36. *Ibid.*, July 31, 1760, May 15, 1769; Hutchinson, *Press-Gang*, pp. 48–49, 200.

37. Sign at "The Anchorage," Baltimore:

"Write Home Often

You'll drift if you slip your moorings":

American Seaman, II (Summer-Fall, 1942), 152.

38. *Post-Boy*, January 21, 1758, December 10, 1767; The King v. Jane the Wife of Thomas Dun, Indictment for Bigamy, filed October 26, 1763, New York Supreme Court: Pleadings K-41.

39. *Post-Boy*, September 30, 1773.

40. See the following wills: Charles Colwell, *Wills*, VII, 148; John Henderson, *ibid.*, VII, 397; Waters Higgins, *ibid.*, VII, 12; Owen Hughes, *ibid.*, XI, 194; William Hughforth, *ibid.*, VI, 111; William Lawler, *ibid.*, VIII, 98; John Moorhead, *ibid.*, VI, 226; Roger Murphy, *ibid.*, VII, 38.

41. This account of the seaman's psychology closely follows Hohman, *Seamen Ashore*, pp. 212–213, 217, 223, 227.

42. The Reverend Hans A. Reinhold, "Christianity and Labor—for Seamen," *American Seaman*, I (Winter-Spring, 1941), 24–26.

II. Impressment of Seamen in Colonial New York

Cheerily, lads, cheerily! there's a ganger hard to wind'ard;
   Cheerily, lads, cheerily! there's a ganger hard a-lee;
Cheerily, lads, cheerily! else 'tis farewell home and kindred,
   And the bosun's mate a-raisin' hell in the King's Navee.
Cheerily, lads, cheerily ho! the warrant's out, the hanger's drawn!
Cheerily, lads, so cheerilee! we'll leave 'em an *R* in pawn!
      — song of seamen fleeing the press-gang.[1]

"A Parsill of Raskills": August 1760

Man-of-War *Winchester* greeted privateer *Sampson* with a shot over
her bow; but instead of bringing to, the Bristol ship hauled up her
foresails, lowered her top gallants, and sailed on through the Narrows.
Winchester fired again, and Captain Hale ordered Third Lieutenant
Frodsham into the ship's boat with thirteen men.[2]

In *Sampson* Captain Greatrakes pleaded with his crew to let the
party aboard, but they locked him in the cabin along with Chief Mate
Josiah Moore, Thomas Cunningham, and the other passengers. The
boat approached on *Sampson*'s bow, and Lieutenant Frodsham hailed
the privateer. The response was a volley of musquetry.[3]

"You are a parsill of Raskills," roared Lieutenant Frodsham,
turning the boat's head. *Sampson*'s inferior officers ordered the men to
stop, but they continued their fire as the boat—now ahead and still
under way—came even closer, despite the oarsmen's efforts. *Winchester*
fired again, sending a shot through *Sampson* just below the fore chains.
A second volley of small arms echoed through the Narrows, and two
men fell overboard from *Winchester*'s boat: sailors John Jackson,
Edward Thurston, and Thomas Scudemore were dead, and Peter Lyel was

mortally wounded. "Crouding all the sail she could," *Sampson* sped on, firing at the boat until it was out of reach of her musquets.[4]

The boat returned to *Winchester*, where Captain Hale ordered the crew northward to the City of New York. There they told their story while the Lieutenant-Governor, the Mayor, and a judge listened. The Mayor immediately issued warrants for the apprehension of *Sampson*'s crew.[5]

Sampson came up within about fifty feet of the end of a dock, but no further. Constables and sheriffs glared across the water at the men they were supposed to arrest. Sixty-seven men glared back, armed themselves with cutlasses, and loaded their swivels. The city officials conferred and decided that they were dealing with "desperate bloody minded fellows" and would need help. At their request Captain Hale weighed anchor and brought *Winchester* into the harbor. When the Man-of-War approached, *Sampson's* crew seized the ship's boats and fled— some headed for the Manhattan shore, some for Long Island, and some upriver.[6]

The men of *Sampson* had fought against and fled what they took to be a threat of impressment. It was August of 1760, England was at war with France in Canada, and the Royal Navy needed men. It was solving its problem in the traditional way: men were being snatched from the decks of ships, from city streets and country roads; there was "a hard Press for Seamen."[7]

In New York the fear of impressment had driven away seamen badly needed to man transport vessels headed north. The Navy had attempted to solve the problem by offering volunteers £6 New York currency in monthly wages and protection from impressment for the duration of their employment. Meanwhile the Navy was having its usual difficulties holding on to those men it had. Late in July the crew of the boat assigned to keep watch around H.M.S. *Norwich* made a run for the Jersey shore, pursued by two boats and booming musquetry. The deserters' boat was hit, and one of them had a leg taken off, but the rest made it to safety and were not heard from again.[8]

So the captains of His Majesty's ships had turned to impressment. They pressed men from market boats and wood-boats; their "acts of severity" roused New York against them and frightened the seamen off into New Jersey and Connecticut. These attempts to solve the labor shortage only exaggerated it, and the Navy kept the hoop spinning by impressing more men. On the morning of August 5 a dress rehearsal for the *Sampson* affair took place. The ship *Minehead* arrived off Sandy Hook with a cargo of salt from Lisbon, and the ship-of-war stationed there—not *Winchester*—sent a boat to demand her men. The crew confined Captain Forrest and his officers in the cabin, seized all the small arms, and refused to receive a boarding party. Three more boats arrived, and the flotilla came under *Minehead*'s stern, firing at the ship and demanding admittance. Captain Forrest from his cabin and the pilot from the deck assured the officers below that their ship was in the crew's control, but the air remained full of grape-shot and langrage. Before the unreasonable assault was ended, *Minehead*'s bowsprit, main topmast, and sails had been damaged considerably, and one man was dead, another wounded.[9]

Late in July H.M.S. *Winchester*, fifty guns, had arrived from Spithead. Captain John Hale was, according to Lieutenant-Governor Cadwallader Colden, "a very humane Gentleman" and he did not, according to the same source, attempt to press anyone. Certainly he needed men. On August 11 he published an exhortation to several of *Winchester*'s seamen who had overstayed their shore leave to come back, promising that they would not be punished. Later in the week the body of seaman Michael Thorp was found floating in the North River: he had died attempting to escape from *Winchester*. On the following Monday, August 18, Captain Hale was still pleading with his men to come back; he had not yet filled up his crew. That afternoon he fired a shot over *Sampson*'s bow and sent Lieutenant Frodsham out to bring her to. It would seem that the Captain's humanity had worn thin. It looked to the privateer's crew like an attempt at impressment and so, despite Colden's assurances, must it appear to us.[10]

As soon as the Council could be called, Colden issued, with their advice, a proclamation calling for the arrest of *Sampson*'s crew and naming fifty-six of them. He ordered a detachment of militia to the city to assist the sheriff and notified governors of provinces as far away as Massachusetts. All of this effort produced only meagre results. Captain Greatrakes and Chief Mate Moore came ashore and were jailed and admitted to bail by Judge Horsmanden. By August 30 only one man had been arrested; by the time the case came to court in October only Third Mate William Mackey and seamen Barney Callahan and Samuel Walker had been added to the list. Since it is not in the seaman's nature to take refuge in the hills, their success in avoiding capture must have been due to the cooperation of the people of the City of New York. And certainly the townspeople—merchants who could not find men for their ships, local boatmen and their relatives—were "distressed" enough by impressment to give the fugitives shelter.[11]

The people took another opportunity to condemn impressment, this time in the legal arena. When indictments were submitted to a grand jury in the October sessions of the Supreme Court they "found the fact to be committed without the body of the County" and refused to vote a true bill. Attorney-General Kempe, an irritated Lieutenant-

Governor hard on his heels, moved that Greatrakes and Moore be handed
over to the Sheriff to answer for "commanding aiding and abetting and
assisting in the said Murder" in whatever court might have jurisdiction.
Kempe came up with a provincial act of 1699 for dealing with pirates—
it had been disallowed in 1700, but no one in New York seemed to
know about it—and a special commission was set up to try the
offenders. But the grand jury returned the indictment endorsed "we are
not Informed of the Facts contained in this Bill," and the prisoners were
discharged. Greatrakes and Moore sailed off in *Sampson* a few hours
after their discharge, but, in a final vindictive outburst, the Council
advised Colden to deliver Mackey, Callahan and Philipse to the captain
of Man-of-War *Dover* for service.[12] The jury had the last word, but only
after populace and seamen had expressed their disapproval of
impressment, the first with judicial weapons, the second by resort to
arms.

Impressment

Impressment of men as a means of supplying the Royal Navy
began in the era of the Saxon kings. The seaman was the "bondsman of
the sea" before *Magna Charta*, and he remained liable to the Crown's
essentially feudal demands until the press-gang died in 1833.[13] Why did
this evil institution endure for so many hundreds of years? Ultimately
the justification for impressment is no nobler than that which its
defenders could offer for American Negro slavery (there are many
parallels): "it had nothing to commend it to posterity, except that it
paid."[14] Doubts there were about its legality[15] and even more about its
morality, but no one ever contended that it would be cheaper for the
Crown of England to hire its sailors at full wages.[16]

What was wrong with the Royal Navy that it had to snatch its men
from the streets, the jails, the marriage-bed? In part, of course, the
question answers itself. The very means which the Navy used to fill out
its ranks—reminiscent as they are of the means of catching Africans for
slavery—suggest that to be in the Navy was to be un-free, and the
service's drawbacks all follow from that fundamental fact. Punishments
were cruel and often irrational, always painful and often mortal. For
obscenity the tongue was scraped with hoop-iron; there were
punishments for smiling in the presence of an officer; one captain put
his sailors' heads in bags for trivial offenses; flogging was universal.[17]

If the merchant seaman had always to consider "the Dangers of the
Seas,"[18] drafted into the Navy, he had additionally to concern himself
with the hazards of battle. If punishment or naval conflict did not get

him, perhaps "the want of wholesome provisions"[19] would;[20] if he survived the food he had yet to contend with fevers, scurvy and incompetent medical care:[21] sickness, Benjamin Franklin tells us, was more common in the Navy than in the merchant service and more frequently fatal.[22]

And so the men deserted. The penalty was hanging or flogging, and there were punishments for those who harbored deserters.[23] As time passed, hanging declined, and in more than one instance captains in New York harbor found themselves forced to offer forgiveness to all men who would return to their ships.[24] Men who had originally arrived in the Navy with the assistance of a press-gang had an additional motive for desertion, and the Navy knew that it could not depend on them in crises.[25] Thus, for diverse reasons, men continued to desert, leaving places to be filled, and these places were filled by newly impressed men who did their best to escape again.

Impressment ceased to exist only in the nineteenth century when the Royal Navy was willing to employ men for work in tolerable conditions and for proper wages. But throughout the eighteenth century the Navy preferred impressing its men to offering them adequate wages. Often the sailor's pay would be deferred—at the time of the mutiny at the Nore there was one ship whose crew had not been paid in fifteen years[26]—either because Parliament had not appropriated enough funds for the Navy or because sailors had been shunted about from ship to ship without ever being officially listed on the books.[27] It was the Navy's theory that a man with wages due would be less likely to desert, but the theory was repeatedly disproved, as in 1711 when a New Yorker noted that " . . . it sometimes happens that one Man, who has three or four years pay due, is as ready to desert as another who has but three or four days."[28] Inevitably, they deserted to higher wages, for, as the same New Yorker saw, "The great wages in all parts of America given to Handicraft Tradsmen [sic] and Labourers on shore, and to those employed in the Merchants service at sea, are a great inducement to sailors to desert Her Majesty's service. . . ."[29] In times of war, privateering lured men away from the Navy,[30] and at any time, peace or war, crimps and innkeepers had the tide of the seaman's will with them when they seduced sailors into the merchant service. The Navy's most imaginative response was sporadic and abortive attempts to limit wages given to merchant seamen, but the inviting differential remained.[31] Finally, when the Navy offered bounties for enlistment, this merely served to induce additional desertions by men who could pick up a month's wages simply for signing up.[32]

Impressment angered and frightened the seaman, but the institution pervaded and disrupted all society, giving many other classes and groups cause to share a common grievance with the press-gang's more direct victims. Anyone connected with trade, and especially merchants, suffered at the hands of the Navy. In an extreme case a ship was wrecked when a press-gang left it with an inadequate crew.[33] Generally impressment drove men away and wages up. Sailings were delayed and cancelled for lack of men; the crew that might have manned the merchant vessels was either incarcerated in a man-of-war or, fearing such a fate, on its way to the freedom of a neighboring colony. "New York and Boston," Benjamin Franklin commented during the French and Indian War, "have so often found the Inconvenience of . . . Station Ships that they are very indifferent about having them: The Pressing of their Men and thereby disappointing Voyages, often hurting their Trade more than the Enemy hurts it."[34]

A New York ferry boat operator lost business when people shunned the city during a press;[35] fishermen were taken from their boats;[36] market boats and fuel boats were frightened away from the city, and the price of wood and food rose, despite official promises that these vessels would be protected from impressment.[37] Thus those who did not lose their liberty to impressment lost their property to it. People of all sorts were frightened, and their fear exacerbated an already bad situation.

Impressment in New York: The Early Period

The history of impressment in New York is, from the very beginning, a tale of venality and vindictiveness. Such, of course, it must be: the press-gang's power—the power freely to deprive a man of his freedom—is inherently tyrannical and will of necessity lead to tyranny and its concomitants in the exercise. By the time of King William's War impressment had been established as the routine method of manning the Navy, and in its operation it had elicited complaints about "irregular proceedings of the Captains of some Ships of War in the pressing of seamen." In response to these complaints, beginning in 1697 needy officers were required to apply to the colonial governors for permission to institute a press, and the Governor's instructions contained a new clause:

> . . . We have thought fit to order and have given directions to our High Admiral . . . , that when any Captain or Commander of any of our Ships of War in any of our . . . Plantations shall have occasion for seamen to serve on board our ships under their Command they do make their application to the Govrs and Commanders in Chief of our Plantations

respectively, to whom as Vice *Admirals*, we are pleased to commit the sole power of impressing seamen in any of our Plantations in America or in sight of any of them. You are therefore hereby required upon such application made to you by any of the Commanders of our said Ships of War within our Province . . . to take care that our said ships of War be furnished with the number of seamen that may be necessary for our service on Board them from time to time.[38]

The reforms at the end of King William's War had little effect on Naval abuses during Queen Anne's War. In the Spring of 1711 William Polhampton of New York complained to the Lords of Trade of certain practices in the Navy. In winter when warships were laid up, desertion was easy; he knew of small ships which had lost as many as sixty men during a winter, thus leaving French privateers in coastal waters unchallenged for want of crews to man the Navy. But instead of entering an "R" ("run") in the ship's books next to the deserters' names, certain commanders—Polhampton did not want to reflect on any one in particular—kept them listed for six, nine, and even more months and pocketed the allowance they were given for provisions. The ships' books were also inhabited by men who had died or been discharged.[39] Captains venal enough to turn desertion to their personal profit did not hesitate to use impressment for the same purpose. Thomas Miles, Captain of a sixth-rater, *Triton's Prize*, pressed men out of incoming vessels and then, "for certain considerations disposed of some of them to some Merchantmen then going out from this Port." On another occasion Miles had dismissed a midshipman who subsequently became a veritable entrepreneur of impressment, setting up shop for himself in a New York-based sloop while Governor Cornbury awaited "the ruin of this place." The people of New York were willing to serve the Queen, but, the Governor reported, "they think it very hard, that the Men must be pressed under pretence of the Queen's service, when indeed there is noe need of it."[40] But even *Triton's* two prizes acted perhaps more honorably than George Fane, Commander of frigate *Lowestaffe*, who waited until the Governor's back was turned to sabotage New York's privateers. Under the pretence that he needed work done on his ship, Fane pressed a carpenter despite the protection which the Governor had had to issue to get the carpenters to work on the ships. When Cornbury returned from New Jersey he ordered Fane to discharge his captive; instead the Commander put him in irons and released him only on the day of *Lowestaffe*'s departure. Fane's action had frightened the rest of the carpenters away, and Cornbury doubted that the merchants would be able to send their ships out that winter. Fane had also pressed some country people who were fishing, so that others were now afraid to come to market. The Governor, at his wits' end, was seriously considering firing on *Lowestaffe*.[41]

In 1708 a Parliament fearful of the effects of impressment on colonial trade passed a law forbidding the practice in America.[42] In New York the response was confused, and the legality of impressment remained a subject of debate. In 1711 Governor Hunter felt himself "pinioned" by the 1708 act; when New York's only ship-of-war was almost unmanned by death, desertion, and sickness Hunter followed his Council's advice and "borrowed" from other ships men their masters said they could spare. But the supercargo of a Bristol brigantine resisted and led the crew in an attack with handspikes on an officer and some soldiers who came to take one-half of the ship's men. One of the soldiers was knocked down and responded by shooting a drunk and especially troublesome seaman. The man died the next day, and the soldiers and officers were convicted of murder by a grand jury.[43] One may suppose that they had difficulty distinguishing between impressing and "borrowing."

Although the fear of impressment did disrupt the life of New York during the wars of the 1740's,[44] the city was a relatively safe haven compared to Boston, where the people complained that the Navy was taking a disproportionate number of men.[45] Here throughout the decade we find repeated instances of brutal press-gangs armed with illegal warrants or with no warrants at all attacking people in the streets and ships, thus creating shortages of seamen and of fuel and injuring trade and privateering. Popular resentment reached a peak in November of 1747 when Commodore Charles Knowles went on an impressment rampage, taking men—without a warrant—from all the vessels in the harbor and from the dock area. During the three days of rioting which followed, the Sheriff was assaulted, the Governor driven to Castle William for refuge, and a mob of several thousand controlled the town. Commodore Knowles was only with difficulty restrained from bombarding Boston to put down "arrant rebellion."[46]

Impressment During the French and Indian War

Hardly had the Treaty of Aix-la-Chapelle been signed when France and Britain resumed the competition left unresolved by the settlement, starting down the path which was to lead to the decisive conflict of French and English imperialism, the Seven Years' War. Commercial rivalry remained in the West Indies, fighting continued in India and erupted in North America early in 1754. Ships and men were needed, and, in England, the press grew hot—so hot that men were taken out of outbound ships, an action which occurred only under extreme circumstances. Special guards were ordered out in case of violent resistance, and all England, landsmen and seamen, trembled. (At Covent Garden "Nancy, or the Parting Lovers" became "The Press-Gang. or Love in Low Life," and Nancy nightly lost her lover to the Navy.)[47]

Early on a spring morning in 1756 the press-gang came back to New York. Marines, armed with clubs and pistols, came ashore at Murray's Wharf and hurried through the Fly Market. Disregarding their orders to press "only such as had the appearance of seafaring or labouring men," they entered houses and grabbed indiscriminately; some people fought back with canes, but most ran in fear; one man's coat was torn off as he was pursued down Wall Street by three sailors who finally tackled him, beat him bloody and unconscious with sticks, bound him and carried him away. As the marines set off in their boats with their captives a few small boys ventured to bombard them with stones.[48]

Late in July of 1756 news arrived of the British declaration of war on the French. Now a new cry was heard in New York. For "All Hearts of Oak, that have an Inclination to make their Fortunes" by "drubbing" the French it was "now or never":[49] *Sturdy Beggar* had "thrown away her Rags and Crutches, intending this Cruise to rigg the Beam, and dress the Gentleman."[50] There were indeed fortunes to be made and, in response, Lieutenant-Governor Delancey observed, "almost a kind of madness to go a privateering."[51] Within a week of the news more than a dozen ships were fitting out; early in September the sloop *Goldfinch* brought in the first prize.[52] By the following spring New York's privateers, captained by such men as Isaac Sears and Alexander McDougall, had brought in £200,000 sterling in prizes.[53] Before the peace of 1763 nearly 20,000 men[54] had sailed from New York hell-bent on drubbing the French—and the Spaniards—and making their fortunes. They did, and in doing so caused great inconvenience to French and Spanish commerce—and also to the Royal Navy.

Throughout the war higher wages and rich prizes lured men into privateers and away from the Navy.[55] New York was "drained of many able bodied men"—gone privateering[56]—and the Navy's business was frequently brought to a standstill for lack of seamen.[57] As in peacetime, men continued to desert—not to the merchant service but to more lucrative privateers. The Navy tried a soft line: all returning deserters "shall be well received, and pardon'd."[58] The Navy tried a hard line: " . . . all Persons, who shall harbour or conceal any Seaman, or other Deserter, belonging to any of his Majesty's Ships, . . . shall be prosecuted with the utmost Rigour of the Law."[59] Neither worked; Jack had found better business.

A license to go privateering could also be used to protect vessels actually engaged in trade with the enemy. The "Mount Trade"[60]—commerce with Cape Francois and Monte Christo—reached its peak in 1760;[61] in July of that year the Reverend Dr. Andrew Burnaby attributed New York's "flourishing" state to its extensive commerce, particularly its trade with the foreign West Indies.[62] But shortly thereafter this "Mungrell Commerce,"[63] as merchant John Watts called it, began to run into serious difficulties. Attempts had been made since the beginning of the war to put a stop to this economically essential but militarily disastrous commerce,[64] but a venal and inept customs service and Navy had accomplished little. (The Captain of privateer *Mars* deceived the Captain of H.M. Sloop *Bonita* and later took pleasure in asserting that his adversary was "as Green as a Leek in being so easily imposed upon.")[65] Besides, the legal status of much of this trade was undefined; New York's lawyers found no statute against it, while the Navy called it illegal. "No two Courts pursue the same Measure," protested John Watts: "A Stranger to form a Judgment . . . would imagine that the Nation in its Jurisdiction had neither Rule Law or probity & yet the Evil is suffer'd to go on without any determination, the Subject is torn to pieces by Robbers, Lawyers & all sorts of Virmin."[66] But with the shift of hostilities to the Caribbean after the fall of Canada late in 1760 the Navy's interpretation of the law began increasingly to make itself felt, until by the spring of 1762 New York's merchants found the West Indian trade, much to their disappointment, "entirely checkt."[67]

As the merchants profited from this trade, so did the seamen. In October of 1759 it was discovered that George Spencer, a bankrupt recently arrived from England, was an informer paid by the government to pass on information about illicit trade. On the evening of November 1 he was "Ill-treated" by several people in a coffeehouse. The following evening, after some of the city's leading merchants had cooked up a pretext to rid themselves of Spencer, Deputy Sheriff Philip Branson arrested him for debt. On their way to jail Branson saw fit to invite his companion to a tavern, where the officer called for wine and liquor. Meanwhile a cart was drawn up to the front of the tavern by a mob of "Sailors and others" who forced him into it and dragged him around the city, huzzaing and—Spencer unhappily recalled from his jail cell two years later—"Paulting me with Mud & Filth of the Streets, in a manner too Notorious to Recite." (" . . . One of the most Base, Cruel, Ignominious Actions . . . ever . . . committed in any Christian Country! Barbarity without Example": after taking refuge in "a

Gentleman's back Apartment out of the way of the Mob," Spencer was again accosted by a pistol-bearing Branson, who forced him onto a horse and rode to jail "like a Madman, huzzaing and Crying-Out He had got the Devil behind him & was riding to Hell.")[68]

As the privateers—the "militia of the sea"[69]—had suffered from normal wartime attrition,[70] some going into the lucrative trade with the foreign West Indies, some to the bottom of the sea, and as illicit traders surrendered the sea to a toughened Royal Navy, yet another source of competition for the limited manpower available to the Navy arose—the land forces.[71] In 1759 not one seaman was among the two hundred thirty-seven men enlisted in New York County companies of the Provincial troops; a £10 bounty and a pay of 1s 3d per day was not enough to lure any away from privateering or illicit trade.[72] The maximum daily pay to an able-bodied seaman, under a 1758 agreement made by the city's merchants, was 5s;[73] this exceeded militia pay and was itself a low figure when contrasted with the rewards of privateering. But in 1759, with the bounty up to £15 and an upstate land grant and the daily pay up an additional shilling, sixty-three of New York County's 301 troops (20.9%) were seamen.[74] Under the same terms of enlistment the percentage of seamen under arms rose in 1760 (114 of 371 or 30.8%)[75] and again in 1761 (91 of 257 or 35.4%).[76] In 1762 a bout between governor and assembly brought a reduction in the bounty to £10[77] and brought the number of seamen down to twenty-three, still 33.8% of the city's 68 men.[78] Although this was once again a hardly significant portion of the 3,552 seamen employed in New York vessels in 1762,[79] it does indicate that what with privateering, illicit commerce, and bounties to troops the Navy had a real manpower shortage on its hands.

The Navy turned to the usual solution—impressment. Throughout the war both impressment and the fear of impressment were constant facts in the lives of New York's seamen.[80] Often a capture was violent enough or involved enough people outside of the maritime community so that we have evidence of specific incidents. We have already presented an account of the incident in the spring of 1756;[81] some of the other incidents in the war years follow.

In the spring of 1757 Lord Loudoun was attempting to assemble a fleet to sail against Louisbourg. New York had cooperated to the extent of producing about one-half of the vessels needed for transport purposes.[82] Seamen were even more scarce, deserting the vessels either to go privateering or to avoid impressment into the Navy.[83] "In Order to prevent such Persons from absenting themselves, and as an Encouragement to them, and others, to engage in the said Service," Governor Charles Hardy assured them "that no Person employed in fitting out, or navigating such Ships or Vessels, shall be impressed into any other Service."[84] Meanwhile the Assembly put additional teeth into the law for apprehension of deserters by providing fines for privateer captains or masters of trading vessels who hired deserters.[85] In March Lord Loudoun sent Captain Falkingham of *Sutherland* to assist in securing hands.[86] Whether Falkingham resorted to the press or contented himself with more tender methods is not known. Regardless, his methods did not work, and in May, his sailing delayed for lack of seamen, Loudoun handed the whole business of recruitment over to Hardy. The Governor found the deserters safely harbored in the city and called on Loudoun for assistance against the tough privateersmen.[87] There followed a massive, efficiently executed operation in which the line between impressment and surprise attack is difficult to perceive.[88] At two in the morning on the twentieth of May Loudoun suddenly surrounded the city with about three thousand men. With this force guarding all escape routes, several parties of sailors under Hardy searched the taverns and other seamen's dives. The seamen found themselves overpowered, and in their dazed state, could make no resistance. The haul came to eight hundred men, including not only seamen but also tradesmen and Negroes; even after one-half had been released there were still enough to fill up the transports and to add to the strength of the men-of-war.

The operation ended in the day's first light, four hours after it had begun. During the night a number of men equal to more than one-quarter of the city's adult male population had been seized.[89] Even with one-half of them returned the city must have found itself crippled. As for the unlucky half: they were loaded on the transports, each of which was guarded by twenty soldiers, a sergeant, and a subaltern to keep the men from getting ashore or from overcoming their captors. Five days later the fleet sailed down to the Hook.[90] This was the crucial moment; many of the men, taken from their families in the dark of night, would never see them again, and they knew it. The vessels squeezed through the Narrows as rapidly as they could without running foul of each other. While this gruesome kidnapping of four hundred men was reaching its culmination, Governor Hardy was issuing new assurances, this time promising boatmen and marketmen bringing provisions to the King's ships that they would not be impressed.[91] Presumably, as on other occasions, they took the Governor at the reverse of his word and headed elsewhere.

In the spring of 1758 another expedition was preparing against Louisbourg. Once again the madness to go privateering and to avoid impressment had caused a shortage of men. Lieutenant-Governor Delancey and Philip Durell, Commander of His Majesty's Ships and

Vessels in North America, tried all the usual methods: promises and penalties. They promised that returned deserters would be pardoned and protected from impressment; they promised that men sailing small provision vessels would not be impressed. People harboring deserters would be punished; those turning them in would be rewarded.[92]

All of this did not prevent impressment of non-maritime personnel and equipment: wagoners, bateau-men, carpenters.[93] And, by mid-April, with sailing but two weeks off, James Montresor noted in his journal: "Arrived in the harbour the Prince of Orange Privateer, her hands pressed as all vessels are when they come in."[94]

At about two o'clock in the morning of Sunday, April 23, Captain Jasper Farmer of the militia led some of his company along the new dock and boarded snow *Charming Jenny* seeking men for the transport service and, possibly, revenge.[95] (A month before Farmer had been in a tavern brawl with some mariners; he thought he heard the word "coward" and charged one of them with a large hickory stick.[96]) He took several men and then turned to four others holed up in the roundhouse and armed with blunderbusses. He tried to entice them out with assurances that he was pressing for the transport service, not for the men-of-war. They replied by firing their guns through the loopholes, one shot hitting Farmer in the neck. Later they surrendered after an officer and a party of regulars came aboard and fired a volley into their fortress.

While Jasper Farmer was languishing—he died at ten Sunday evening and was buried and fittingly eulogized early in the week— another party of militia was out hunting for seamen. At about five in the morning in a house on the outskirts of the city they came upon nine sleeping Dutchmen; they had recently been brought in by some privateers. The Dutchmen refused to surrender; when an officer and more men were brought up as reinforcements, two of the men reconsidered while the seven others took shelter in the garret. The reconsideration was fatal: the officer ordered his men to fire up through an open trap-door, and they wounded one, killing the other with a ball which entered under his chin and emerged from the top of his head. Thus before the sun rose two murders had been committed in the process of impressing men for the transports in the harbor.

Recalling the events of August 1760[97] we can safely conclude that war-time impressment in New York had been a matter of armed attack and armed resistance, of pistols and clubs, blunderbusses, cutlasses and musquets, grape-shot, langrage and rocks. In the major known incidents a total of seven men were killed and many were brutally wounded; perfect information presumably would indicate a higher total. This naval warfare inevitably involved the land population. Much of the impressment took place on land amid a society deeply irritated by the disruption of its normal workings which responded with sympathy for the victims of impressment, sheltering seamen and refusing to consider as criminals those who fought back. And New York observed and considered: were the rights of man safe when men were impressed, day or night, off incoming or outgoing vessels? Were the rights of Englishmen safe when all this was done in contradiction to the clear statement of the law?

The Peace-Time War: New York vs. the Royal Navy

With the return of peace in 1763 New York's seamen thought the continuation of impressment unlikely.[98] Their minds were burdened with other problems. Twenty thousand seamen were being discharged from the Navy;[99] privateering was now a dead profession, its former practitioners able to find employment only in street mobs;[100] another group formerly employed on merchant vessels found jobs more and more difficult to get as a trade depression began.[101] Throughout the period from the Peace of Paris to the Declaration of Independence work at sea was to be scarce.[102]

The situation was worsened by a series of new trade regulations and practices[103] which interfered with the "circuity [sic] of commerce"[104] upon which New York's prosperity depended. New laws and new rigor in the enforcement of old laws seemed to spell doom for the vital West Indies trade, and what was bad for commerce was bad for seamen. Early in 1764 a widely printed "Essay on the Trade of the Northern Colonies" claimed that the new regulations had put twenty thousand seamen and fishermen out of work,[105] and New York's merchants worried that discharged men would have "no means of Subsistence, but by entering into, and augmenting a foreign Marine."[106]

The new regulations gave the Navy a new function: it was to take a vigorous role in the enforcement of customs regulations: "Whereas for the more effectual prevention of the infamous practice of smuggling, it may be necessary to employ several of the ships and vessels of war belonging to his Majesty," an act of 1763 sought to encourage officers and crews by ordering the division of proceeds of seized vessels and goods among them.[107] The King in Council supplemented this by specifically providing for the distribution of shares to trumpeters, quarter-gunners, carpenters, stewards, stewards' mates, cooks, cooks' mates, gunsmiths, ordinary trumpeters, barbers, able seamen, ordinary seamen, and swabbers.[108] In short, everyone from the swabber to the barber to the Ruler of the King's Navee was to have a share of the loot.

The Treasury pointed out "The Advantages of a Sea Guard," the Privy Council concurred,[109] and shortly a new squadron under a new commander inaugurated a coastal patrol.[110]

In June of 1764, Admiral Colville dispatched four vessels to raise men in the principal harbors between Casco Bay and Cape Henlopen,[111] that is, within the limits of the central four of the nine North American stations.[112] Lieutenant Thomas Laugharne's armed sloop *Chaleur* left Halifax and sailed down the coast without success until July 10. On that day he found five vessels anchored in a small Long Island bay. Suspecting illicit trade and hoping to recruit some men, Laugharne ordered his boat out with instructions to see if the vessels were well-manned and could spare a man apiece without endangering their safety. The boat returned with five men. On the following morning Laugharne stopped out of *Chaleur*'s moses boat on Manhattan Island, where he was greeted by a mob which immediately seized the boat. The mob advised Laugharne that he had taken fishermen; he lamely replied that they should have told him so, that he had not had the least intention of pressing men from market-boats or fishing-boats, and of course he would release them, if the mob would only leave his boat alone. He went into the coffeehouse and wrote out a note which he gave to the mob's leaders. By the time they had returned with the fishermen Laugharne had gone into hiding after receiving a message from Captain O'Brien of H.M.S. *Juno* that his life was in danger. The mob pulled the boat through the streets until they reached the front of the City Hall; there, to the sound of great shouts, *Chaleur*'s boat was burned. Then the mob dispersed just before the Mayor arrived. Only two men were apprehended; a court discovered that by afternoon everyone had forgotten everything; two weeks later a grand jury gave up the pursuit.[113]

So New York learned that the return of peace did not mean an end to impressment. The city met its continuation with a violent response and would continue to do so in the troubled decade following. Meanwhile New Yorkers' conduct served as a model for others: in June of 1765 "a Mob consisteing chiefly of Sailors, Boys and Negroes, to the Number of above Five Hundred" responded to H.M.S. *Maidstone*'s pressing the entire crew of a brigantine in Newport harbor by hauling the ship's boat onto the Common and burning it. Thus ended a month during which Captain Antrobus and his "Set of Myrmidons" had impressed not only from incoming vessels of every sort—thus driving seamen's wages up and frightening fuel-laden coasters away—but also "in the very Bowels of the Town."[114]

New Yorkers read about Newport's troubles[115] with one eye on their own myrmidons. Sloop *Hawke*, whose station was supposed to be "the Coasts of the Province of New York and New England between

Nantucket & Sandy Hook" was lounging in New York Bay taking men indiscriminately from sea vessels, coasters, and market boats. "Tis strange," the *New York Gazette; or, The Weekly Post-Boy* commented, "there should be such a Want of Hands in this Time of Peace." When one of *Hawke*'s officers made the mistake of pursuing a vessel right up to town, he was manhandled on the deck by a mob. This "mannerly Usage" was enough to keep Naval officers out of the city but not enough to evict them from the bay.[116]

Almost five months passed before cold weather forced *Hawke* and her companion vessel into winter quarters, where, commented a New Yorker, "they will no longer be able to act as Enemies to the Trade of this Place."[117] During that period the Royal Navy found itself on the losing side in a major battle which began early in September when *Hawke* was sent down to the Hook to await the arrival of New York's first shipment of stamps under the Stamp Act.[118] In the months of turmoil which followed, both common seamen and the Royal Navy played central roles.

The New York Stamp Act riots were led by privateer captains—men such as Isaac Sears and Alexander McDougall—and large numbers of seamen.[119] These men had been the victims—some indirectly, some quite directly—of impressment and thus had a real grievance against the Navy and the civilian administration which had cooperated with it. With the end of the war the privateersmen had lost their jobs, and since then they had had difficulty getting new ones. They blamed the new British legislation for their plight and took aggressive action against the Stamp Act, the latest link in a chain forged by a government which seemed to treat the Sons of Neptune little better than slaves.

The Navy's action during the height of the crisis was severely limited. Frigate *Coventry*, twenty-eight guns, one hundred sixty men,[120] was on hand; but her twenty-eight guns could do little more than fire noisy signals, for most of her one hundred sixty men were impressed and could not be relied upon. In a real sense these men functioned in support of their fellows ashore: Captain Kennedy could not risk sending more than twenty-four marines ashore as reinforcements lest his men desert,[121] and *Coventry* could not be considered a safe place to store the stamps because of her natural fifth column.[122]

But as November passed on to December and the more immediate crisis ended, the Navy found itself a role. As was so often the case, it involved conflict with the patterns of commerce preferred by New York's merchants and seamen. The latter wished to nullify the Stamp Act by proceeding with business as usual without stamps. They did so; under pressure of the continuation of trade without stamps, and fearing what action increasing numbers of seamen might take, the New York Custom House began to issue unstamped clearances early in December.[123] But the Navy was not so ready to throw the law over the side. Captain Kennedy declared that he would not allow the outward passage of vessels with unstamped clearances or without let-passes;[124] he had *Coventry* and *Garland* weigh anchor and move from the North to the East River.[125] Thus a naval comedy developed in which ships meeting all of the customs officers' requirements would set out, only to be stopped and turned back by the Navy. Some few sneaked through at night—ten had escaped unstamped by December 24—but in general commerce continued to stagnate.[126]

The people acted—they burned Colville's effigy[127] and advertised their intent to destroy the effects of the captains of the men-of-war[128]— but only the weather put an end to the Navy's private blockade.[129] With the vessels in winter quarters a new source of conflict arose: the captains of the ships allowed their men to hire themselves out for various waterfront jobs, and the men were willing to work for lower wages than those demanded by New Yorkers.[130] Some of the civil-naval antagonisms were given vent when Lieutenant Hallam of Man-of-War *Garland* told Captain Normand Tolmie that New Yorkers were traitors, that anyone who opposed the Stamp Act deserved a halter around his neck and that he—the Lieutenant—might take on the job. Captain Tolmie advised Lieutenant Hallam to watch his language, lest he find a halter around his own neck. To which Hallam replied "that they might be damn'd and might kiss his Arse." This was the last thing the Sons of Liberty were prepared to do, and a committee boarded the *Garland* to demand that Hallam backtrack. He denied that he had ever said anything, but when the committee returned with affidavits sworn to by Tolmie and other witnesses he ordered them ashore. A mob offered Hallam some of his own advice: " . . . bring the Lieut. ashore with a Halter about his Neck." The following day the Sons of Liberty assembled to assault *Garland* and stopped only out of respect for the powder and cartridges newly loaded (or, as they put it, because they refused to commit an outrage against the Crown.) Hallam, they promised, would remain safe only so long as he kept himself on board *Garland*.[131]

When the ice cleared, Captain St. John was thirsty for revenge, and *Garland*, along with *Coventry*, returned to the old game of impressment.[132] On April 21 Garland fired several shots at ship *Prince George*, in from Bristol in nine weeks, and at an unnamed brig in from Oporto in thirteen weeks, to bring them to. The brig obeyed, and the men from *Garland*'s boat boarded her; but in *Prince George* the crew had taken command from the captain and officers and would neither bring the ship to nor allow the boat to board her. *Garland* was forced to retire after one of the men in her boat was seriously wounded in an attempt to shoot their way on board *Prince George*.[133] Impressment continued, and New Yorkers yearned to take the captains to court.[134]

His Majesty's Navy continued to employ itself in "distressing the trade of the colonies"[135] up to and, of course, during the Revolution.[136] Impressment continued throughout the colonies, and the response was, if anything, more violent. In 1768 H.M.S. *Romney* pressed in Boston Harbor, causing a riot in which a customs collector's boat was burned.[137] In 1769 a party from Frigate *Rose* boarded the Marblehead brigantine *Pitt Packet* in pursuit of four men. The seamen retreated to the forepeak, swearing they would not be taken alive; when the battle was over two of the seamen were seriously wounded, and Lieutenant Panton of *Rose* was dead, his jugular vein pierced by a harpoon. A court called the killing justifiable homicide.[138]

The Navy's conduct grew more vindictive, less rational, and more brutal.[139] An Admiral punished Marblehead for the detention of a shipment of wax candles imported for his own personal use by issuing press warrants.[140] In July of 1773 the crew of brig *Mary* deserted to avoid impressment by Frigate *Lively*, anchored off Staten Island. Seemingly angered by his failure to catch them, the captain of *Lively* sent a boat to harass the brig. The captain, the mate, and a few passengers, in response to some arbitrary commands, were doing the best job they could with the sails, but it was not good enough, and the boat opened fire—"unnaturally, unjustly, and brutally," as one New Yorker saw it. One ball whistled past the captain as he stood at the helm, and another went between the mate's legs. The whole attack seemed motivated by an urge to compete in brutality with the late *Gaspee*; it was a flagrant breach, "not only of our invaluable constitution, but even of the Law of Nature."[141] *Lively* went on impressing.[142]

This intensification of the attack on American shipping was part of what Oliver M. Dickerson calls "customs racketeering."[143] Lured by profits from confiscation and sometimes, it would seem, simply by the opportunity to exercise tyrannical power, the "Marmadonian Ravens" of the Royal Navy engaged in a war on many fronts. All of their activities hurt seamen by hurting trade, but seamen were especially victimized by impressment and, after 1768, by new practices which interfered with their traditional right to import petty items as private ventures, separate from the cargo and from the captain's concern.[144] So firmly was this custom established that it was generally accepted that the seaman who did not engage in such importations had a right to the freight charges which a cargo would have brought.[145] But the new Board of Customs Commissioners challenged the ancient custom by considering the seaman's importations, even the contents of his sea-chest—traditionally unlocked[146]—as part of the cargo, and thus subject to confiscation if not listed in the cockets. The Board advised owners of vessels "to suppress the Custom of suffering the Seaman to take in private ventures,"[147] and the Navy proceeded to confiscate what was, by ancient custom, the seaman's property. Thus the seaman whose person was not impressed increasingly ran the risk of having his personal possessions impressed into the coffers of a Naval officer.

Jack Tar's Life, Liberty, and Property

The impressment of seamen in America had been illegal since 1708. Not until after the outbreak of fighting in America—and for reasons totally unconnected with that fighting—did Parliament repeal the act known as "the sixth of Anne."[148] That act, more formally "An Act for the Encouragement of the Trade to America," had said:

> no marriner or other person who shall serve on Board, or be retained to serve on Board, any Privateer or Trading Ship or Vessel that shall be employed in any Part of America, nor any mariner or other person, being on shore in any part thereof, shall be liable to be Impressed or taken away or shall be impressed or taken away, by any Officer or Officers of, or belonging to any of Her Majesty's Ships of War, Empowered by the Lord High Admiral, or any other person whatsoever, unless such mariner shall have before deserted from such ship of War, belonging to her Majesty at any time after the Fourteenth day of February one thousand seven hundred & seven upon pain that any officer or officers so Impressing or taking away, or causing to be Impressed or taken away any Mariner or other person contrary to the tenour and true meaning of this Act, shall forfeit to the Master or Owner or Owners of any such Ship or Vessel twenty pounds for every man he or they shall so impress or take, to be recovered with full costs of suit in any Court within any Part of Her Majesty's Dominions.[149]

This act was passed largely to protect valuable American commerce against the disruption caused by impressment. As we have seen it did not succeed; impressment continued under the act as before, and during the sixty-seven years between passage and repeal the central item of debate was not whether impressment ought to stop but whether an act exempting America from the press did indeed exist.

In June of 1709 a captain asked Lieutenant-Governer Ingoldsby of New York for seamen. This followed the practice in existence since 1697[150] and suggested a possible conflict of laws: did the sixth of Anne over-rule that section of the governor's instructions directing him to provide seamen when needed, or did the 1708 act merely prohibit officers of the Navy from impressing, leaving civil authorities a free hand? On June 18 the Council passed the question to the Chief Justice and the Attorney-General of the Province.[151] Two weeks later Chief Justice Mompesson offered a ringing opinion which harked back to a glorious age only two decades before.[152] "An Act declaring the Rights and Liberties of the Subjects," passed in the first year of the reign of William and Mary, declared

> That the pretended power of suspending laws or the execution of laws by the Royal Authority without Consent of Parliament, is illegal.
>
> That the pretended power of dispensing with laws by Regal Authority as it hath been assumed & exercised of late, is illegal.

What did this have to do with the impressment of seamen in America? Mompesson's reading of the sixth of Anne was utterly straightforward, totally unclouded by any equivocal legalism: "the prohibition is general as to all on shoar. . . ." Thus impressment by the governor would be regal usurpation, punishable by indictment "or by action of the Statute by the party grieved. . . ."[153]

Had all the officers of the Crown been so sensitive to Parliamentary supremacy, governors and Naval officers would have deferred to the clear intent of Parliament, and there would have been no impressment problem in America. The Governor's Council sensed the weight of Mompesson's opinion and concurred (although they expressed some doubt as to whether "the Act exempts persons on shoar *not* belonging to any merchant ship or privatier from being impressed by the Civill Magistrate.")[154] But in so concluding the Council had disagreed with Attorney-General Rayner, a man far more attentive to giving "all possible obedience . . . to her Majesty's Commands . . ." and thus to the governor's instructions. These instructions, he noted, were supported by the Admiralty's orders to captains to apply to the colonial governors for men, and these directions had continued to be issued after the passage of the 1708 act; "I take it that the late Act of Parliament only intended to secure the ships and vessels here, their men, and not to tye up the hands of government from making provisions for men of War. . . ."[155] In England the Queen's Attorney-General[156] and Solicitor-General were equally devoted to untying the hands of government, and they sided with Rayner. "Now 'tis my humble Opinion," announced Solicitor-General Robert Eyre concerning the crucial section of the sixth of Anne,

> that this Clause Extends only to the Officers of Her Majesty's Ships of War, who are apt to [be] Irregular in the Execution of this Power and not to restrain the Sovereign Authority from Impressing Men for the public Service by Civil Officers; For Officers of or belonging to Her Majesty's Ships of War are the only persons prohibited, and the Penalty extends to no others; The Prohibition is not general, neither can any person be punished for transgression of this Act, but an officer of or belonging to Her Majesty's Ships of War; And taking all the Parts of the clause together, it can't be imagined that it was Design'd to take away a Prerogative of the Crown, in which the common security of the Plantations is so much concern'd, by depriving the Govr. in America, of the power of providing the necessary Supplies of Men, for her Majesty's Ships of War, sent for the protection of Trade, and the Defence of the Plantations.[157]

This conflict of interpretations left the true meaning of the act of 1708 a moot question indeed. But activites of other crown agencies helped to clarify it. Late in 1709, after consultation with the Secretary of State, the Board of Trade decided to omit the clause directing governors to impress men for her Majesty's service from the instructions sent to Robert Hunter, New York's new Governor.[158] Meanwhile the Admiralty, which had always acknowledged the clear prohibition against its impressment activities, instructed commanders in America to comply with the sixth of Anne. With the government's hands tied up—"pinioned," as Governor Hunter saw it—new expedients had to be found. One ingenious scheme was to "borrow" men from merchant vessels, to be returned on conclusion of a voyage. Perhaps this contented masters who, in 1711, were restricted by an embargo anyway, but to the men it was indistinguishable from impressment.[159]

With the return of peace in 1713 the question arose whether the sixth of Anne was only a wartime measure. Certainly there is nothing in the act to indicate that it should expire upon the cessation of hostilities, but it was so interpreted by Crown officers such as the Attorney-General, who declared in 1716, "I am of opinion the whole

American Act was intended, and appears to have been intended only for the War." The Admiralty did not agree, and its instructions to American commanders continued to refer to the Act. Then, in 1723, the Admiralty decided that it did agree, and began to omit the prohibition of impressment from its instructions. But colonial governors' instructions continued to treat the act as valid. Thus all was confusion, and confusion gave license for renewed impressment. As far as anyone in America knew—including Governor Shirley of Massachusetts—the sixth of Anne was still in force, and impressment was as illegal as it was universal.

Impressment produced mobs and riots during the wars of the 'forties, during the French and Indian War, and, as we have seen, it did not end with the Peace of Paris. With an inconsistency for which "paradox" is but a weak description and "faith" but a partial explanation, belief persisted in the legality of the sixth of Anne. In 1766 some members of the House of Lords opposed the repeal of the Stamp Act because colonists already exempt from impressment might seek exemption from paying for their own defense. Two years later, after *Romney*'s attempt to press in Boston Harbor brought a violent response, John Adams expressed the will of the people of Boston when he drew up special instructions to their respresentatives, quoting the 1708 act and reminding them that impressment was a violation of that act.[160] In 1769 Adams defended the seamen charged with killing Lieutenant Panton of H.M.S. *Rose*.[161] During the trial his copy of the volume of the *Statutes at Large*—the only one in Boston—containing the sixth of Anne lay on the table before him. It was Adams' intention to read the relevent sections of the act and thus to demonstrate the illegality of impressment. Sensing the danger, Governor Hutchinson swiftly and suddenly ordered the court adjourned. The next morning the decision—justifiable homicide in necessary self-defence—was announced, and the government successfully avoided embarrassment. Many years afterwards Adams explained the trial's rapid conclusion by the court's dread of having the statute publicized.

The repeal of the sixth of Anne in 1775 is, of course, final and conclusive evidence that it had been on the books—if nowhere else— since 1708. But since impressment had in fact continued largely unhindered throughout the act's paper existence, one wonders about the legality of impressment on a broader geographical scale. Was it legal in England? Certainly. But this is not to say that its legality was unchallenged. Blackstone—and Lord Mansfield—deplored it, finding it justifiable only on grounds of public necessity.[162] But earlier Coke had declared it illegal for the King to impress men to serve him in his wars.[163] Strong support, and consistent action, came from John Wilkes,

New York's favorite radical. In 1768 thousands of sailors demonstrated their support of "Wilkes and Liberty" while striking for higher wages, all amidst great violence and culminating in a mass march on Parliament.[164] Late in 1770 and in January of 1771, while an extremely hot press was in progress throughout England,[165] the Alderman obstructed impressment in the City of London—calling it a "suspension of *Magna Charta*"[166]—by refusing to back warrants and by discharging men snatched up by that "set of lawless ruffians,"[167] the press-gang. Under Wilkes' leadership the Common Council decided to prosecute, in the name of the victims of impressment, any justices of the peace who granted or backed press warrants and all constables who executed them.[168] In New York the Sons of Liberty, gathered for their annual celebration of the repeal of the Stamp Act, toasted "The spirited Corporation of the City of London."[169]

Unhappily for Great Britain, Wilkes was wrong when he asserted that impressment violated *Magna Charta*. The practice was well established before 1215, and it continued uninterrupted after the sealing of the Charter; *Nullus liber homo capiatur* did not apply to seamen.[170] Thus, far from being unconstitutional, the existence of impressment indicated a grave defect in the English Constitution. Viewing England from Geneva in 1771, the democrat Jean Louis Delolme saw some flaws in an otherwise praiseworthy constitution: he especially noted the impressment of seamen.[171] Benjamin Franklin had not law enough to dispute its legality, but he was certain impressment was inequitable. Cite modern practice, or cite ancient precedents, "Both the one and the other only show that the constitution is yet imperfect, since in so general a case it doth not secure liberty, but destroys it . . .": "If impressing seamen is of right by common law in Britain, slavery is then of right by common law there; there being no slavery worse than that sailors are subjected to."[172]

No one ever stopped a seaman running "like Hell out of A Great Gun"[173] to ask him how he justified his flight from the press-gang. He was running to save his skin. Law could not protect him, nor could the Constitution itself. He ran to preserve his life, his liberty, his property, and in his desperate sprint he was many decades ahead of the rest of the American population; only later, and under similar pressures, would his fellows ashore realize that they had no protection for their natural rights as British subjects. Sometimes others, more articulate than the seaman, sensed the meaning of his flight, as in 1754, when a New York newspaper reprinted from a London paper a comment on the "cruel and tyrannic" institution of impressment:

That the hardy Sailor, who has just survived the Fury of
the Seas, and the Rage of Elements, should be immediately
torn from the Bosom of his Friends and Family, and, without
the least Prospect of Honour or Advantage, compelled to re-
visit barbarous Shores, is inconsistent with Civil Liberty, and
the natural Rights of Mankind.[174]

When Americans finally took to arms to defend their natural rights,
their act was not without precedent, for in their midst were men with an
ancient tradition of violent resistance to British tyranny based not on
the rights of Englishmen—for to be an Englishman was not to be free
of impressment—but on the rights of man.

* * * * * * *

In the Summer of 1814 Marinus Willett, former sea captain and
hero of the Revolution, now aged threescore and fourteen, came to City
Hall Park to plead for unity against "the haughty, cruel, and
gasconading nation that makes war against us." He recalled for his
audience an earlier day: "Fifty-eight years now are passed since I was a
witness of press-gangs traversing these streets, and dragging men from
their houses on board of ships of war!"[175] Once again that gasconading
nation was trying to enslave free Americans. The scene was the same—
off New York Harbor, within sight of Sandy Hook. Now it was
Leander, or *Guerriere*, instead of *Winchester* or *Chaleur*; not *Sampson*,
but *Spitfire*. But the issues were remarkably similar, and a folk memory
of tyranny at sea played a role whose significance can only be
guessed.[176]

Marinus Willett, Alexander McDougall, and Isaac Sears saw British
tyranny at first hand through impressment.[177] Thousands of others,
American seamen who sailed under these and other captains, suffered
more directly, and this helps to explain their patriotism in 1776 and in
the years following. Other thousands who never set foot in a ship knew
that their fuel was more expensive or their food more limited because of
that man-of-war off the Hook. And every man (and some men who were
little more than children) knew that they were not free so long as that
ship was there. Thus it was that an old sailor's song became the
common property of the whole population:

Hearts of oak we are still;
For we're sons of those men
    Who always are ready —
    Steady, boys, steady —
To fight for freedom again and again.[178]

Notes

1. A seaman who deserted his ship would have an "R"—for "run"—written against his name. For the song see Hutchinson, *Press-Gang*, p. 151.

2. The King v. Ship *Sampson*, Examination of Hugh Mode, Pilot, taken August 19, 1760, New York Supreme Court: Pleadings K-304; *New-York Gazette*, August 25, 1760 (hereafter cited as *Gazette*); Cadwallader Colden to Lords of Trade, August 30, 1760: *N Y Col Docs*, VII, 446; Council Session, August 20, 1760: *Calendar of Council Minutes, 1668–1783* (New York State Library, *Bulletin 58* [March, 1902]), p. 449 (hereafter cited as *Calendar of Council Minutes*).

3. The King v. Ship *Sampson*, Examination of Hugh Mode, Pilot, taken August 19, 1760, New York Supreme Court: Pleadings K-304; *Gazette*, August 25, 1760; The King v. Osborn Greatrakes, October 30, 1760, New York Supreme Court: Minute Book (1756–1761), p. 215, Office of County Clerk, Hall of Records, New York City; The King v. Gatrap [Greatrakes] Recognizance of Thomas Cunningham, August 27, 1760, New York Supreme Court: Pleadings K-375; Cadwallader Colden to Lords of Trade, August 30, 1760: *N Y Col Docs*, VII, 446.

4. The King v. Ship *Sampson*, Examination of Hugh Mode, Pilot, taken August 19, 1760, New York Supreme Court: Pleadings K-304; *Post-Boy*, August 21, 1760; *Gazette*, August 25, 1760; Cadwallader Colden to Lords of Trade, August 30, 1760: *N Y Col Docs*, VII, 446.

5. *Ibid.*; *Gazette*, August 25, 1760.

6. *Ibid.*; Cadwallader Colden to Thomas Boone, August 21, 1760: *The Colden Letter Books, 1760–1775* (New-York Historical Society, *Collections*, 1876–1877 [New York, 1877–1878]), I, 11 (hereafter cited as *Colden Letter Books*).

7. *Post-Boy*, April 28, 1760.

8. *Ibid.*, April 28, July 31, 1760; *New-York Mercury*, August 4, 1760 (hereafter cited as *Mercury*).

9. Cadwallader Colden to Lords of Trade, August 30, 1760: *N Y Col Docs*, VII, 446; *Post-Boy*, August 7, 1760. One must exercise a certain skepticism toward these supposed mutinies. They were often staged with the cooperation of the captain and officers. See Hutchinson, *Press-Gang*, pp. 144–145.

10. *Gazette*, July 28, August 11, 18, 1760; *Mercury*, August 18, 1760; Cadwallader Colden to Thomas Boone, August 21, 1760: *Colden Letter Books*, I, 11; Cadwallader Colden to Lords of Trade, August 30, 1760: *N Y Col Docs*, VII, 446.

11. *Ibid.*; Cadwallader Colden to Lords of Trade, February 18, 1761: *ibid.*, VII, 454; Council Sessions, August 20, 21, 1760: *Calendar of Council Minutes*, p. 449; *Gazette*, August 25, 1760; Cadwallader Colden to Thomas Boone, Ausust 21, 1760: *Colden Letter Books*, I, 11–12; Francis Bernard to Cadwallader Colden, September 6, 1760: *The Letters and Papers of Cadwallader Colden, 1711–1775* (New-York Historical Society, *Collections*, 1917–1923, 1934–1935 [New York, 1918–1937]), V, 334 (hereafter cited as *Colden Letters and Papers*); J. T. Kempe to Cadwallader Colden, [October 11, 1760]: *ibid.*, V, 345. Henry B. Dawson, *The Sons of Liberty in New-York* (New York, 1859), p. 53 states outright that the townspeople gave *Sampson's* crew shelter. This is probably so, but the sources only justify a slightly more cautious statement. (Hereafter cited as Dawson, *Sons of Liberty*.)

12. Cadwallader Colden to Lords of Trade, February 18, 1761: *N Y Col Docs*, VII, 454–455; The King v. Osborn Greatrakes and The King v. Josiah Moore, October 24, 28, 30, November 11–17, 1760, New York Supreme Court: Minute Book (1756–1761), pp. 1–6, 200, 209, 215; Cadwallader Colden to J. T. Kempe, October 11, 1760: *Colden Letter Books*, I, 30; Cadwallader Colden to J. T. Kempe, October 15, 1760: *Colden Letters and Papers*, V, 348; Council Sessions, November 4, 5, December 3, 1760: *Calendar of Council Minutes*, pp. 450–451; Edmund B. O'Callaghan, ed., *Calendar of New York Colonial Commissions, 1680–1770* (New York, 1929), p. 43. On the question of jurisdiction see Julius Goebel, Jr., and T. Raymond Naughton, *Law Enforcement in Colonial New York: A Study in Criminal Procedure, 1664–1776* (New York, 1944), pp. 307–309. Hereafter cited as Goebel and Naughton, *Law Enforcement*.

13. Hutchinson, *Press-Gang*, pp. 6–7, 311. Anyone fortunate enough to be familiar with this magnificent and delightfully written book will see my indebtedness to Hutchinson for this general account of impressment. Unfortunately Hutchinson's interest is restricted almost entirely to England, and much of the book deals with the history of impressment after the American Revolution. I have also used Dora Mae Clark, "The Impressment of Seamen in the American Colonies" in *Essays in Colonial History Presented to Charles McLean Andrews by his Students* (New Haven, 1931), pp. 198–224. Hereafter cited as Clark, "Impressment," *Andrews Essays*. This is an excellent account of the laws regarding impressment in America, and as such it is indispensable. But in neglecting the moral and human aspects of the institution and the resistance to it, Clark misses what must have been its major significance to those who suffered by it. Also useful was R. Pares, "The Manning of the Navy in the West Indies, 1702–63" in Royal Historical Society, *Transactions*, fourth series, XX (1937), 31–60. Hereafter cited as Pares, "Manning the Navy." Despite the limitations of its title, this essay was enlightening in regard to developments elsewhere.

14. Kenneth Stampp, *The Peculiar Institution: Slavery in the Ante-Bellum South* (New York, 1956), p. 422.

[15.] See above, pp. 31–36.

[16.] Nonetheless many correctly contended that the work could be done more efficiently by adequately paid and freely employed men.

[17.] Hutchinson, *Press-Gang*, pp. 31–36.

[18.] Will of James Nelson: *Wills*, VII, 64.

[19.] *Post-Boy*, June 2, 1755.

[20.] See Hutchinson, *Press-Gang*, pp. 36–40.

[21.] *Ibid.*, pp. 40–41.

[22.] Remarks on Judge Foster's Argument in Favor of Impressing Seamen: Jared Sparks, ed., *The Works of Benjamin Franklin* (Boston, 1837–44), II, 333. Hereafter cited as Sparks, *Works of Franklin*. Sparks gives this no date; John Bigelow, *The Complete Works of Benjamin Franklin* (New York, 1887–88), IV, 70 dates it 1767; Helen C. Boatfield of the Mason-Franklin Collection, Yale University Library speculates that it may be from the period 1782–83. Although it would be helpful to establish a precise date, the substance of Franklin's comments remains relevant, regardless of date.

[23.] Hutchinson, *Press-Gang*, p. 46; *Post-Boy*, April 17, 1758, December 5, 1768.

[24.] *Ibid.*, March 27, 1758; *Gazette*, August 11, 1760; Hutchinson, *Press-Gang*, p. 46.

[25.] Archibald Kennedy to Cadwallader Colden, November 1, 1765: *Colden Letters and Papers*, VII, 86.

[26.] Hutchinson, *Press-Gang*, p. 44.

[27.] Pares, "Manning the Navy," in Royal Historical Society, *Transactions*, fourth series, XX (1937), 31–38.

[28.] *Ibid.*, p. 38; William Polhampton to Lords of Trade, March 6, 1711; *N Y Col Docs*, V, 194.

[29.] *Ibid.*

[30.] During the Revolution the American Navy had the same problem. See Morison, *John Paul Jones*, p. 68.

[31.] Pares, "Manning the Navy," in Royal Historical Society, *Transactions*, fourth series, XX (1937), 33–34; Hutchinson, *Press-Gang*, pp. 48–49; *Post-Boy*, March 11, 1771; Benjamin Franklin, Remarks on Judge Foster's Argument in Favor of Impressing Seamen; Sparks, *Works of Franklin*, II, 333. Franklin states that pressed men served for 25s per month as against £3 15s per month in the merchant service.

[32.] Hutchinson, *Press-Gang*, p. 22; for some bounty notices see *Post-Boy*, March 31, April 21, 1755, January 14, 1771; *Journal*, June 10, 1773.

[33.] *Post-Boy*, January 14, 1771.

34. *Ibid.*, June 27, 1765; Benjamin Franklin to Joseph Galloway, April 7, 1759: ms. #226, Mason-Franklin Collection, Yale University Library; Cadwallader Colden to Lords of Trade, August 30, 1760: *N Y Col Docs*, VII, 446.

35. Richard B. Morris, *Government and Labor in Early America* (New York, 1946), p. 274. Hereafter cited as Morris, *Government and Labor*.

36. *Post-Boy*, July 12, 1764.

37. Cadwallader Colden to Lords of Trade, August 30, 1760: *N Y Col Docs*, VII, 446.

38. Instructions to Lord Bellomont, August 31, 1697: *ibid.*, IV, 287; Instructions to Lord Lovelace, [n.d.]: *ibid.*, V, 101.

39. William Polhampton to Lords of Trade, March 6, 1711: *ibid.*, V, 194.

40. Lord Cornbury to Lords of Trade, October 3, 1706: *ibid.*, IV, 1172, 1183–1184.

41. Lord Cornbury to Lords of Trade, December 14, 1706: *ibid.*, IV, 1190–1191. Fane later publicly declared that he hated the whole Province and would not help a New York vessel in distress at sea if he met one: Lord Cornbury to Lords of Trade, July 1, 1708: *ibid.*, V, 60. For an instance of Naval insubordination to the Crown in Boston see Clark, "Impressment," *Andrews Essays*, p. 205.

42. 6 Anne, c. 37, known as "the sixth of Anne." For a discussion of the act and of the legality of impressment, see below, pp. 31–36.

43. Governor Hunter to Secretary St. John, September 12, 1711: *N Y Col Docs*, V, 254–255.

44. *Post-Boy*, October 1, 1744.

45. Morris, *Government and Labor*, p. 276; Clark, "Impressment," *Andrews Essays*, p. 218.

46. For accounts of impressment in Boston in the 1740's see Bridenbaugh, *Cities in Revolt*, pp. 26, 114–117; Clark, "Impressment," *Andrews Essays*, pp. 215–218.

47. *Ibid.*, pp. 199n.–200n.; *Post-Boy*, April 8, 15, 1754, March 31, 1755; Hutchinson, *Press-Gang*, p. 261.

48. William M. Willett, *A Narrative of the Military Actions of Colonel Marinus Willett, Taken Chiefly from his own Manuscript* (New York, 1831), pp. 9–10, 149–150 (hereafter cited as Willett, *Narrative*); Howard Thomas, *Marinus Willett* (Prospect, New York, 1954), pp. 2–4 (hereafter cited as Thomas, *Willett*).

49. This attempt to recruit men for a voyage—actually, against the *Spanish*—appeared in *Post-Boy*, June 24, 1762. Similar exhortations— none so delightfully phrased— appeared throughout the war. See *ibid.*, August 2, 1756.

50. *Ibid.*, October 2, 1758.

51. Lieutenant-Governor Delancey to Secretary Pitt, March 17, 1758: *N Y Col Docs*, VII, 343.

52. Stuyvesant Fish, *The New York Privateers, 1756–1763: King George's Private Ships of War which cruised against the King's Enemies* (New York, 1945), pp. 4, 7, 88. Hereafter cited as Fish, *New York Privateers.*

53. Lord Loudoun to Pitt, May 30, 1757: Gertrude Selwyn Kimball, ed., *Correspondence of William Pitt* (New York, 1906), I, 69. Hereafter cited as Kimball, *Pitt Correspondence.*

54. Fish, *New York Privateers*, p. 4.

55. Lord Loudoun to Pitt, May 30, 1757: Kimball, *Pitt Correspondence*, I, 69. The Continental Navy had to cope with the same problem during the Revolution: Morison, *John Paul Jones*, p. 34.

56. Lieutenant-Governor Delancey to Secretary Pitt, March 17, 1758; *N Y Col Docs*, VII, 343.

57. Lord Loudoun to Pitt, March 10, May 30, 1757: Kimball, *Pitt Correspondence*, I, 19, 69. The Admiralty was desperate enough so that on one occasion it sought, without success, to hire German mercenaries as marines: see Lords of Admiralty to Lord Halifax, July 22, 1763: James Redington, ed., *Calendar of Home Office Papers of the Reign of George III* (London, 1878–1879), I, 296. Hereafter cited as Redington, *Calendar of Home Office Papers.*

58. *Post-Boy*, March 27, 1758.

59. *Ibid.*, April 17, 1758.

60. John Watts to Isaac Barre, February 28, 1762: *Letter Book of John Watts, Merchant and Councillor of New York: January 1, 1762–December 22, 1765* (New-York Historical Society, *Collections*, 1928 [New York, 1928]), p. 27. Hereafter cited as *Watts Letter Book.*

61. George L. Beer, *British Colonial Policy, 1754–65* (New York, 1907), p. 131. Hereafter cited as Beer, *British Colonial Policy.*

62. Andrew Burnaby, *Travels through the Middle Settlements in North-America. In the Years 1759 and 1760. With Observations upon the State of the Colonies* (Ithaca, New York, 1960), 81. Hereafter cited as Burnaby, *Travels.*

63. John Watts to Isaac Barre, February 28, 1762: *Watts Letter Book*, p. 27.

64. Lords of Trade to Governors in America, October 9, 1756: *N Y Col Docs*, VII, 162; Beer, *British Colonial Policy*, p. 78.

65. New York Supreme Court, pleadings K-1051.

66. John Watts to Isaac Barre, February 28, 1762: *Watts Letter Book*, p. 27.

[67.] John Watts to John Erving, May 30, 1762: *ibid.*, p. 60. An interesting measure of the Navy's increased strength is found in the decline of marine insurance rates from 15% in 1757 to 6–7% in 1761: Philip L. White, *The Beekmans of New York in Politics and Commerce, 1647–1877* (New York, 1956), p. 373. Hereafter cited as White, *Beekmans.*

[68.] Petition of George Spencer, November 25, 1761: *Colden Letters and Papers*, VI, 93–94. For details of the case see also Milton M. Klein, "The Rise of the New York Bar: The Legal Career of William Livingston," *William and Mary Quarterly*, third series, XV (July, 1958), 348–349; Goebel and Naughton, *Law Enforcement*, pp. 280–283.

[69.] Howard M. Chapin, *Privateer Ships and Sailors: The First Century of American Colonial Privateering, 1625–1725* (Toulon, France, 1926), p. 7.

[70.] As of June 16, 1760 only two New York privateers were on cruise: Stuyvesent Fish, "Log of Cruises of New York Privateer Duke of Cumberland, Capt. James Lilley, 1758–1760," New-York Historical Society, *Quarterly Bulletin*, XXIX (July, 1945), 169.

[71.] Again, this was another problem with which the Continental Navy would have to cope: Morison, *John Paul Jones*, p. 55.

[72.] The same situation held true throughout the Province in 1758; figures for seamen out of total enlisted in other counties are: Dutchess, 0/80 or 0%; Queens, 5/269 or 1.9%; Westchester, 3/381 or .8%. These figures are derived from *Muster Rolls*, pp. 54–135. Information about bounties and wages in *ibid.*, p. 51. The *Muster Rolls* give no professional identifications before 1758.

[73.] *Post-Boy*, August 7, 1758.

[74.] *Muster Rolls*, pp. 134–213, 515–517.

[75.] *Ibid.*, pp. 212–341, 523–524.

[76.] *Ibid.*, pp. 342–419, 530–531.

[77.] Cadwallader Colden to Lord Egremont, April 7, 1762: *Colden Letter Books*, I, 192–193; *Journal of the Votes and Proceedings of the General Assembly of the Colony of New-York. Began the 8th Day of November 1743; and Ended the 23d of December, 1765* (New York, 1766), II, 690–691, 701. Hereafter cited as *Assembly Journal.*

[78.] *Muster Rolls*, pp. 421–481, 533–534.

[79.] Report of Governor Tryon on the Province of New York, June 11, 1774: *N Y Col Docs*, VIII, 446.

[80.] Lack of evidence of impressment in the year 1759 might indicate simply that there was no newsworthy violence in connection with what had become a routine operation. Certainly it would seem unlikely that the press-gang should take a year off in the midst of the war and then return to its business. In addition it must always be remembered that we are dealing with a situation in which the victims usually left no reports and the perpetrators had no desire to publicize their activities.

81. See above, p. 21.

82. Lord Loudoun to Pitt, March 10, 1757: Kimball, *Pitt Correspondence*, I, 19.

83. Lord Loudoun to Pitt, May 30, 1757: *ibid.*, I, 69.

84. *Post-Boy*, March 7, 1757.

85. *Ibid.*, March 14, 1757.

86. Lord Loudoun to Pitt, March 10, 1757: Kimball, *Pitt Correspondence*, I, 19.

87. Lord Loudoun to Pitt, May 30, 1757: *ibid.*, I, 69.

88. The following account is based on *ibid.*; Paul Leicester Ford, ed., *The Journals of Hugh Gaine, Printer* (New York, 1902), II, 8–9 (hereafter cited as *Gaine Journals*); *The Montresor Journals* (New-York Historical Society, *Collections*, 1881 [New York, 1882]), pp. 150–151 (hereafter cited as *Montresor Journals*.)

89. See 1756 census figures for white and Negro males sixteen and over (total: 3,154) in Evarts B. Greene and Virginia D. Harrington, *American Population before the Federal Census of 1790* (New York, 1932). Hereafter cited as Greene and Harrington, *Population.*

90. I.N.P. Stokes, ed., *The Iconography of Manhattan Island, 1498–1909* (New York, 1895–1928), IV, 691. Hereafter cited as Stokes, *Iconography.*

91. *Post-Boy*, May 30, 1757.

92. Lieutenant-Governor Delancy to Secretary Pitt, March 17, 1758: *N Y Col Docs*, VII, 343; *Post-Boy*, March 20, 27, April 3, 10, 17, 1758; Council Session, May 17, 1758: *Calendar of Council Minutes*, p. 439.

93. Council Session, May 17, 1758: *ibid.*, p. 439; Lieutenant-Governor Delancey to Secretary Pitt, March 17, 1758: *N Y Col Docs*, VII, 343; Stokes, *Iconography*, IV, 697.

94. *Montresor Journals*, p. 152.

95. For the following accounts of the two press-gangs see *Post-Boy*, May 1, 1758.

96. *Ibid.*, March 21, 1757.

97. See above, pp. 13–16.

98. For amazement at impressment "in this Time of Peace" see *Post-Boy*, July 18, 1765.

99. *Ibid.*, May 19, 1763.

100. Cadwallader Colden to Secretary Conway, November 5, 1765: *N Y Col Docs*, VII, 171.

[101.] See below, pp. 51–53.

[102.] As late as January 1776 Thomas Paine argued in *Common Sense* that the unemployment of seamen and shipwrights would make the organization of an American Navy an easy task: Harry Hayden Clark, ed., *Thomas Paine: Representative Selections* (New York, 1944), p. 37.

[103.] 3 Geo. III, c. 22: Danby Pickering, ed., *The Statutes at Large from Magna Charta to [46 George III]* (London, 1762–1807), XXV, 345–351 (hereafter cited as Pickering, *Statutes at Large*); Lord Egremont to Cadwallader Colden, July 9, 1763: *Colden Letters and Papers*, VI, 222–225; James Munro, ed., *Acts of the Privy Council of England: Colonial Series* (Hereford, 1908–1912), IV, 569–572 (hereafter cited as Munro, *Acts of Privy Council*); *Journal of the Commissioners for Trade and Plantations* (London, 1920–38), XI, 389–390.

[104.] *Post-Boy*, February 9, 1764.

[105.] *Ibid.*; for an account of the various printings of this essay see Frederick Bernays Wiener, "The Rhode Island Merchants and the Sugar Act," *New England Quarterly*, III (July, 1930), 482.

[106.] Merchants' petition, April 20, 1764: *Assembly Journal*, II, 742–743.

[107.] 3 Geo. III, c. 22, sec. iv: Pickering, *Statutes at Large*, XXV, 347–348.

[108.] Munro, *Acts of Privy Council*, IV, 561–562.

[109.] *Ibid.*, IV, 571.

[110.] Admiral Alexander Colville to Cadwallader Colden, October 14, 1763: *Colden Letters and Papers*, VI, 240. For a list of His Majesty's Ships stationed in North America see *New-York Gazette*, October 10, 1763 (hereafter cited as *Gazette*). For the arrival of some of these at New York see *Post-Boy*, October 13, 20, November 3, 1763.

[111.] Lord Colville to Mr. Stepens [sic], July 26, 1764 (extract): J. R. Bartlett, ed., *Records of the Colony of Rhode Island and Providence Plantations in New England (1636–1792)* (Providence, 1856–1865), VI, 428. Bernhard Knollenberg, *Origin of the American Revolution: 1759–1766* (2d ed. rev.; New York, 1961), p. 180 says the orders were "to raise men by enlistment, if possible, but, if not, to impress them," but the option is not justified by the source, which merely says "raise." Hereafter cited as Knollenberg, *Origin of the American Revolution*. One of the four vessels, *St. John*, was involved in a serious impressment incident in Rhode Island; see Edmund S. Morgan and Helen M. Morgan, *The Stamp Act Crisis: Prologue to Revolution* (Chapel Hill, 1953), pp. 43–44. Hereafter cited as Morgans, *Stamp Act Crisis*.

[112.] *Gazette*, October 10, 1763.

[113.] *Post-Boy*, July 12, 1764; Lieutenant Laugharne to Lord Colville, August 11, 1764: Monro, *Acts of Privy Council*, VI, 384–385, 714; Council Session, July 8, 1765: *Calendar of Council Minutes*, p. 468; Stokes,

Iconography, IV, 742; Report of Grand Jury, August 2, 1764, New York Supreme Court: Minute Book (July 31, 1764–October 28, 1767), p. 7. On the same day the Grand Jury reported on the case of Thomas Tyrel, "late Lieutenant of Marines on board his Majesty's Sloop Jamaica." On an unspecified date Tyrel had been killed—murdered, the Jury concluded—by a rock thrown by an unknown person "the said Thomas Tyrrel being then in a certain Boat with divers other persons belonging to the . . . sloop [*Jamaica*] in order to press Men for the said Vessel." The Jury reported that it was unable to discover anyone involved. There is reason to suppose, although not enough evidence to justify such a speculation, that *Jamaica* was accompanying *Chaleur*, and that the mob which attacked Lt. Laugharne was seeking revenge for more than the aforementioned impressment of five seamen. None of the secondary accounts of the events of July 10–11 mentions the murder of Tyrel, which could not have taken place too long after these events, possibly on the same day. See Dawson, *Sons of Liberty*, pp. 54–55; Knollenberg, *Origin of the American Revolution*, p. 180.

[114.] *Post-Boy*, June 27, 1765; Bridenbaugh, *Cities in Revolt*, pp. 309–310.

[115.] *Post-Boy*, June 27, 1765.

[116.] *Ibid.*, July 18, 1765; *Gazette*, July 15, 1765; "A List of His Majesty's Ships and Vessels Stationed in North America, under the Command of the Right Hon'ble The Lord Colville, [1765]: *Colden Letters and Papers*, VII, 131.

[117.] *Post-Boy*, January 2, 1766; *Montresor Journals*, p. 344.

[118.] *Ibid.*, p. 328; Cadwallader Colden to Captain Kennedy, September 3, 1765: *Colden Letter Books*, II, 29–30.

[119.] See below, pp. 88–92.

[120.] *Post-Boy*, October 20, 1763; "A List of His Majesty's Ships . . . ," [1765]: *Colden Letters and Papers*, VII, 131.

[121.] Archibald Kennedy to Cadwallader Colden, November 1, 1765: *ibid.*, p. 86.

[122.] Cadwallader Colden to Secretary Conway, March 28, 1766: *N Y Col Docs*, VII, 823.

[123.] General Gage to Secretary Conway, December 21, 1765: Clarence Edwin Carter, ed., *The Correspondence of General Thomas Gage with the Secretaries of State, 1763–1775* (New Haven, 1931), I, 78 (hereafter cited as Carter, *Gage Correspondence*); Collector and Comptroller of New York to Commissioners of Customs, December 4, 1765; quoted in Morgans, *Stamp Act Crisis*, p. 162.

[124.] *Montresor Journals*, p. 342.

[125.] *Ibid.*, p. 341.

[126.] General Gage to Secretary Conway, December 21, 1765: Carter, *Cage Correspondence*, I, 78; John Watts to Robert Monckton, December 30,

1765: *The Aspinwall Papers* (Massachusetts Historical Society, *Collections*, fourth series [Boston, 1871], X, 587) (hereafter cited as *Aspinwall Papers*); Henry Moore to Secretary Conway, December 21, 1765: *N Y Col. Docs*, VII, 802; *Montresor Journals*, p. 343.

127. *Ibid.*, pp. 342–343.

128. *Ibid.*, pp. 343–344.

129. *Ibid.*, p. 344. For the lifting of the "blockade," see below p. 102.

130. *Ibid.*, p. 346. For the further development of this major issue, see below, p. 124ff.

131. *Ibid.*, pp. 354–355; Deposition of John and James Abeel, March 19, 1766, Deposition of Isaac Sears et al., March 20, 1766: Lamb Papers, #22, #24, #25 in folder dated January 26, 1762 to December 16, 1773, New-York Historical Society; *Post-Boy*, March 27, 1766.

132. *Montresor Journals*, p. 367.

133. *Ibid.*, p. 361; *Post-Boy*, April 24, 1766.

134. *Montresor Journals*, p. 367.

135. *Post-Boy*, July 27, 1772.

136. Elizabeth Cometti, "Impressment during the American Revolution" in Vera Largent, ed., *The Walter Clinton Jackson Essays in the Social Sciences* (Chapel Hill, 1942), pp. 97–109. Hereafter cited as Cometti, "Impressment," Largent, *Jackson Essays*.

137. Massachusetts Historical Society, *Proceedings*, LV (October 1921-June 1922), 250–255.

138. Lawrence S. Mayo, ed., *The History of the Colony and Province of Massachusetts-Bay by Thomas Hutchinson* (Cambridge, 1936), II, 167n. (hereafter cited as Mayo, *Hutchinson's History*); "Testimony taken in case of Michael Corbet," Massachusetts Historical Society, *Proceedings*, XLIV (October 1910–June 1911), 429–452.

139. For a cruise involving all three but not impressment see *Journal*, June 3, 1773.

140. Margaret Wheeler Willard, ed., *Letters on the American Revolution, 1774–1776* (Boston, 1925), p. 65. Hereafter cited as Willard, *Letters on American Revolution*.

141. *Journal*, July 8, 1773.

142. *Ibid.*, February 23, 1775.

143. Oliver M. Dickerson, *The Navigation Acts and the American Revolution* (Philadelphia, 1951), pp. 208–265. Hereafter cited as Dickerson, *Navigation Acts*.

144. *Ibid.*, pp. 218–219.

145. Morris, *Government and Labor*, p. 239.

146. C. W. Jenkins, "Answers," *American Neptune*, I (July, 1941), 312.

147. *Post-Boy*, May 15, 1769. Although there is no justifying the Commissioners' conduct, it should be noted that the custom was potentially a mask for unauthorized importation; the master discovered importing goods not listed on his cocket could always claim that they were a seaman's private venture.

148. Clark, "Impressment," *Andrews Essays*, pp. 222–223. In the following account, except where otherwise noted, quotations and information about the legality of impressment are derived from Clark.

149. 6 Anne, c. 37, sec. ix: *N Y Col Docs*, V, 99.

150. See above, p. 18–19.

151. *Calendar of Council Minutes*, p. 229.

152. Council Session, July 2, 1709: *ibid.*, p. 230; Stokes, *Iconography*, IV, 465.

153. June 30, 1709: *N Y Col Docs*, V, 100.

154. July 3, 1709: *ibid.*, V, 102; Stokes, *Iconography*, IV, 973 (italics mine).

155. June 21, 1709: *ibid.*, V, 100–101.

156. September 15, 1709: *ibid.*, V, 101.

157. September 17, 1709: *ibid.*, V, 99–100.

158. *Ibid.*, V, 124–153.

159. *Ibid.*, V, 224–225. See above, p. 20.

160. See above, p. 30.

161. See above, *ibid.*

162. *Post-Boy*, December 10, 1770; Morris, *Government and Labor*, p. 273.

163. Hutchinson, *Press-Gang*, p. 15.

164. *London Daily Advertiser*, May 12, 1768; *Post-Boy*, August 1, 8, 1768; R. W. Postgate, *That Devil Wilkes* (New York, 1929), pp. 167–168 (hereafter cited as Postgate, *Wilkes*).

165. *Post-Boy*, November 19, 26, 1770, March 25, 1771.

166. *Ibid.*, December 31, 1770.

167. *Annual Register . . . for 1771* (London, 1772), p. 68.

168. *Ibid.*, pp. 67, 68, 70–71; Postgate, *Wilkes*, p. 182; Percy Fitzgerald, *Life of John Wilkes* (London, 1888), II, 120.

169. The Sons of Liberty found time for thirty-nine other toasts: *Post-Boy*, March 25, 1771. Throughout the 'sixties and 'seventies New Yorkers

followed Wilkes' activities with avid interest and ardent support. On August 8, 1763 William Weyman remarked in the *Gazette* after one of the many Wilkes items published in the years following 1762: "(So much has lately been published relating to Mr. Wilkes's Affair in England, that we are afraid it has become fulsome to the Publick . . .)" But the public did not tire of "the furious Tribune" (John Watts to Gedney Clarke, August 9, 1763: *Watts Letter Book*, p. 166), and in 1770 ex-privateer Alexander McDougall capitalized on this popularity by presenting himself as "the American Wilkes." See Dorothy Rita Dillon, *The New York Triumvirate: A Study of the Legal and Political Careers of William Livingston, John Morin Scott, William Smith, Jr.* (New York, 1949), pp. 106–124 (hereafter cited as Dillon, *New York Triumvirate*). See also below, pp. 78–79.

170. Hutchinson, *Press-Gang*, pp. 5–7.

171. Delolme, *La Constitution de l'Angleterre* (Amsterdam, 1771), cited in Robert R. Palmer, *The Age of the Democratic Revolution: A Political History of Europe and America, 1760–1800* (Princeton, 1959), p. 148.

172. Benjamin Franklin, Remarks on Judge Foster's Argument in Favor of Impressing Seamen, Sparks, *Works*, II, 337, 338, 334.

173. Described as "A sea Term" in E. Carther to _____, November 2, 1765: *New York City during the American Revolution, Being a Collection of Original Papers (Now First Published) from the Manuscripts in the Possession of the Mercantile Library Association of New York City* (New York, 1861), p. 42. Hereafter cited as *New York during the Revolution*.

174. *Post-Boy*, August 12, 1754.

175. Willett, *Narrative*, pp. 149–151.

176. But one may speculate that this memory did play a significant role. It is unreasonable to suppose that New York's harsh experience with impressment in the British Empire would be forgotten when the same nation committed the same offense in the same place in the next century. I think that much of the strength of impressment as a grievance in 1812 is connected with the fact that it was a repetition of an ancient pre-revolutionary grievance. One account of the impressment of American seamen treats the institution as practically non-existent before the Revolution. It gives the pre-revolutionary phenomenon only the briefest consideration—in footnotes—and concludes, on the basis of speculative evidence, that impressment was rare in the colonies. The author does not understand the sixth of Anne and thinks that it was repealed in 1769: James Fulton Zimmerman, *Impressment of American Seamen* (New York, 1925), *passim* and especially pp. 11–17.

177. George Athan Billias, *General John Glover and his Marblehead Mariners* (New York, 1960), p. 31 would add Glover to the group whose patriotism grew partly out of reaction to impressment. Hereafter cited as Billias, *Glover*.

178. *Boston Post-Boy & Advertiser*, April 14, 1766, quoted in Philip Davidson, *Propaganda and the American Revolution, 1763–1783* (Chapel Hill, 1941), p. 189. Hereafter cited as Davidson, *Propaganda*.

III. Jack Tar on the Beach: The Birth of the Mob

Unemployment was the natural condition of New York's seamen in the decade and one-half preceding the American Revolution. The transition from maritime prosperity to poverty began with the close of the French and Indian War. The termination of hostilities brought a decisive end to privateering, one of New York's major war industries. Thousands of men, habituated to the regular receipt of prize money from the captains of hundreds of vessels, suddenly saw their jobs and their incomes eliminated.[1]

Unemployed privateersmen naturally turned to the trade they knew best, the one which had employed them before the war—merchant shipping. But the merchant marine could not begin to absorb the returning seamen, for it was reeling under the stricter enforcement of the Molasses Act of 1733. Beginning in 1763 a series of new regulations, enforced, it will be recalled, by the Royal Navy, interferred with long-established trade patterns and exacerbated the rigors of transition from an economy of war to an economy of peace; trade suffered, shipping became a depressed industry, and seamen found it harder to get work.[2]

The passage of the Stamp Act dealt a further blow to the confidence of New York's trading community, and months before the act went into effect maritime commerce had fallen into inactivity. With the act actually functioning in the fall of 1765 the strategy of opposition chosen by New York's liberal leadership could not have had a worse effect on the seamen. To lessen the community's dependence on English goods, leading citizens promoted the expansion of domestic manufactures. A promotional society was founded, and goods such as shoes, hose, linen, caps, and gloves were sold in a newly established marketplace. "All Ranks of People"—including seamen, no doubt—took "a laudable Pride in wearing what is made among themselves," but every item manufactured locally meant one less item of import and thus fewer ships and fewer jobs. The total strategy reinforced this effect by purposely aiming at "a total stagnation of all business"; rather than make use of the stamps required under the act, New York's leaders at first proposed simply to stop importing goods from England. The measure of non-importation's success is the measure of the failure of New York's seamen to find jobs.[3]

Throughout the remainder of the 'sixties and on into the following decade British regulations combined with American strategy to make maritime employment a rare experience for the seaman. When he came ashore to look for work in an already flooded labor market he found himself competing with off-duty English soldiers and sailors who consistently undercut his wage demands.[4] And recurrently the seaman's employment problem was worsened by the strategy of non-importation.

The end of privateering, more rigid enforcement of the acts of trade, the Stamp Act and the strategy of opposition to it—all combined to produce an acute maritime employment problem. At the end of the War there had been great concern among a group of younger lieutenants over the problem of what was to be done with the twenty thousand seamen and officers about to be discharged from a Navy which had undergone great enlargement during the fighting. The problem was not only one of keeping the Navy properly manned but also of keeping English seamen from floating into foreign navies. The lieutenants suggested a government-promoted expansion of the whale fishery—this would be "the best seminary for seamen" and would occupy the newly unemployed. But senior officers in the Admiralty took no action; seamen did float into foreign navies, and in America conversion to a peacetime economy combined with the new trade regulations to put thousands of seamen and fishermen out of work.[5]

New York was one of the communities most heavily hit by postwar maritime unemployment. During the war a total of nearly twenty thousand men had sailed 224 privateers out of New York; in 1759, 5,670 New Yorkers had been employed on privateers. Many of these men were out of work, each competing with the other for one of the 3,000 places in merchant vessels. After the war the merchant service contracted rather than expanding: in 1762 New York's seamen numbered 3,552; ten years later, coming out of the slough of the Stamp Act and non-importation, the number had been reduced to 3,374.[6]

Under these conditions those seamen who did find berths clung all the more firmly to their two or three pounds monthly wages.[7] Seamen appeared more frequently as plaintiffs in suits for wages, winning with great frequency both in Vice-Admiralty Courts and in courts of common law.[8] They sharpened their ingenuity, discovering new ways both within and without the law to get more pay for less work. Their skill was recognized in an act passed by the New York Assembly "for the

Better Government & Regulation of Seamen in the merchants Service."
Seamen, the act said, would wait until a ship was just ready to clear out
and then demand higher wages to keep them at their posts. Or they
would desert and then bring suit for wages earned between the time they
shipped themselves and the time they quit. Another of the seaman's
favorite devices was to arrange to have himself sued when the vessel
was about to sail; in order to stop the suit and retain the use of his
seamen the master would be forced to advance wages before they were
due.[9]

Disgusted with the legal quibbles which sailors constantly
discovered, John Watts complained that New York was "without Doubt
the worst port in the English Dominions for Seamen." Part of the
problem had its origin in the increasingly close connection between
lawyers and common seamen. "Such a Number of Pettifoggers," Watts
wrote, "are allways ready to disturb the Minds of Seamen and puzzell
[sic] the Laws, which are far from being explicit with respect to
Commerce . . ."[10] This relationship was to take on greatly increased
significance in the years to come. Needing lawyers as they did, and
generally gaining by their relationship with them, we may suppose that
seamen had less of the common colonial bias against the men of the
law. Later when lawyers assumed leadership of the growing
revolutionary movement the seamen would be predisposed to view legal
leadership in a sympathetic way.

Thus depression produced unemployment, and unemployment
produced genuine poverty. Business stagnated, New Yorkers actually
saw grass growing in the streets, and far from looking for clerks or
seamen, merchants looked for ways to employ their own idle hours.[11]
The poverty was real: if no one starved to death, it was only because
there were always fish and oysters to fill the bellies of the poor. If one
New Yorker exaggerated when he advised his fellows to "See our poor,
starving!" this is not to deny that many were in a "starving condition."
The poor grumbled about "those who live on the Sweat of others" and
made grim prophecies: "In the Year 1776, the English will be the
richest people in the Universe, for before that time all the *poor* will be
starved to death."[12]

To whom might the seaman turn for aid when he was unemployed
and in a starving condition? The poor seaman's problem was worse than
that of his land counterpart, aggravated as it was by special health
problems. For if to be a seaman in the 1760's and '70's often meant to
be unemployed, it always meant to be unhealthy, to be a sufferer from
fevers, fits, pains, scurvy, and other diseases.[13] Partially compensating
for the special dangers of his occupation was a government medical
program whose scope, on paper, is unmatched by twentieth-century

legislation. In 1696, hoping to protect and encourage one of Britain's richest resources, her seamen, Parliament had passed an act providing for a 6 d a month levy on the wages of all seamen—both in the Navy and in merchant vessels and coasters—for the maintenance of a hospital at Greenwich. The disabled seaman was entitled to care at the hospital and, if he should die, his widow and children were to be maintained at government expense and his children to be educated. In 1729 this act was extended to America, and the colonial governments were ordered to collect 6 d a month from all British seamen entering or clearing American ports.[14]

During the French and Indian War the first evidence appears of a reluctance on the part of American seamen and their employers to pay the naval sixpence. A successful privateering cruise could produce more than £400 for the Greenwich Hospital. Having made the deduction, masters and owners naturally were reluctant to throw such large sums into the sea.[15] And as far as the seaman was concerned, the money was a monthly six pence thrown into the sea, for few American seamen ever saw Greenwich Hospital, no matter how serious their physical condition. This single hospital—together with a new one established at Liverpool in 1749[16]—could not possibly care for more than a fraction of the medical problems of the seamen of the world's leading maritime nation. In addition the Hospital was all but inaccessible to American seamen; it was almost the turn of the century before another government, more friendly to American seamen, established such facilities on American shores. Meanwhile, in the decades preceding the Revolution, seamen could reasonably view Greenwich Hospital money as taxation without representation and, equally bad, taxation without benefit.[17]

Benefiting little from the charity of the Empire, the seaman in trouble in New York was forced to throw himself on the mercies of the municipality. Here he fared only slightly better. What public charity existed was poorly administered, and legislation aimed more at keeping the poor out of town than at relieving their poverty. Generally New York's charity was more limited than that of the other major cities in America.[18]

Unlike the Empire as a whole, New York could not afford to do without good medical care for seamen; an imported disease was a real threat to the City's existence. In June of 1738 a temporary quarantine was established on Bedloe's Island (now Liberty Island) to protect New York from a small-pox epidemic in other colonies. Pilots were required to bring all suspected vessels to the Island where a doctor passed judgment on the condition of passengers and crew. The temporary practice became permanent, and in 1754 a tax was imposed on incoming seamen to pay the expenses of the quarantine system. In 1758 the City purchased all of Bedloe's Island and proceeded to erect a pesthouse for bearers of contagious diseases and a hospital for sick and wounded seamen. These two building were, according to a visitor in 1759, "the most noted public buildings in and about the city."[19] In 1769 Dr. Samuel Bard, Professor of Medicine at King's College, began a movement to add a regular hospital for the poor in the city. Construction began in 1773, but the nearly completed building was destroyed by fire in 1775, and when it was rebuilt it was more useful to Hessian troops than to American seamen.[20]

Outside of the area of medical care New York's record of public charity was dismal. The Almshouse, built in 1736 in the Fields, gave shelter to paupers and served as a workhouse (mariner John Cregier [sic] once applied for a job as keeper). When the workhouse overflowed as it did in February of 1771, the poor were supported or assisted at their own places of residence. Finally, the Almshouse served as a house of correction.[21]

One of the institutions most familiar to seamen was the jail. Until 1759 the basement of the City Hall served that function, but the turbulence of the period of the French and Indian War necessitated expansion, and in that year the New Gaol was constructed in the Fields. An English visitor reported that it was "one of the finest prisons I have ever seen." So it might have appeared from the outside, but the overcrowding which gave the New Gaol birth made it almost immediately obsolete. More than half a century before, the Court of General Sessions had informed the Common Council of the "Absolute Necessity that a Bridewell be built and Maintained within the City of New York for the better Suppressing of Vice and Maintainance of the poor. . . ." Finally, in November of 1765 the Common Council appointed a committee to plan such an institution which would take over one of the jail's functions by serving as a workhouse and house of correction for the poor and vagrant. Two years later, as a temporary measure, two rooms were set aside as a bridewell in the New Gaol. The building was finally completed in 1775, just in time to house captured Americans during the Revolution.[22]

Seamen unfortunate enough to find themselves inside one of the city's jails must have found the experience somewhat similar to being impressed into the British Navy. The administration was poor, sometimes venal, and often condemned by respected authorities. One jailer was charged with mistreating prisoners and indicted for extortion but nonetheless allowed to retain his position. Mariner William Dobbs became bridewell keeper on condition that he could pocket any profits arising from hiring out prisoners. The jails were overcrowded, unsanitary, and unhealthy. In Winter the prisoners lacked fuel and "the common Necessaries of Life" and were forced to solicit aid through newspaper advertisements: "Besides our Misfortune of Confinement, we are under great Necessity for want of Firing, not having at this time one Stick to burn: nor have not had for several days, and unless we are relieved by some charitably disposed Persons, we must unavoidably perish in this Place."[23]

Under extraordinary circumstances the Common Council would appropriate emergency funds for the relief of those who would otherwise "unavoidably perish"[24] or would rent extra houses to care for the poor.[25] These emergency moves were as inadequate as the more permanent programs, and the seaman in trouble had to depend more on private charity than on the generosity of the municipality. Thus the inmates in the jail were assisted by private individuals who either subscribed directly to their assistance or staged theatrical benefits.[26] Later the prisoners' plight became involved in the central political question of the day: the Sons of Liberty made it their practice to contribute the remains of their annual dinner in celebration of the Stamp Act's repeal, along with barrels of beer, to the prisoners.[27] Various clergymen preached charity sermons and passed on their collections to the poor, in and out of jail; sometimes there were strings attached, as in 1767 when the consistory of the Dutch Church passed a resolution that "no one shall be taken up as a poor person to be supported by the Church, unless on condition that whatever may be bequeathed to them shall fall to the Church."[28]

A major attempt to palliate the worsening economic position of men who derived their living from the sea came with the foundation of the New York Marine Society. The Boston Marine Society had been founded in 1754 to spread maritime knowledge and to assist the families of poor mariners. In the same year nineteen Newport sea captains formed a society to promote their mutual interests. In 1765 the Sea Captain's Club of Philadelphia was founded as a "Society for the Relief of Poor and Distressed Masters of Ships, their Widows, and Children." Finally in November of 1769, a meeting of New York sea captains took the first steps toward organizing a similar society; it received its charter in the Spring of 1770 (over the objection of William Smith who worried that the Society might "increase the Wantoness [sic] of the Populace.")[29]

The Marine Society held quarterly meetings, elected officers, collected dues and donations, and distributed funds to the widows and orphans of members. It was a mutual assistance association, not a group of radical dissidents, and the limitations which ultimately made it irrelevent to the problems of the common seaman show through its title: "The New-York Marine Society, for promoting Maritime Knowledge, and for Relief of distressed Masters of Ships, their Widows, and Orphan Children." For every master out of work several common seamen shared the same plight, but along with the Boston, Newport, and Philadelphia organizations, the New York Society did nothing for the latter. New York's mariners claimed that their Society was founded in imitation of the Greenwich Hospital; insofar as both institutions were of little use to American common seamen the parallel was ironically correct.[30]

For the seaman in New York the only welfare agency which really functioned was the "public house"—the bar. In these houses the seaman was free of the authoritarian atmosphere of the ship and the alien ways of the landman. Here, among his fellows, the unemployed or unpaid seaman could drink his frustrations away, sure that his credit was good. Here were women, cards, and dice. Here too was information about jobs, and advice on such technical problems as making out a will. Between proprietor and seaman there was sometimes enmity but always mutual need, a fact expressed more than once in the powers of attorney of seamen authorizing proprietors to act in their interest while they were at sea, or, if they were privateers, to receive their share of prize money.[31]

New York sprouted taverns as rapidly as any nineteenth-century frontier town. In 1766 there were 282 licensed innholders; there were 396 in 1773. Thus there was one licensed bar for every sixty people, not to speak of the many other bars which did not bother to have themselves licensed.[32] But not all of these entertained seamen. A common seaman might be seen from time to time—especially during periods of political stress—at Bardin's, or its successor, Montagnies', at the Long-Room, or even at the merchants' coffeehouses; but he found the atmosphere more congenial at Daniel Sullivan's "Bunch of Grapes" or at any of the several houses nearby in the Fields, such as Quaker Fan's or, in the West Ward, James or Thomas Dunn's, or in Montgomerie Ward, Sarah Dyllon's.[33] Although the Dock Ward was home territory for seamen, their haunts were to be found wherever the prostitutes drew them—"in every quarter of the metropolis."[34]

The proprietors of these houses, as can be seen, were often women. Mary Allen was murdered by the mate of a naval vessel who got drunk and had his pocket emptied of nine guineas in her establishment.[35] Kate Crow, keeper of "a Place of noted ill Fame," was fined £100 and sent to jail for a year after a mariner and a plasterer fractured the skull of a shopkeeper in her place in 1767.[36] Fanny Bambridge, a noted prostitute known as "Quaker Fan," died in her bed in 1768; the coroner attributed her death to excessive drinking.[37] Sarah Dyllon was indicted in 1774 for keeping a "disorderly house for her own lucre & gain [and for having] procured women of ill fame who gathered drinking tipling . . . etc."[38] Some women took their business to their clients; a prostitute who boarded a privateer received a ducking from the yardarm and a tarring and feathering from the skipper; another, in a naval vessel, drank too much and killed herself in a fall from the main deck into the hold.[39] A pair of free Negroes named Peter and Elizabeth were indicted for keeping a disorderly house in 1766.[40] Two years later Mary Mulvaney was convicted of keeping a disorderly house along with three men and was fined £3 and sent to prison for three days.[41] Jane Dunn ran a disorderly house along with her husband Thomas until she left him for a laborer after nine years of happy and, we may suppose, prosperous married life.[42]

The activities in these houses were best summarized in a 1767 indictment: "drinking, typling, quarelling, fighting, whoring, and misbehaving."[43] Here the undersocialized seaman[44] came, either unemployed and discontented or, fresh in from a voyage, seeking dissipation after long hours of boredom mixed with danger, physical hardship, and mental subjection.[45] The seamen drank and fought with one another and sometimes tried the patience of the innholders; one tar nearly died as the result of some cuts in the head delivered by an angry proprietress.[46]

Almost inevitably the seaman emerged from the public house with three sheets in the wind. Sometimes he fell asleep before he returned to his vessel and froze to death;[47] or he made it back, fell overboard and drowned.[48] Then as now the drunken sailor was a cliché, as easily recognized in the streets as in the theatre;[49] when a sober seaman drowned in the dark there was cause for special notice that he had not been "in liquor."[50]

On his way home the seaman carried some of the violence of the tavern out into the streets with him. Some of the people responded with sympathy, especially for "those poor unfortunate prostitutes, whose audacity calls aloud for justice, and whose misfortunes demand a pitiful eye . . . "[51] More frequently the response indicated an understandable lack of sympathy with local low-life: build a bridewell, lock them up, put the law on them; the whores were whipped before a great crowd and given forty-eight hours to get out of town.[52] Throughout the 'sixties and 'seventies, as the number of houses grew and the seamen found more and more time for them, respectable opinion continued its attack on "those infamous houses, which to the great scandal of our wholesome laws, are suffered to exist as so many receptacles for loose and disorderly people:"[53]

These houses are generally great Nuisances to Society, and while they afford a disorderly, uncomfortable Subsistence to one Family, are the Means of Destruction to 20.

These abominable houses are too frequently the avenues to every vice; from these the road is easily and too commonly found, even by the youngest, to the scenes of lewdness, debauchery, disease and ruin, with which the invirons [sic] of this city very much abound. . . .

The Suppression of these Houses, which subsist only by furnishing the Means of Drunkenness and Debauchery to Servants and mean disorderly People, would be highly agreeable to the Inhabitants in general.[54]

Having failed to produce an adequate program of public or private charity, New Yorkers looked with horror on a situation for which they were partially responsible and could find no better solution than the formation of a "Society for Reformation of Manners, and Suppression of Vice"[55]—an approach which looked more towards the obliteration of effects than the removal of causes. But disapproval of the seaman's way of life by the community—or at least by the trading segment—had a far more subtle manifestation in legislation which attempted to loose the bonds that joined seamen and innkeepers.

Sometimes the connection between innkeeper and seaman was of a personal sort; some innkeepers and keepers of disorderly houses were former mariners.[56] Always the relationship was one of mutual need: the seaman needed credit, and the innkeeper needed his business. Often personal and business relations combined with the mutual interdependence of seaman and proprietor in a manner which displeased the seaman's employer. On the simplest level, this might mean that drunken seamen were no good to their employers. On a more complex level there might be collusion between seaman and innkeeper to milk a master of his money.[57]

The laws which dealt with these situations favored the master over the seaman or proprietor; the employer, equally capable of subterfuge, was left unhindered. As early as 1638 Dutch ordinances had outlawed the sale of wine outside of the store-house of the West India Company and penalized those who harbored seamen on shore overnight without permission of the director-general. In other words seamen were to be kept as sober as possible at all times, immediately available to their employers. In 1647 two seamen tore a copy of the ordinance from the mainmast of their ship; they were sentenced to be chained to a wheelbarrow and employed at hard labor for three months, subsisting on bread and water.[58]

Under English administration, New York's laws pertaining to seamen ashore followed the same pattern. The preamble to a 1691 order of the Common Council stated the purpose frankly, without reference to seamen causing disturbances in the City:

> Whereas great Inconveniency doth arise by trusting of Saylers whereby they Neglect thier [sic] Attendance on board greatly to the hinderance of Trade
>
> Ordered that if any publicq house or any other person Shall trust any Sayler belonging to any Shipp or Vessell shall forfeit all that hee Shall so trust him with and Shall have no benefitt of the Law for the Recovery of the Same.[59]

Clearly the purpose here was primarily to keep seamen available to their masters and only secondarily to protect the city against violence. An order of the Mayor's Court a few months later forbade tappers and innkeepers from selling drinks to seamen unless the master or merchant had "posted his word" for payment. Thus employers could control their men's drinking on shore and be certain of not losing their men to suits for debt when the vessel was about to sail.[60]

An order of the Common Council of 1694 harked back to the earlier Dutch ordinance in dealing with the question of seamen's overnight berths:

> Order'd that no Taphouse or Victualler doe Receive or Entertaine any Seamen or Saylors to Lodge in their houses whereby they may neglect their Masters or Imployers Service upon Penalty of twenty Shilings [sic] for each Default one halfe for the use of the Citty the Other halfe to the Informer and that noe Victualler or Taphouse within this Citty as Aforesaid does trust any Saylor or Seaman belonging to Any Vessel within this Roade or Harbour Above the Sum of Six Shilings [sic].[61]

An Act of the provincial legislature of 1695 expanded on the final clause of the 1694 order by stating that no suit could be instituted against an employed seaman for the recovery of more than 6s or against one who is out of work for more than 12d.[62] Over the years certain refinements were added to the basic law: any attempt at evasion by taking a bond or a bill from seamen was to be void; no tavern-keeper was to entertain any seaman after ten o'clock at night; innkeepers were not to sell strong liquors to common seamen nor to allow them to play with cards or dice.[63]

An act of 1760, later disallowed, illustrates the general tenor of the New York Assembly's attitude toward seamen ashore in the period immediately before the Revolution. Noting that New York's prosperity depended on trade and that trade had been hampered by employers' continuing inability to depend on their seamen's presence when a vessel was about to sail, the act listed the abuses discussed earlier. The new law provided that masters make written contracts with all seamen except apprentices, and that seamen sign their contracts within three days of entering into a ship's service. Seamen deserting or refusing to proceed were to forfeit all wages due. Seamen going against their contracts were subject to the warrant of the Justices of the Peace; if they could not satisfy the Justices, they were to be kept at hard labor at the house of correction and delivered to the ship when it was about to sail. Seamen absent without leave were to forfeit three days' pay for every day's absence. Seamen leaving their ship before it was unladen were to forfeit one month's pay. To prevent collusive suits, plaintiffs in suits against seamen had to sign an affidavit that the debt was bona fide due. Tavernkeepers or innholders could not sue seamen for debts over 10s—a slight liberalization over the previous 6s—and tavernkeepers procuring obligatory bills or other security from seamen as a means of evading this requirement were to be penalized.[64]

The intent of the act, as of the ones which preceeded it, was to preserve a ready maritime labor force for masters and merchants, and although some clauses—such as that requiring written contracts—might work in the seaman's favor, the act was clearly framed without regard to their interests. Why, it might be inquired, with legislatures and municipal bodies so frequently acting against their interests, did not the seamen vote the rascals out? The answer seems to be that most seamen could not vote and some did not care to. Many seamen who made New York a second home and were much concerned in its affairs were necessarily without the franchise because of their non-residence. For residents qualification for the franchise was a simple enough operation. One had to purchase the freedom of the city from the Common Council for a fee ranging from £5 for a merchant or shopkeeper down to 20s for an artisan. Apprentices were eligible for the freedom without fee after seven years apprenticeship, and often the Common Council admitted those who were unable to pay without cost. Sometimes the freedom was given as an honor as in the case of three seamen who received it as a reward for putting out a dangerous fire. Having been chosen by the city authorities and having taken an oath of fidelity to the city the candidate would pay the fees, if any, and be registered as a freeman.[65]

But the fact is that many common seamen were not franchised. One-fifth of the "mariners" listed among those granted freedoms were actually masters; the same was true, with much greater regularity, of "mariners" who served on juries. Perhaps seamen were apathetic, unconcerned about bettering themselves by political action. It seems more likely that, as the lowest rung in one of the more rigidly structured class societies in America, they were uninformed about their prerogatives or victims of subtle pressures by an upper class sensitive to maintaining its position and quite capable of controlling the seaman's fortunes.[66] That such pressures did exist was frequently testified to during the campaign for the secret ballot, a campaign, according to one partisan, against "the great and the mighty, and the rich, and the long Wiggs and the Squaretoes, and all manner of Wickedness in high places" who tried "to over-awe and intimidate . . . by the very Appearance of their Magnosities." According to the same source,

> many of the poorer People have[e] deeply felt the Aristocratic Power, or rather the intollerable Tyranny of the great and opulent, who (such is the shocking Depravity of the Times, and their utter Contempt of all public Virtue and Patriotism) have openly threatened them with the Loss of their Employment, and to arrest them for Debt, unless they gave their Voices as they were directed. . . .[67]

It is relevant to note that one of the leaders in this campaign was former privateer Captain Alexander McDougall, a man who had the seamen's confidence and often led them in their activities ashore in the troubled days of the 'sixties and 'seventies.[68]

The New York seaman's unhappy situation after the French and Indian War has been described; he had serious troubles and just about no one to help him. So it happened that the seaman worked out a new relationship with the society around him: he met that society on dishonest, even criminal, terms and became accustomed to expressing himself in violent ways. This response, so apparently irrational in its manifestations, was in fact his only means of expression.

Some of this dishonesty was petty and hardly a novelty in the 'sixties. Seamen were indicted for passing counterfeit bills of credit and counterfeit Spanish quarter-dollars,[69] but they had done this before, sometimes with greater skill.[70] Seamen continued to desert their vessels and to jump bail.[71] But seamen stole more frequently. They stole from laborers, women, the church, and each other. Some of the items they stole were clearly for resale: silver buckles and buttons, watches. Others were for use: money, tobacco, tea, and clothes of all sorts: shirts, coats, stockings, trousers.[72] Some stole repeatedly: in April of 1771 Adam Smith was indicted for stealing trousers, a jacket, and money from Jacob Spragge, a shirt, some tea, some cotton, a chest, cups and saucers, tobacco, and silver knee buckles from James Churchward, and a blanket, sheet, rug, pillow, and Bible from Cornelius Disesway. He pled guilty, sought benefit of clergy, and was burned on the left hand. Barely a month later he stole silver buckles, a watch, and a hat from Edward Tinker. In November he was indicted for stealing another watch and some money from Tunis Van Pelt. A year later he was free to make another large haul, this time what must have been every stitch of clothing owned by Zebulon Waterman.[73]

Perhaps the rationale of this apparently irrational conduct can best be understood in connection with the many thefts from ships and their masters. Seaman John Forster admitted breaking into Captain Robert Elder's vessel and stealing some clothes and other items; he had gotten no more than forty or fifty yards from the vessel when he was apprehended by the Captain.[74] William Pollitt, a twenty-five year old seaman from England, spent his first night in New York in his berth in the brig *Jamaica*, Henry McKibben Master; the following night he lodged in town but returned to the vessel between ten and eleven at night, and finding no one on board, went to the cabin and broke open a chest. He was apprehended the next morning, still in possession of some of the silver and gold coins which he had taken.[75] Other seamen made off with such items as sails, rope, and cable.[76] A man who steals from his employer can hardly be considered content with his job, and these thefts would seem to express in an unorganized way some of the discontents which are expressed in the twentieth century by a strike.

The seaman did violence to the law but also, and more seriously, to individuals. Sometimes that violence was aimed at himself, as when he committed suicide.[77] More frequently his aggressions turned outward. This happened increasingly among all seamen in the 'sixties and 'seventies, regardless of whether they were American merchant seamen or British sailors.[78] Sometimes robberies were combined with assaults: Samuel Doren took advantage of the darkness of a January night to beat George Ball and make off with his beaver hat.[79] Seamen assaulted each other,[80] and they assaulted women—sometimes other men's wives.[81] It was in the nature of their situation that seamen should frequently attack law enforcement officials: Nathaniel Cooley assaulted jailer Francis Child;[82] Anthony O'Neal, previously indicted for keeping a disorderly house, attacked constable Abraham Van North with a knife, leaving him in a desperate condition with a wound in his belly and another across the side of his face and ear between his eye and his mouth.[83] Often the assaults seem to express grievances deeper than violence for the sake of violence, as when seamen assaulted prominent citizens such as Gerard J. Beekman[84] or masters such as Captain Mooney.[85]

Inevitably some of the violence reached the point of murder or manslaughter. Public houses produced their share of fractured skulls and "horrid murders,"[86] and women were often the victims.[87] Seamen killed each other, the pettiness of the cause probably indicating something of the tensions of their way of life: Moses Vinter of schooner *Speedwell* found his breeches missing and concluded that since Richard Cope of sloop *Mary Flower* had stolen a knife from *Speedwell* he had also taken the breeches, and he announced his contention to the world. Some days later Cope and Vinter met on the dock near the Albany Pier; Cope stripped to the waist and they fell to blows. In less than a minute Cope fell to the dock, calling out that he had enough, that he was sick and had been sick before. He was carried aboard *Mary Flower* where he died.[88]

The crimes discussed above were of types committed by many people, seamen and non-seamen; they are of interest here only insofar as they express dissatisfactions which the seamen had in common with the rest of the population and special grievances which he had against his employer. A final type of crime was most pregnant with meaning in the broad perspective of events in the pre-Revolutionary era. This was the riot directed against people who had roused the seamen's ire, including merchants and tavern-keepers. Armed with sticks, stones, staves, clubs, swords, "and other offensive weapons" seamen would band together, sometimes with great numbers of other seamen, sometimes with people who will never be identified, to storm the houses of their enemies. The pattern was frequently repeated: a mob of seamen would gather in front of the home of someone they had reason to dislike, shower it with stones and insults, and then parade in to threaten and rough up the occupant and, perhaps, his wife.[89]

Illegality had thus become an accepted part of seamen's daily lives, a means of expression in a society whose institutions and customs seemed in many ways planned to worsen their very difficult lot. Increasingly illegality meant violence, and frequently violence meant mob action. Seamen became accustomed to such conduct and were prepared to use it in a calculated way against the agents of a nation they thought responsible for their troubles. As politics flowed into violence, violence *became* politics. Conversely, the use of what had once been illegality as a political technique blinded British eyes, leading them to confuse the new politics of the street with the older non-political violence which had been its training ground.[90] It was a costly confusion.

Notes

[1] See above, pp. 21–22, 26.

[2] See above, pp. 26–27.

[3] *Post-Boy*, October 10, 24, November 7, 1765.

[4] See below, p. 125ff.

[5] *Post-Boy*, May 19, 1763, February 9, 1764, November 18, 1771.

[6] Fish, *New York Privateers*, pp. 4, 54–82; Bridenbaugh, *Cities in Revolt*, p. 62; Governor Tryon: Report on Province of New York, June 11, 1774: *N Y Col Docs*, VIII, 446. In their protest of April 20, 1764 (*Assembly Journal*, II, 742–743) New York's merchants estimated 2,400 seamen were employed annually in the period 1757–1763, but this is based on eight men to every 100 tons in an annual total of 30,000 tons. I have used Forrest McDonald's more accurate estimate of one seaman for every ten tons of shipping: *We the People: The Economic Origins of the Constitution* (Chicago, 1958), p. 190.

[7] Wages varied greatly with experience. Common seamen could make more than two or three pounds, but generally the range was from £1 10s up to £3. *Post-Boy*, January 14, 1754; Gurney Teneyck v. William Ward, Complaint, filed September 12, 1763, Mayor's Court: Pleadings, file drawer (1760–1765), Office of County Clerk, Hall of Records, New York City; Morris, *Government and Labor*, pp. 236n., 238n.

[8] The law allowed such suits in either type of court, and procedure in each court had certain attractive features to the seaman. See Carl Ubbelohde, *The Vice-Admiralty Courts and the American Revolution* (Chapel Hill, 1960), pp. 13–14, 19, 20, 131–133, 156, 159–160; Morris, *Government and Labor*, pp. 230–262. For some cases involving seamen's wages see the following complaints in Mayor's Court: John Clarke v. Robert Stockton, filed January 28, 1763; Alexander Irvin v. Cornelius Haight, filed May 31, 1763; Francis Doyle v. Cornelius Haight, filed June 8, 1763; Gurney Teneyck v. William Ward, filed September 12, 1763; John Haycraft v. John Rockett, filed March 6, 1764. All above in Pleadings, file drawer (1760–1765). See also Abraham Warner v. Jacob Banks, Narration on Bail Bond, filed December 21, 1767, Mayor's Court: Pleadings, file drawer (1766–1774).

[9.] *The Colonial Laws of New York from the Year 1664 to the Revolution including the Charters to the Duke of York, The Commissions and Instructions to Colonial Governors, the Duke's Laws, The Laws of the Dongan and Leisler Assemblies, The Charters of Albany and New York and the Acts of the Colonial Legislatures from 1691 to 1775* (Albany, 1894), IV, 483–490 (hereafter cited as *Colonial Laws of New York*); Cadwallader Colden to Lords Commissioners for Trade and Plantations, January 8, 1761: *Colden Letter Books*, I, 54; Council Session, June 11, 1762: *Calendar of Council Minutes*, p. 407; John Watts to John Erving, June 14, 1762: *Watts Letter Book*, pp. 61–62. For some of John Paul Jones' wage troubles with his men see Morison, *John Paul Jones*, pp. 23–26. For the provisions of the act discussed here see below, p. 61.

[10.] John Watts to John Erving, June 14, December 29, 1762: *Watts Letter Book*, pp. 62, 112.

[11.] Stokes, *Iconography*, IV, 749, 759.

[12.] *Post-Boy*, October 17, 1765, February 13, November 13, 1766, June 26, 1769.

[13.] *Ibid.*, November 3, 1763, March 28, 1768; Hutchinson, *Press-Gang*, p. 40; *Mariner's Mirror*, XXXIX (February, 1953), 69.

[14.] D. Macloed, "Answers": "Naval Sixpence," *ibid.*, XXXIX (February, 1953), 1; W. R. Chapin, "A Seventeenth-Century Chart Publisher: Being an Account of the Present Firm of Smith & Ebbs, Ltd., Printers and Stationers, Who have a Continuity in Business of 300 Years," *American Neptune*, VIII (October, 1948), 315; Morris, *Government and Labor*, p. 252n; Robert Straus, *Medical Care for Seamen: The Origin of Public Medical Service in the United States* (New Haven, 1950), pp. 18, 20 (hereafter cited as Straus, *Medical Care*); Allyn B. Forbes, "Greenwich Hospital Money," *New England Quarterly*, III (July, 1930), 519–526.

[15.] *Post-Boy*, June 20, 1757, March 27, 1758; John Watts to Christopher Kilby, November 15, 1763: *Watts Letter Book*, p. 197. These sources indicate that privateers paid the "naval sixpence" in the form of a proportion of the take rather than in deductions from wages.

[16.] Straus, *Medical Care*, p. 20.

[17.] *Debates and Proceedings in the Congress of the United States, Fifth Congress* (Washington, 1851), pp. 1386–1393; Billias, *Glover*, p. 29.

[18.] Edwards, *New York as Eighteenth Century Municipality*, p. 100; David M. Schneider, *The History of Public Welfare in New York State* (Chicago, 1938–41), I, 61 (hereafter cited as Schneider, *Public Welfare*); Bridenbaugh, *Cities in Revolt*, p. 324.

[19.] *Minutes of Common Council*, IV, 429, VI, 124–125; *Post-Boy*, April 24, 1758, November 19, 1770; Cadwallader Colden to Sir Jeffrey Amherst, May 26, 1762: *Colden Letter Books*, I, 210–211; "Journal of a French Traveller in the Colonies, 1765," *American Historical Review*, XXVII

(October, 1921), 82 (hereafter cited as "Journal of French Traveller"; Burnaby, *Travels*, p. 76; Edwards, *New York as Eighteenth Century Municipality*, pp. 100–101; Stokes, *Iconography*, IV, 309, 703.

20. *Journal*, May 25, 1769, September 2, 1773; Edwards, *New York as Eighteenth Century Municipality*, p. 102.

21. *Minutes of Common Council*, IV, 307; *Post-Boy*, February 11, 1771. For Cregier see *Minutes of Common Council*, IV, 474, VI, 161; *Wills*, VII, 56.

22. *Minutes of Common Council*, IV, 325, VI, 449, VII, 46, 87; Burnaby, *Travels*, p. 76; Stokes, *Iconography*, IV, 458; Edwards, *New York as Eighteenth Century Municipality*, pp. 103–104.

23. *Ibid.*, pp. 104–106; *Post-Boy*, March 11, 1751; *Journal*, February 6, 1772; Stokes, *Iconography*, IV, 756.

24. *Minutes of Common Council*, IV, 403.

25. *Ibid.*, VII, 66.

26. *Post-Boy*, March 18, 1751; *Mercury*, September 17, 1753.

27. *Ibid.*, March 25, 1771; *Journal*, March 23, 1769, April 5, 1770.

28. *Post-Boy*, January 1, 1767, February 6, 1772; Stokes, *Iconography*, IV, 777.

29. *Ibid.*, IV, 809; Bridenbaugh, *Cities in Revolt*, pp. 127, 322; *Mercury*, November 13, December 11, 1769, January 1, 15, 1770; *Post-Boy*, November 20, December 11, 1769; William H. W. Sabine, ed., *Historical Memoirs from 16 March 1763 to 9 July 1776 of William Smith* (New York, 1956), p. 80 (hereafter cited as Sabine, *Smith Memoirs*).

30. *Post-Boy*, December 11, 1769, October 8, November 5, 1770, January 7, April 1, 1771; J. H. French, *Gazetteer of the State of New York: Embracing a Comprehensive View of the Geography, Geology, and General History of the State and a Complete History and Description of Every County, City, Town, Village, and Locality. With Full Tables of Statistics* (Syracuse, 1860), p. 434. In 1747 a charter was given to the English "Merchant Seamen's Corporation." I have been unable to discover anything about this organization except that it was founded "for the relief and support of disabled seamen, their widows and children, in the Merchant Service." H.T.A.B., "Query," *Mariner's Mirror*, VII (October, 1921), 319.

31. Henry Collins Brown, ed., *Valentine's Manual of Old New York*, no. 12, New Series (New York, 1928), p. 61. Hereafter cited as Brown, *Valentine's Manual*.

32. Bridenbaugh, *Cities in Revolt*, p. 358. For population figures see *ibid.*, pp. 5, 216; Greene and Harrington, *Population*, pp. 102–103; Burnaby, *Travels*, p. 75.

33. Brown, *Valentine's Manual*, p. 60; *Post-Boy*, October 23, 1766, March 28, 1768; The King v. James Dunn, Indictment, filed November 5, 1767,

Court of General Quarter Sessions: in Mayor's Court Pleadings, file drawer (1766–1774); The King v. Thomas Dunn and Jane his Wife, Indictment for Keeping a Disorderly House, filed August 9, 1770, Court of General Quarter Sessions: Pleadings K-519.

34. Edwards, *New York as Eighteenth Century Municipality*, p. 343; *Post-Boy*, June 4, 1767.

35. Cadwallader Colden to Pitt, December 4, 1760: *Colden Letter Books*, I, 43–44.

36. *Post-Boy*, October 22, November 5, 1767.

37. *Ibid.*, March 28, 1768.

38. The King v. Sarah Dyllon, Indictment for Keeping a Disorderly House, filed July Term, 1774, New York Supreme Court: Pleadings K-856.

39. *Mercury*, November 5, 1764; Bridenbaugh, *Cities in Revolt*, p. 121.

40. The King v. Peter and Elizabeth, Indictment for Keeping a Disorderly House, filed October 31, 1766, New York Supreme Court: Minute Book (July 31, 1764 - October 28, 1767), p. 192.

41. *Post-Boy*, April 11, 1768.

42. The King v. Thomas Dunn and Jane his Wife, Indictment for Keeping a Disorderly House, filed August 9, 1770, Court of General Quarter Sessions: Pleadings K-519; also The King v. Jane the Wife of Thomas Dunn, Indictment for Bigamy, filed October 26, 1773, New York Supreme Court: Pleadings K-41.

43. The King v. James Dunn, Indictment, filed November 5, 1767, Court of General Quarter Sessions: in Mayor's Court Pleadings, file drawer (1766–1774).

44. This term is used in Straus, *Medical Care*, pp. 12–13.

45. Hohman, *Seamen Ashore*, pp. 211–230 and the same author's "Seamen" in *Encyclopedia of the Social Sciences* (New York, 1934), XIII, 611–616.

46. *Post-Boy*, July 9, 1770; Bridenbaugh, *Cities in Revolt*, p. 160.

47. *Post-Boy*, March 30, 1772.

48. *Ibid.*, October 3, 1765, August 22, 1768; *Mercury*, August 18, 1760.

49. *Post-Boy*, April 21, 1768.

50. *Ibid.*, December 25, 1766.

51. *Ibid.*, June 4, 1767.

52. *Ibid.*, June 25, November 12, 1767, August 12, 1771; *Mercury*, July 23, 1753.

53. *Post-Boy*, October 23, 1766.

54. *Ibid.*, July 25, 1765, November 9, 1772; *Journal*, September 23, 1773.

55. *Post-Boy*, September 23, 1769.

56. See James Dunn: *Muster Rolls*, pp. 164–165; The King v. Thomas Dunn and Jane his Wife, Indictment for Keeping a Disorderly House, filed August 9, 1770, Court of General Quarter Sessions: Pleadings K-519; Daniel Sullivan: Joseph Forman v. The King, Demurrer, filed April 30, 1761, New York Supreme Court: Pleadings K-729; John Campbell: The King v. John Campbell, Indictment for Keeping a Disorderly House, filed February 9, 1769, Court of General Quarter Sessions: Pleadings K-469; The King v. Thomas Farinscomb: Indictment for Receiving Stolen Goods, filed January 19, 1770, New York Supreme Court: Pleadings K-266.

57. *Colonial Laws of New York*, IV, 489.

58. Stokes, *Iconography*, IV, 86, 88.

59. *Minutes of Common Council*, I, 223.

60. Stokes, *Iconography*, IV, 281.

61. *Minutes of Common Council*, I, 372.

62. *Colonial Laws of New York*, I, 345–348.

63. *Ibid.*, I, 866–867, II, 952.

64. *Ibid.*, IV, 483–491.

65. Edwards, *New York as Eighteenth Century Municipality*, 85–86; *Freemen*, pp. 532–533.

66. On New York as a class society see Staughton Lynd, "Who Should Rule at Home? Dutchess County, New York, in the American Revolution," *William and Mary Quarterly*, third series, XVIII (July, 1961), 330–359, especially 340–341. On the franchise: of forty-eight men listed as "mariners" in *Freemen*, ten are identifiable as captains after comparison with such sources as the Loyalist Transcripts, *Post-Boy*, and the especially valuable list of privateer captains in Fish, *New York Privateers*, pp. 83–90. As to juries: here the £60 freehold requirement (see three orders for panels of jurors dated January 19, 1765, New York Supreme Court: Pleadings K-814) must have acted to exclude common seamen. Certainly there is no indication that it was ignored. One panel contains fifty-two names, of which ten are "mariners"; all but three of these are identifiable as captains on the basis of the sort of comparison indicated above: Panel of Jurors, n.d., New York Supreme Court: Pleadings P-2689.

67. *Post-Boy*, January 8, 1770.

68. See below, pp. 91–92, 130–131.

69. The King v. Nicholas Bassong, Indictment, filed April Term, 1775, New York Supreme Court: Pleadings K-12; The King v. Felix Meigs, Indictment, filed July 30, 1772, New York Supreme Court: Pleadings K-518.

70. *Post-Boy*, May 10, 17, 1756.

71. *Ibid.*, October 14, December 16, 1762, December 5, 1765.

[72.] The King v. Jacob Abrahams, Indictment for Grand Larceny, filed January Term, 1775, New York Supreme Court: Pleadings K-15; The King v. Levy Barnet, Indictment for Grand Larceny, filed October 26, 1767, New York Supreme Court: Pleadings K-300; The King v. Thomas Farinscomb, Indictment for Receiving Stolen Goods, filed January 19, 1770, New York Supreme Court: Pleadings K-266; The King v. John McCume, Indictment for Petty Larceny, filed February 9, 1769, Court of General Quarter Sessions: Pleadings K-478; The King v. Thomas Norton, Indictment for Grand Larceny, filed October 27, 1767, New York Supreme Court: Pleadings K-175; The King v. Adam Smith, Indictments for Larceny, New York Supreme Court, filed April 22, July 20, August 2, 1771: Pleadings K-317, Parchment 127-E-6, Pleadings K-263; The King v. William Smith, Indictment for Grand Larceny, filed October 29, 1773, New York Supreme Court: Pleadings K-28; *Post-Boy*, February 11, 1760, February 20, July 24, 1769.

[73.] The King v. Adam Smith: Indictment for Grand Larceny, filed April 22, 1771, New York Supreme Court: Pleadings K-317; The King v. Adam Smith, Indictment, filed July 20, 1771, New York Supreme Court: Parchments 127-E-6; The King v. Adam Smith, Indictment for Larceny, filed August 2, 1771, New York Supreme Court: Pleadings K-263; The King v. Adam Smith, Indictment for Petty Larceny, filed January 23, 1772, New York Supreme Court: Pleadings K-498; The King v. Adam Smith, Indictment for Grand Larceny, filed January 23, 1772, New York Supreme Court: Pleadings K-374.

[74.] The King v. John Forster, Indictment for Petty Larceny, filed October 23, 1772, New York Supreme Court: Pleadings K-495; Deposition of Captain Elder and Examination of John Forster, sworn October 20, 1772, New York Supreme Court: Pleadings K-457.

[75.] The King v. William Pollitt, Examination, taken June 14, 1775, New York Supreme Court: Pleadings K-42.

[76.] The King v. Jacob Catus, Examination, New York Supreme Court, taken April 9, 1765; Pleadings K-274; The King v. Edward Grant, Indictment for Grand Larceny, filed October 24, 1767, New York Supreme Court: Pleadings K-239.

[77.] *Post-Boy*, September 30, 1773.

[78.] Cadwallader Colden to Pitt, December 4, 1760: *Colden Letter Books*, I, 43; The King v. Lt. William Jones, Indictment for a Riot, filed February 8, 1769, Court of General Quarter Sessions: Pleadings K-515; The King v. William Mahawn, Indictment for Beating one of the City Watch, filed February 9, 1769, Court of General Quarter Sessions: Pleadings K-731.

[79.] The King v. Samuel Doren, Indictment, filed January 23, 1772: Pleadings K-529; Presentment in same case: Pleadings K-851.

[80.] Andrew Moriarty v. David Beaton, September 23, 1766, Mayor's Court: Minute Book (January 25, 1763 - October 29, 1765), pp. 155, 157.

[81.] The King v. Edward Waddon, Indictment for Assault and Battery, filed October 22, 1765, New York Supreme Court: Pleadings K-783; The King v. John Bogert, Jr., Indictment for Assault and Battery, filed October 23, 1772, New York Supreme Court: Pleadings K-393.

[82.] The King v. Nathaniel Cooley, Indictment for assaulting Gaoler, filed October 25, 1763, New York Supreme Court: Pleadings K-27.

[83.] The King v. Anthony O'Neal, Indictment for Keeping a Disorderly House, filed January 22, 1764, New York Supreme Court: Pleadings K-744; The King v. Anthony O'Neal, Indictment for Assaulting and Wounding a Constable, filed October Term, 1763, New York Supreme Court: Pleadings K-793.

[84.] The King v. John Kendall, Indictment for Assault and Battery, filed April Term, 1775, New York Supreme Court: Pleadings K-868.

[85.] *Post-Boy*, February 2, 1764.

[86.] *Ibid.*, October 22, 1767, July 9, 1770.

[87.] The King v. Bryan Mullen and Mathew Sweetman, Indictment for Murder with a Chair, filed March Term, 1755, New York Supreme Court: Pleadings K-577; *Post-Boy*, June 27, 1765.

[88.] *Ibid.*, November 13, 1760; The King v. Moses Vinter, Depositions of Jonathan Hibbs, Arthur McNeil, Charles Geere, and James Richetts and Inquisition of Richard Cope, taken January 20, 1761, New York Supreme Court: Pleadings K-1834 and K-370.

[89.] The King v. Daniel McCarty et al., Information for a Riot, filed October 29, 1763, New York Supreme Court: Pleadings K-754; The King v. Thomas Martin and Edward Groomes, Indictment, filed April Term, 1765, New York Supreme Court: Pleading K-797; The King v. William McMon et al., Indictment for a Riot, filed January Term, 1771, New York Supreme Court: Pleadings K-346; The King v. Thomas Clarke, Jr. and John Kendal, Indictment for a Riot and Breaking of Windows, filed April 24, 1771, New York Supreme Court: Pleadings K-384.

[90.] See below, pp. 89–90.

IV. Jack Tar in the Streets: The Stamp Act Crisis

Strange Ballast

Captain Davis[1] gazed mockingly as he closed the brig on his port bow. "Whither bound?" From Newcastle to Philadelphia—and fighting the Gulf Stream all the way. William Davis knew the North Atlantic better: he kept *Edward* to the cold green water and sailed on for New York.[2] The Captain was in a hurry, and although they did not share his motive, the crew would cooperate if it meant an earlier exchange of the cold sea for the warmth of Kate Crow's or Quaker Fan's.[3]

Below, in the warmth of the cabin, the passengers continued their stale discussion of what had been fresh news in London nine weeks before. Mrs. Cary and Mrs. Nichols talked about the birth of a third prince; the soldiers—Mr. Webb and Major Cary of the Royal Americans—discussed the Stamp Act with merchant Kendrick and Mr. Brownjohn of New York. On his last voyage Captain Davis had brought New York the news that the Stamp Act had passed; now he listened with more than ordinary interest as he heard that one could get one hundred guineas to ten in London coffee houses that the Act would be repealed as soon as Parliament met the next month. At last the ladies and the gentlemen found common ground for conversation in the recent death of the Emperor of Germany. . . .[4]

Below the water-line, below goods intended for perhaps one hundred different shippers, even below six barrels of pippins destined for Colonel Amherst,[5] deep in the hold rested three packages. Their weight helped to keep *Edward* upright against the October gale. Two of them were marked "No. 1, J. McE., NEW YORK," and on a third was written, "No. 1, J.I. CONNECTICUT." Inside these—and seven more like them scattered through the ship's hold—were more than two tons of paper. Paper, parchment, and vellum: all of it bearing the same embossed stamp of the royal arms.[6]

Captain Davis knew his cargo, but up above, in the cabin, the passengers talked on, unaware of *Edward*'s paper ballast.[7]

On the evening of Tuesday, October 22, 1765, after six weeks and three days at sea, *Edward* sighted the Highlands of Neversink.[8] Ahead lay the new Sandy Hook lighthouse, a full nine stories high.[9] Captain Davis sailed ahead in ten fathoms of water, carefully avoiding the bar. When the lighthouse bore west a half point south and Mount Pleasant appeared midway between the light and the cedar trees on the Hook, *Edward* sailed over the bar. Safe in six fathoms, Captain Davis awaited the pilot.[10] Then, shortly after the middle of the first watch, a blast from one of sloop *Hawke*'s ten cannon echoed through Raritan Bay and rolled like thunder northward through the Narrows, past Bedloe's Island, and on to Manhattan.[11]

Hawke was one of three warships which had been awaiting some "Ship or Vessell"[12]—their captains knew not which—since shortly before *Edward* had sailed from England. In the Narrows, midway between Manhattan and *Hawke*'s station at the Hook, lay the frigate *Garland*, twenty guns; before the town lay *Coventry*, commanded by Archibald Kennedy.[13] Before that time and subsequently Captain Kennedy would send his ships out to the same stations to stock the King's Navy with unwilling seamen lifted off incoming vessels;[14] this time the warships were there at the special request of Lieutenant-Governor Cadwallader Colden. Their mission was to protect William Davis and his cargo from the people of New York City and to deliver a note to the Captain. The note spoke of "violent and riotous proceedings" and directed Davis to put himself under the protection of His Majesty's Ships of War until further notice.[15]

The kind of violent and riotous proceedings which Cadwallader Colden hoped to avoid were those which had taken place in Boston where stamp-distributor Andrew Oliver had been forced by mob action to resign his commission even before it had arrived.[16] James McEvers of New York was especially concerned about such proceedings. McEvers—a store-keeper with close to £20,000 worth of such diverse stock as wine, china, hose, and shoes[17]—had been appointed stamp distributor for New York (apparently without having sought the job),[18] had accepted, and had entered into bonds for the execution of the office.[19] New York seemed to talk only of what had happened at Boston—a bit jealously.[20] McEvers' enemies suggested that he insure his house; his friends offered no consolation: a storm was rising, they told him, and it was headed his way.[21] It all added up to a hardly subtle suggestion that McEvers resign. So he resigned and—amid thunder and lightning[22]—threw the ball to Colden.[23] The Old Man[24] caught it at Spring Hill, about two hours out on Long Island, away from New

York's heat and small pox.[25] This was, he claimed, the first he had heard of the "seditious . . . Temper" of the people of New York: he was on cool terms with the members of his Council, meeting them only when necessary, and neither the councillors nor the municipal authorities had bothered to inform him.[26] He immediately resolved to return to town, then vacillated, and finally responded to his son's urgent call.[27]

As the men of *Coventry*'s boat moved him closer to the Manhattan shore and Fort George,[28] Colden's thoughts moved in the age-old patterns of unsuccessful colonial governors under pressure: military force is the thing . . . the only way to prevent trouble is to have enough military force to discourage all opposition to the laws . . . military weakness is an invitation to sedition . . . a battalion may be necessary. . . .[29] In the spring he had fretted when General Gage had set out for the south, leaving him with a handful of invalids to guard the Fort. What if a mob should attack the Fort? What if the slaves should rebel, as they had done before, with bloody results?[30] Late in July General Gage ordered a company of the second battalion of the Royal Americans from Crown Point to the Fort. After McEvers' resignation Major James had taken it upon himself to move into the Fort two howitzers and two royals with their ammunition and had posted a sentry on the Fort's northwest bastion to observe the town. And, on the same day that Colden returned to the Fort, an ordinance transport arrived with another two companies of artillery; they were immediately marched into the Fort.[31]

The Fort was enough to produce despair in the military mind; anyone else would have laughed. Built by the Dutch in 1614, it had clearly not been designed to hold off effectively an attack from the town. A square set at the southwestern tip of the island, its job was to protect the city from hostile vessels. (It did this poorly; its ninety-two twenty-four pounders were almost level with the water, and ships could easily stay beyond their reach; the fortification also failed to cover the harbor in the East River.)[32] Thus only two sides of the square had any relevance at all to the town, one facing Broadway and the other Stone Street. The works were entirely *en barbette*, that is, the guns were so mounted as to fire over a parapet and not through embrasures; thus they were exposed and could be commanded from the rising ground towards the north. Captain Kennedy's home, at the bottom of Broadway, commanded the two sides and would be a danger if taken. But in addition to all these problems of construction were difficulties caused by the governors' way of life. The governor's residence—three stories high and facing west—lay inside the fort, and the fort and its environs had become simply an instrument for his family's pleasure and convenience. Firewood was piled up against the wall, and wherever the guns pointed there seemed to be a building—a stable, or some more imposing structure—erected for the governor's use. Thus everything military had been allowed to go to pot: there was no ammunition in the fort, the guns were honeycombed, their carriages rotten. In this state the fort could not withstand one hundred resolute men.[33]

"I shall not be intimidated": such was Colden's response to McEvers' resignation,[34] and his actions throughout the fall fairly shrieked the words at the populace. On September 5 Colonel John Montresor was asked to make an inconspicuous survey of the fort to determine how it might be strengthened. The firewood must be removed; railings must be lined with oak planking to furnish a base for additional fire; the many windows must be crenelated and the gorges of the four bastions must be closed; artillery positions must be changed; a stink pot is needed; some of the exits must be blocked; crow's feet must be provided to cover the salients and sally ports; two frigates must be so placed that their fire will intersect at the northeast salient, and another frigate must be placed at Turtle Bay.[35] The movement of tools, ammunition, oak planking, and men into the fort[36] and of ships about the bay and rivers[37] could not escape the public's attention. Soon the fort was so crowded with men and supplies that Colden began to wonder where he would put the object of all the fuss—the stamps themselves.[38] Howitzers on the curtains, cannon facing the gates and Broadway: it looked as if Montcalm himself were at Kingsbridge,[39] and Colden was terrified.

The people interpreted every one of these moves as a clear provocation. The preparations were extraordinary and unprecedented, they were ostentatiously performed, and their intent was patently hostile.[40] The Council, the Mayor, and the Magistrates all agreed that the people abhorred violence and the government's safest policy would be to show confidence in the people rather than to provoke them by calling in special assistance.[41] At one point General Gage tried to check the ostentatious show, and when a new governor arrived in November he was mortified by the preparations.[42] But the General did carry the job through, and the new governor privately suggested that firing on the mob was the best solution.[43] And Sir William Johnson twice congratulated Colden on his firmness and resolution.[44] Certainly the Old Man was stupid and the effect of his actions provocative. But to make too much of this is to imply that the people's subsequent rage might not have occurred had a more sensitive man been running things. And to say this would be to belittle the intensity of feelings demonstrated in the days that followed.

After spending the night anchored off the Hook, *Edward* sailed on, conducted by *Coventry* and *Garland*, through the Narrows, where porpoises played on the surface of the water, past the hospital for sick and wounded seamen and the quarantine on Bedloe's Island. In the harbor *Edward*—or rather her cargo—was greeted by lowered color signifying mourning, lamentation, and woe. Two thousand people stood at the Battery, enraged at the sea-borne procession. *Edward* dropped anchor in the North River under Fort George's ninety-two guns.[45]

While *Edward* lay at anchor and debate proceeded in the Council Chamber over what to do with her, another sort of debate was about to reach its conclusion less than one-half mile to the north. There twenty-seven men, representing nine provinces, had held moderate and reasonable discussions for a little more than two weeks. Among the Declarations of this Stamp Act Congress were the following: that Americans were entitled "to all the inherent Rights and Liberties of . . . Subjects within the Kingdom of *Great-Britain*"; that among the basic rights of Englishmen were freedom from all taxes imposed without their consent; that Americans were not and could not be represented in Parliament; that the Stamp Act thus had "a manifest Tendency to subvert the Rights and Liberties of the Colonists"; and finally,

> That it is the indispensable Duty of these Colonies, to the best of Sovereigns, to the Mother Country, and to themselves, to endeavour by a loyal and dutiful Address to his Majesty, and humble Applications to both Houses of Parliament, to procure the Repeal of the Act for granting and applying certain Stamp Duties. . . .[46]

The twenty-seven men who emerged for the last time from New York's Town Hall on October 25, 1765 had completed a structure which would endure for a decade—a long time on the stormy seas of revolutionary times. The Sugar Act had "set people a thinking, in six months, more than they had done in their whole lives before;"[47] when they were done thinking about the Sugar Act and the Stamp Act they had accepted Parliament's right to legislate for them but denied its authority to tax them in any way. They would be content with this position for a decade, until they found themselves too cramped by the rights of Englishmen and would be content with nothing less than the rights of man.[48]

Riots: Left vs. Right

The Congress had completed its work: "The Stamp Act has been so fully, and so frequently proved to be inconsistent with the first principles of the *English* constitution, that little more is necessary to be said on that head."[49] Whatever the result of the Stamp Act Congress' proceedings, wrote a New Yorker shortly after its close, "the Generality of the Friends of Liberty, did not choose that it should ever once be thought that the Enjoyment of their Rights depended merely upon the Success of these Representations or the Courtesy of those to whom they were made."[50] The mere assertion of right would have little effect, either in England or America. The search for principles had, for the time being, ended; the best minds would now devote themselves to the search for tactics.

One way of fighting the Stamp Act was to stop all activities which required the use of stamps. Newspapers could stop publishing, lawyers could refuse to do business, merchants could boycott English goods. This was the policy decided upon by more than two hundred New York merchants who met at Burns' City Arms Tavern late in the afternoon of October 31, a few hours before the Stamp Act was to take effect. They resolved to cancel all orders for English goods and to refuse to sell all goods shipped from England after January 1. The shopkeepers plugged potential loopholes by pledging not to buy goods shipped from England after the New Year.[51]

While the merchants were meeting in George Burns' Long Room, something happened outside which suggested a quite different strategy of opposition to the Stamp Act. A group of children and seamen appeared, drawn by the rumor that a ceremonial burying of Liberty was to take place. When the meeting broke up and the merchants went home without a burial, the children and seamen set out through the streets, hooting and yelling. They proceeded to the fort, then broke up into three squads. The magistrates tried unsuccessfully to disperse them, but they ran on through the streets, shouting "liberty," threatening to destroy the homes of certain individuals and to bury Major James alive, destroying lamps and, before they were done, a few thousand windows.[52]

The spirit of John Wilkes was abroad in the streets of the City of New York.[53] That spirit had been present when McEvers had resigned and, more recently, when a feverish and aguey escaped Maryland stamp distributor had been forced to flee his bed and take refuge in the fort.[54] It had been present when "the voice of the people" had dared any man to distribute or use stamps under pain of destruction of his house and person.[55] The spirit of John Wilkes had been there every time a seaman had battled for his freedom against impressment by the English Navy. Now, once again, the sailors fought: once again for freedom against English tyranny, and, again, with violence.

On November first New York's seamen left their ships at the docks and came into Manhattan.[56] The city was wild with rumor: houses would be destroyed, Major James would be buried alive, there would be a larger mob than the night before, there would be a riot. Shoemaker John Ketcham told John Bridge; Bridge told Colden; Colden told Mayor Cruger; Cruger told the aldermen. The municipal authorities confirmed the rumors and sent them back to Colden. The Lieutenant-Governor sent Colonel Montresor to inspect the fort, now ready for gunfire. Colden worried about how he could put down a mob and also hold the fort with the troops available; he asked Captain Kennedy for some marines. Kennedy sent a lieutenant and twenty-four marines; this left him without sentries and worried: "as most of our men are imprest there is a great risque of their deserting."[57]

Shortly before seven in the evening a stranger rushed up to the fort gate with a note which was immediately rushed in to Colden. The same note—or a similar one—had been posted at the coffeehouse most of the day. Signed simply "New York," it addressed Colden as the "Chief Murderer of their Rights and Privileges" and "an enemy to Your King and Country, to Liberty and Mankind" (he had earned these epithets by taking the oath to support the Stamp Act the day before). The Stamp Act would not take effect so long as they lived to defend their country; indeed Colden would see his own blood shed if he did not take another oath that very night—an oath to prevent the functioning of the Act and to seek its repeal in England. And if he fired on the town—as it was rumored he would if there were a riot—his associates would be killed and the gray-haired Lieutenant-Governor would be hanged on a signpost—"a martir to your own villainy."[58]

As Colden finished the note a distant roar carried his eyes out over the town. Up by the Fields a bright light could be seen against the sky. It was the light of a great many candles—perhaps six hundred. Colden followed the lights down the Fly: at every corner a cheer, and then a pause for a few minutes at the coffeehouse.[59]

The Mayor and Aldermen were the first to try to cope with the mob. They went into the street—accompanied by constables—and were confronted by a huge procession, its way lit by candles and torches. At the head was a seaman. On the seaman's head was an old chair, and seated in the chair was a paper effigy of Cadwallader Colden. The constables marched up to the seaman and threw the effigy to the ground. With great restraint the mob picked it up, put it back in its place, and, "in the most magisterial manner," offered the Mayor and his associates safety if they would get out of the way. The mob proceeded, its numbers constantly increasing, without destroying anything. From time to time someone unloaded his pistol at the effigy.[60]

The mob arrived at the walls of the fort a few minutes later. The men inside tensed for an assault. They witnessed the scene before them with confusion and, finally, relief. For the present the mob was content to break into Colden's carriage house and pull out his coach. They set their effigy of its owner on the coach's seat, pulled it through the city, and returned to the Fields.[61]

In the Fields another group had been hard at work while the procession had made its way through the town. They had been erecting a gallows. From the gallows hung some lanterns and two figures— Colden and, to his right, the Devil with a boot in his hand. The Devil was whispering into Colden's ear, "as 'tis suppos'd it was intirely at his Instigation he acted. . . ." In Colden's right hand was a stamped bill of lading, "which he seemed to court the People to receive." A drum—"the Badge of his Profession"—was fixed to his back, and on his chest there was a piece of paper bearing the words, *"The Rebel Drummer in the Year 1715."*[62]

Now the two mobs met and silence was called for. Someone stood up to proclaim the rules the protest would follow: no stones were to be thrown, no windows broken, and no one was to be injured. Then, with Colden's coach in the lead, followed by the gallows with the effigies, the procession headed for the fort.[63] At the gate they knocked and demanded to be let in. They raised their effigies above the gate and hooted obscenely.[64]

The soldiers watched all this from the ramparts. Some of the people threw bricks and stones; others placed their hands on top of the ramparts and seemed about to climb into the fort. They were trying to provoke gunfire, but their obscenities were greeted with silence, and their actions produced no fire. The garrison's restraint was grounded in fear. Despite all the provocative preparations, the fort was not ready to withstand an attack by a mob of one hundred, much less the two thousand who were there. Major James felt that he could have killed nine hundred by firing on the mob, but both he and General Gage knew the garrison would be massacred in the ensuing civil war. In the mob were three hundred carpenters ready to cut down the gate at the first shot. There were also others "acquainted with military Affairs," notably four or five hundred seamen. So the garrison froze in inactivity: "not a single return, in words or otherwise was made from any Man in the Fort. . . ."[65]

Unable to arouse the garrison, they set out for the Bowling Green. In the middle of the Green, under the muzzles of the fort's guns one hundred yards away, they built a bonfire, using for kindling the Green's palisades (which they had destroyed during their march) and the planks of the Broadway face of the the fort's fence, which had been torn down by the garrison to expose attackers to the fort's fire (this was a hostile action which the people had taken as a provocation). They cut the effigies down and threw them into the fire: "Such," we are told they shouted, "are the entertainments the people bestow on the friends of stamps!" Then into the fire went everything that had not been nailed down in the coach-house: Colden's chariot, a single horse chaise belonging to someone else, two sleighs, some carriages belonging to Colden's friends, and all the stable furniture. All burned to ashes, to the accompaniment of "every Expression of the most inveterate Hatred & Contempt." All this was observed by a crowd of thousands, probably including Colden on the nearby rampart.[66]

Whatever leaders the mob might have had had lost control: their direction against destroying property had been flagrantly disobeyed. Now the mob was fully its own master, and it had an account to settle with Major James, one of the men on whom they pinned the responsibility for strengthening the fort and pointng the artillery at the town—in short, for being "over officious in his duty." He was the sort of man who was proud to be so charged, and he later boasted before Parliament that he had indeed ostentatiously burned an unstamped almanac; that he had sent some ladies and gentlemen off the ramparts of the fort so they could not see the works he was carrying on; that "I threatened to cram the Stamps down their Throats with the End of my Sword"; that he had said "If they attempted to rise I would drive them all out of the town for a pack of Rascals, with four and twenty men."[67]

So now a detachment of volunteers set out for the Hudson River and Vaux-Hall, the house Major James had rented for a three year period with a promise to return it in as good condition as he received it. They marched in an orderly way, singlemindedly intent upon the destruction of an enemy to liberty. The house had recently been redecorated and it had a handsome garden and a fine library and good furniture. Into this elegant establishment poured the angry mob, breaking through the front door. When they were finished the Major and his lady would have only the clothes on their backs. Into a bonfire in front of the doorway went tables, chairs, desks, trunks, chests—everything that would burn. They cut the featherbeds open and scattered the contents about. Nine and one-quarter casks of wine kept their enthusiasm high, and they destroyed what they did not drink. Into the fire went all the family's clothes, a library of three hundred "choice books," glass, china, official papers, manuscripts, linen, antiques, and mathematical instruments. Having destroyed everything moveable, they turned on the house itself; they broke every window, cut down the sashes and shutters and destroyed the partitions, leaving a shell where Vaux-Hall had stood. They tore down the summer houses, tore up the garden, and trooped off with the regimental colors and Major James' military trophies.[68]

At two in the morning the light of the bonfire that was Vaux-Hall revealed a mob that had been in action for seven hours, trooping off to the sound of ringing church bells, doubtless with the regimental colors in the lead, towards the Fields where they had begun. There they entertained themselves at the sailors' whorehouses for another two hours and called it a night at four o'clock.[69]

We Will Have the Stamps!

Far from being a time for sober planning, the morning after held promise of a repetition of the night before. On Friday the mob had attacked people connected with the stamps; Saturday's concern would be the stamps themselves.

On Saturday morning a man climbed to the balcony of the coffeehouse. He read a paper which called on the people to be peaceable and indeed to turn out with arms to quell any breach of the peace. When the speaker was done, Isaac Sears, a former privateer captain, stood up and commented on the paper just read. Its intention, he told the crowd, was to keep them from having the stamps. Do not listen to these timid warnings, he added; "we will have them within four and twenty hours." With a flourish of his hat he cried out, "Huzza, my lads," and they cheered in reply. Sears turned aside to some gentlemen who had been watching the meeting and told them what they must have suspected: "Your best way, as you may now see, will be to advise Lieutenant-Governor Colden to send the stamp papers from the fort to the inhabitants."[70]

By word of mouth and by note Colden got many messages: he must not distribute the stamps, he must hand them over to the people or they would attack and set fire to the fort, he must move the stamps from the fort to a ship in the harbor.[71] Colden called his Council together; they discussed the previous day's troubles, and he informed them of the latest threats. Did they not think the fort ought to be further strengthened? Well, they were no judges of military affairs—that was a matter for specialists—they thought the fort perfectly safe—but if something had to be done it ought to be done. With this ambiguous mandate Colden sent the engineers out for another survey, and since only five Council members had been able to make it, called another session for the afternoon.[72]

The Mayor and Aldermen met at the City Hall in the afternoon, and "despondency and irresolution prevailed over all." Bowed heads raised as Mayor Cruger introduced Leading Citizen Robert R. Livingston, who had come to offer his help. Suggestions were made that they raise a posse, form an association, call out the militia. They slumped back into their stupor. Finally one genius, more resolute than the rest, came up with a plan: they would do nothing until they heard from the Council.[73]

The Council advised Colden to pass the buck, and he did it with enthusiasm. Some time before he had thought it all out, and he might well have avoided his troubles had he had the courage to announce his timidity then. Captain Davis had brought no instructions of any sort, not even a bill of lading for the stamps, and he had not even received an official copy of the act; clearly, thought this man of otherwise dictatorial temperament, clearly he had no authority to distribute the stamps in place of McEvers. He would wait for the arrival of Henry Moore, the new Governor, who was expected daily. ("No man," Colden had written, "can more earnestly desire your speedy arrival than I do." "If ever he was sincere," wrote a Council member of Colden, he is sincere when he "wishes for the arrival of the new Governor. . . .") Now, with Moore expected hourly, the Council told Colden what he wanted to hear: he could not distribute the stamps, and he should declare that he would do nothing until Moore's arrival; "he intirely acquiesced," with the proviso that he would distribute no stamps unless they were called for.[74]

Meanwhile Robert R. Livingston was concerned to prevent an assault on the fort by the mob which was reassembling. James Duane had a plan which, Livingston later observed, "contributed more than any other thing to success." Who, Duane asked, had begun the trouble the night before? The seamen. Among whom would it probably begin again? The seamen. The best way to quiet the seamen, thought Duane, would be to enlist the support of the privateer captains. Easier said than done, for several of them were "much inflamed" and by no means willing to cooperate in putting down a movement which they approved. They found one, who seems to have served more as guide than as liaison with the seamen. Touring the town they found the seamen filled with resentment against Colden, many of them intent upon attacking the fort. But the Leading Citizens could find no group about to carry through the plan and after talking to many people, they convinced themselves that they had split the mob. Peace reigned, and the gentlemen set out to examine the ruins of Vaux-Hall.[75]

Suddenly seven or eight men rushed out of a house opposite the Commons, carrying lighted candles and an effigy made out of a barber's block and a pole and dressed in rags. The peacemakers ran towards them and stopped a few. But it began increasingly to look like the night before all over again, and Livingston finally realized that they meant it. A "strange sett" poured in from all sides, and the gentlemen were soon surrounded by more than two hundred men. They convinced some that the Lieutenant-Governor's concession was satisfactory, but hostile expressions clearly indicated that the mob was minutes away from marching on the fort, sea captains or no sea captains.[76]

Just at this moment Colden's declaration arrived: "The Lieutenant-Governor declares he will do nothing in Relation to the STAMPS, but leave it to SIR HENRY MOORE, to do as he pleases, on his Arrival." This was official and more unqualified than the information they had. Once again the mob demonstrated its devotion to political ends rather than to violence as an end in itself. The concession divided them, and the assault was cancelled. But some suspected deception, and their satisfaction was only temporary.[77]

Sunday saw no cease-fire in the campaign to gain possession of the stamps. The morning's crop of notes was as belligerent as ever. An oyster shell, dropped at the fort gate, advised Colden that his life depended on the efforts he took to get the Stamp Act repealed and upon a clear declaration under oath that he would never, in any way, "Countenance, or assist, in the Execution of the Stamp Act, or anything belonging to it." "John Hamden" tossed a note into printer John Holt's doorway, warning him of his imminent destruction; the customs officers received a similar warning.[78]

Among the notes posted at the coffeehouse was one which indicated the failure of Livingston's and Duane's mission to the seamen. *"The Sons of Neptune"* advised readers to pay no mind to the "peaceable orators" who had kept them from the fort the night before. The note set a new date for the attack—Tuesday, November fifth—and, in a clear reference to former privateersmen, advised the attackers to "be resolute, they would be commanded by men, who had given proofs of their courage, in the defense of their country."[79]

Robert Livingston looked at this and decided it was high time for those who wanted to keep the peace to "rouse their sleeping courage." The uproar continued and William Davis, his life threatened, found the courage to flee. The military roused its courage, barricaded the fort's front gate, and, while the people were "in Commotion," spiked the guns on the battery and many belonging to merchants so they could not be used in an assault.[80] Livingston called a meeting at the coffeehouse for ten the following morning, Monday.[81]

Before the meeting on Monday a blue-ribbon delegation consisting of Livingston, Mayor Cruger, Beverly Robinson, and John Stevens consulted with the Lieutenant-Governor. He reaffirmed his statement of November 2 and added a more explicit pledge "that he would not issue, nor suffer to be issued, any of the STAMPS now in Fort-George." Then they went on to the meeting, where the tensions of three days of rioting had their effect: although everyone agreed that something had to be done, none could find the courage to speak until Livingston urged them to action, warning them of the terrors of mob rule. When he was done some of his audience was worried by his audacity, but they found the courage to agree that since they were satisfied that the stamps were not to be issued, they were determined "to keep the Peace of the City, at all Events, except they should have other Cause of Complaint." Colden's original statement, his new corollary, and the meeting's statement of satisfaction were printed on a broadside and distributed through the town.[82]

On Monday evening some of those who had been present at the morning meeting took it upon themselves to go to the Common to keep the peace. But by then the failure of the day's activities was clear. A broadside had been issued calling a meeting in the Fields at five on Tuesday; it advised the people to come armed. With the fort "pretty well under cover" General Gage pooled his intelligence and concluded that the people's two pieces of artillery were unconfirmed rumor, but that they were armed with clubs and such weapons—all the traditional instruments of the popular assault. The "Insurrection," as he called it, was composed of New Yorkers and inhabitants of neighboring counties and even neighboring provinces, and "great number of Sailors headed by Captains of Privateers, and other Ships." John Montresor confirmed the presence of armed country people—some from Connecticut—and Robert Livingston qualified Gage's information by reporting the night-time meeting of "several Captains of Vessels" who "sent word to the Mayor and Corporation, that they were resolved to join in the design to keep the peace." This was all to the good, for they were clearly needed to calm the seamen.[83]

Meanwhile the final surrender was being prepared in the first round of New York's battle against the Stamp Act. Colden's declaration in the Council on Saturday afternoon had not been entirely acceptable. There was feeling among some councillors that all provocation might be removed by transferring the stamps out of the fort and into *Coventry*. Colden disapproved. He thought the stamps at least as safe in the fort as they would be in the ship, for with winter approaching the ship would have to be brought to one of the town's wharfs, its guns would be put on shore, and the disloyalty of the seamen would become a factor; they would either desert or join with the townspeople—"it is well known sailors easily may be seduced"—especially, Colden should have noted, impressed sailors. Colden also disapproved for other reasons: he suspected that once the stamps were in Captain Kennedy's ship the townspeople would blackmail him into surrendering them by threatening to destroy some of his extensive property holdings in the town. And finally Colden thought the whole idea an insult to the government.[84]

For these reasons Colden refused to ask Kennedy directly, but he was willing to *relay* the Council's request to the Captain over his signature; he told them he would put the stamps in *Coventry* if Kennedy would take them. He did this in a delicately worded note which received an equally delicately worded reply. Kennedy was aware of the blackmail possibility, and while not explicitly refusing he clearly indicated that he thought such a move unwise.[85]

On the evening of November 4 Archibald Kennedy was offered the stamps once again. The sea captains who had volunteered their help asked Colden to reconsider the plan and went themselves to ask Kennedy. Once again Kennedy rejected the idea: *Coventry* was good enough for Colden's family—which he was protecting on board by this time—but he would have no stamps.[86]

Tuesday November 5—Guy Fawkes Day—offered only two alternatives: surrender or fight. All the intermediate choices had been tried and had failed. The mob planned to celebrate the day by storming the fort under the pretense of burning the Pope and the Pretender. Colden expected them and did everything in his power to prepare a "warm reception."[87]

The Common Council met in the morning and sent a delegation to Colden with a new offer: the stamps should be transferred to the City Hall where they would be guarded by the city watch, and the Corporation would make good the value of all stamps which might be lost, destroyed, or carried away. Colden was privately pleased with the offer, but he must have felt the need for some official truculence to save face, for he told the Council that if the Corporation could protect the stamps alone, certainly the corporation plus the garrison—the *status quo*—would be preferable. If he gave in on this point, who knew where the populace would stop? Besides, he said with a concern which had not bothered him until now, it would be a breach of his oath.[88]

The Council played its part. It painted a bleak picture of mob rule and civil war and advised Colden to "catch at the Expediente [sic]." The script required coyness on Colden's part here: he would have to ask General Gage's opinion before he could decide. The Council left and Colden sent a copy of their minutes to the General with a request for a quick reply.[89]

At this point Colden had all but surrendered the reins of government, but his insistence on retaining the petty remnants of his authority in the crisis—and using them irrationally—drove other more rational officials to the brink of terror, and they all descended on General Gage, the latest recipient of Cadwallader Colden's buck. The Mayor, the Corporation, and other leading citizens trooped into Gage's office and begged that he intervene "to save their families from Ruin, and their City from Destruction." Gage, as sensitive as Colden to the proprieties of a crumbling empire, refused to act until he heard directly from the Lieutenant-Governor. Despair, fear, frights, and threats. Finally, much later, the Old Man's note arrived, accompanied by Nicholas Bayard, who told the truth when he said that Colden merely awaited a concurrence but later had to suffer a dressing down for being so blunt.[90] Gage sat down and advised Colden to take the offer, citing the possibility of civil war if he should be forced to fire on the inhabitants, country people, and seamen.[91]

At four o'clock the mob in front of City Hall felt the ground shake as two guns called the Men-of-War to their stations. Would they have to fight? They were ready; but Colden was not. The sun sank and fifty troops just in from Detroit and the Western Communication marched into the fort. Finally, having waited for darkness to cover his shame, Cadwallader Colden sent a convoy of carts containing his seven boxes of stamps through the angry crowd of five thousand and into City Hall.[92]

After five days of rioting something like peace returned to New York. Signs went up announcing *"Peace Proclaimed."* The Governor's family left its shelter in *Coventry*. Major James boarded *Edward*, advised Colden to leave the country, and sailed away, escorted to the Hook by *Gaspee*. The ship that had brought the stamps was gone, headed back to England bearing diverse and conflicting accounts of the trouble it had brought.[93]

A week later *Minerva*, Captain Tillet, sailed into the bay with a long-overdue cargo. The old cannon on the ramparts finally let loose, firing seventeen times to welcome Governor Moore. Sir Harry, "extremely mortified" to find the fort so belligerently decked out ("To be sure," wrote John Watts, "the old Gentleman fortified as if he had been at Bergen-op-Zoom, when the French besieged it with a hundred thousand men. . . ."), immediately ordered the gates thrown open and the fortification dismantled.[94]

Lieutenant-Governor Colden elbowed his way out through the crowds swarming through the fort's open gate, fretting at the new Governor's policies. Some thought he was leaving the country, but he was only headed for his grandson's house. After five days there he

returned to Spring Hill, where he had been when the trouble began.
Thus along with Major James and Captain Davis he had left the stage
on which he had played his role in the Stamp Act crisis. But he would
return one day to enact an even more desperate role, and only death
would prevent him from participating in the Empire's final collapse.[95]

Who and Why

The swift return of peace surprised Colden not a bit. That the mob
should disappear as soon as the stamps were in the City Hall was a clue
to the identity of those responsible for the rioting: " . . . the Lawyers
of this Place are the Authors, Promoters and Leaders. . . ." When
McEvers resigned the Lieutenant-Governor had realized that "a few
Men" were stirring up the people of New York. Thereafter the
newspapers were filled with articles "exciting the People to disobedience
of the Laws and sedition. . . . I am persuaded some of the most
popular lawyers are the Authors of the seditious Papers. . . ." The
Lawyers stirred up the lower classes—they were "easily . . .
seduced"—and now it was questionable whether the lawyers could
protect themselves against the destructive forces which they had
aroused.[96]

Colden's theory was in part a reflection of, and in part a source of,
what came to be the English official view of the Stamp Act riots. The
theory had three aspects. First, the real leaders were members of the
upper class: "several Persons of Consequence" (Sir William Johnson);
"the wiser and better Sort" (General Gage); "some Gentlemen of
Property" (Colden); Moore doubted that the apparent leaders were the
real leaders, for they were not of enough "Consequence." And among
the upper class it was the Lawyers who were "Planners and
Incendiaries": so John Montresor's friends told him. Second, the people
were somewhat cynically used by these "Ringleaders," who "excited"
and "fomented" the mobs. Finally, since the lower class was originally
misled toward violent action in behalf of a cause in which they had no
real interest, they easily turned to violence for its own sake, thus
frightening and disaffecting the upper class which had aroused them.
This was the theory of the Stamp Act riots on which the British
government acted. It was summarized by General Gage:

> The Plan of the People of Property has been to raise the
> lower Class to prevent the Exertion of the Laws, and as far as
> Riots and Tumults went against Stamp-Masters and other
> Obstructions to the Issuing of the Stamps, they encouraged,

and many perhaps Joined them. But when they tended towards Proceedings which might be deemed Treasonable or Rebellious, Persons and Propertys being then in Danger, they have endeavored to restrain them.[97]

When Colden spoke of popular lawyers, there was no mistaking whom he meant. "Three popular lawyers"—William Livingston, John Morin Scott, and William Smith, Jr.—had come from Yale (that "nursery of sedition," according to a conservative) to oppose him on every major public issue of the mid-century period. The New York Triumvirate ("the wicked triumvirate" to Dr. Samuel Johnson of King's College) were Colden's candidates for leadership, but he could not have been more wrong. Livingston's position, for instance, was a liberal one, but it stopped far short of the radicalism necessary to promote an attack on the King's Fort. When Colden spoke of papers in which the people were excited to sedition, he meant especially Livingston's series, "The Sentinel," in the *Post-Boy*, in which Livingston did indeed, as Colden said, oppose Parliament's right to lay internal taxes. And having denied that right, what method of opposition did Livingston choose? "Let us oppose arbitrary rule in every shape by every lawful method in our power." By every lawful method—not by armed assault. Livingston, in the words of his biographer, "emphatically disapproved the terrorist tactics" used in the Stamp Act riots and subsequently. Livingston would continue his theoretical opposition to British policy, but we must look elsewhere for leaders of mobs.[98]

Why did Colden make this mistake? The reasons are worthy of brief examination, for they underlay much of the failure of British policy in the 'sixties and 'seventies. For many years the Lieutenant-Governor had taken "high pet" at the conduct of New York's "Insolent" and "Petulant" set of lawyers. He had grown paranoid, exaggerating their power, seeing them in everything, and imagining them always out to get him. Their dominance was unopposed, matched in its strength only by that of priests in former times. They controlled the Assembly by deluding it, and they tried to ruin him. Shortly before the Stamp Act troubles he had done battle with the triumvirate over the issue of writs of error.[99] He had trodden heavily on the lawyers' constitutional sensitivity, had inflamed them, and had become inflamed himself. Thus he naturally blamed his traditional enemies for the rioting, although, as it turned out, they had no connection with it. This fatal blindness was rooted in Colden's dedication to the old politics, in which all significant events took place in the Assembly or in the courtroom. Wherever he went—and he did not go far beyond such places—he saw lawyers, and they opposed him. But the old politics were being replaced by a new

politics, in which significant events took place in the streets. Colden
had not the least comprehension of the new politics. When events
which displeased him took place in the streets, he understood them only
in his own limited frame of reference. Transforming events to that
frame, he saw only his old enemies of the Assembly-Chamber. It was
this inability to see that the new politics had replaced the old, that the
legislature had taken a back seat to the mob, that led Colden to see
lawyers where they were not.

Although it is true, as John Watts said in another context, that
lawyers were always ready to stir up seamen,[100] it should be clear that
the lawyers were not pulling the strings at the time of the Stamp Act
riots. And indeed, must there be anyone pulling the strings, of whatever
profession? Is it true, as the official theory would have it, that an
uninterested mob had to be artificially aroused—created—to function as
the tool of more directly interested groups?

"The Sailors," who were, to General Gage, "the only People who
may be properly Stiled Mob," came out in great numbers. The only
numerical estimate which we have—four or five hundred of a *total* New
York merchant marine of about 3,500 in a mob of two thousand—is
significant enough, and the prominence which seamen as a professional
group have above all others in accounts of the riots may indicate that
this is low.[101] Of course one reason for the presence of so many seamen
is simply that they were unemployed. This further suggests another
problem. Seamen have a very direct interest in the volume of trade, for
if ships do not sail they do not work. Ships had been sailing with much
less frequency since 1763 under the impact of British legislation.
Perhaps the seamen's interests were as directly affected by the strategy
of opposition to the Stamp Act as were the merchants' and the
lawyers'.

Aside from the directly economic, which we shall examine below,
the seamen had other perfectly valid reasons for rioting. Along with the
rest of New York, they too had been offended by military preparations
at the Fort and by Major James' arrogant statements. But in reaching a
judgment on the question of whether a mob which had no interests at
stake was aroused from above we need not resort to such
generalizations, for history has furnished us with a control experiment.
The official theory is that although its leaders had political interests, the
mob itself was merely out to plunder. "A great part of the Mob," said
Colden, "consists of Men who had been privateers and disbanded
soldiers whose view it is to plunder the town." When his more
enlightened replacement arrived, he too decided that the mobs were
merely out for plunder and that political grievances were mere
pretense.[102] If this were so we would expect an uncontrolled mob to

engage in nothing but aimless destruction. When the mob's leaders lost control, as all testimony agrees that they did on the night of November first, what did the mob do? Did it turn to aimless and unreasonable plundering? No; although they were in the center of town, in the midst of an area rich for plunder, they chose to march, in a disciplined way, clear across town—from the present City Hall to the Hudson River—in order to attack the logical political scapegoat, Thomas James. They considered their assault on his goods a "Sacrifice to Liberty,"[103] and indeed all the evening's activities might be so described. The whole affair had been performed with what could rightly be described as "the greatest Decency and good Order."[104] How could this be said? Perfectly reasonably: no one had been killed or wounded, and the mob had focused all its ire on the attainment of political goals. Drunk as many of them were, they might have simply destroyed whatever happened to be in their way—and indeed their performance did give pause to men of property. But the mob's conduct on the night of November first made it clear that only those who allied themselves with British tyranny had anything to fear. Such discriminating conduct is hardly that of a group of unthinking puppets.

To dismantle the puppet show is not, however, to do away with the whole concept of leadership. It is merely to redefine it. Instead of instigators, men who stirred violence and retreated when it got out of hand, we must look for planners, men who directed the actions of a group of people who knew very well what they wanted but whose energy would have been wasted had there not been some leadership to give them direction. And this direction was probably of the most rudimentary sort, a question of setting times, of priorities, and, in the heat of the riot, of getting from street A to street B in the quickest way possible.

It was General Gage's conclusion that "This Insurrection is composed of great numbers of Sailors headed by Captains of Privateers, and other Ships." Although in his hunt for privateer commanders to calm the sailors R. R. Livingston found one, he also found many who were "much inflamed." Who were the sea captains who directed the seamen in the New York Stamp Act riots? Isaac Sears, the only man named as a riot leader in any source claiming to have more or less first-hand knowledge, had been a privateer, Captain of sloop *Catherine*, dogger *Decoy*, and ship *Belle Isle*. Other New York sea captains who shortly revealed themselves as active members of the Sons of Liberty were Marinus Willett and "the American Wilkes," Alexander McDougall. A host of other sea captains, Normand Tolmie for one, displayed warm patriot sympathies, and we may reasonably guess that they were on the scene at the riots.[105] For the present, then, we may conclude that New York's seamen played a significant role in the Stamp Act riots (both as participants and, as possible deserters, in limiting Archibald Kennedy's freedom), that they were directed by the familiar voices of sea captains, and outstanding among these were definitely Isaac Sears, and probably Alexander McDougall and Marinus Willett.

Factions: Left vs. Left

"Perfect tranquillity (as to appearances)." The diarist stated the situation precisely: peace had returned to New York. But there was a tranquillity of a more ominous sort. This was the tranquillity of empty streets and stowed sails. New York had grown used to this since the departure of wartime prosperity after 1760. The new trade regulations beginning in 1763 had worsened the situation: trade had deteriorated, and the price of labor had fallen. By the summer of 1765 anticipation of the Stamp Act had dealt commerce another blow. With the coming of the Stamp Act the twin prongs of liberal opposition—non-importation and home manufacture—operated so as purposely to aggravate an already stagnant trade situation. By late November John Watts could report that there was "nothing . . . done in the Commercial way"; by year's end importations from Great Britain had fallen off by twenty-six percent.[106]

Except for a few wealthy merchants who profited heavily from the artificial monopolies produced by the boycott, the Stamp Act meant financial troubles for all and, for some, poverty. First among the sufferers were the seamen. Nautical labor had been in surplus supply ever since the Navy had discharged twenty thousand sailors in 1763. A decline in trade meant fewer ship sailings; fewer sailings meant fewer jobs for seamen; as simply as that the Sugar and Stamp Acts plunged maritime labor into depression. But things were just as bad in Massachusetts—where Governor Bernard worried about "an Insurrection of the Poor against the rich"—and in Philadelphia, where a society was formed for the relief of poor and distressed shipmasters, their widows, and children, and where Benjamin Rush found "Our tradesmen Clamorous for want of employment. Our city is full of sailors who cannot procure berths, and who knows what the united resentments of these too numerous People may accomplish?"[107]

Who would speak for the poor, for the prisoners in the City Gaol who could not hope for release so long as legal business ceased? Who would speak for the hungry, the seamen, and longshoremen? Not William Livingston, a founder of the New York Society for the Promotion of Arts, Agriculture and Oeconomy, who saw salvation in home manufacture, industry, and frugality. Certainly not the Stamp Act

Congress, which made so bold as to hint that the Stamp Act was unconstitutional and proposed to fight it by calling it names. Not any assembly on the continent, except that of Rhode Island, which had forthrightly resolved:

> ... That the Inhabitants of this Colony, are not bound to yield Obedience to any Law or Ordinance, designed to impose any internal Taxation whatsoever upon them, other than the Laws or Ordinances of the General Assembly. ...
>
> ... That all the Officers in this Colony, appointed by the Authority thereof, be, and they are hereby directed to proceed in the Execution of their respective Offices, in the same Manner as usual: And that this Assembly will indemnify and save harmless all the said Officers on Account of their Conduct, agreeable to this Resolution.[108]

The "Perfect tranquillity" was indeed only "as to appearances." The first public evidence of this was an advertisement posted on Monday, the twenty-fifth of November. Headed "LIBERTY, PROPERTY, AND NO STAMPS" it called for a general meeting of freeholders, freemen, and inhabitants the next afternoon between three and four at Burns' City Arms. The purpose of the meeting was to draw up instructions for their representatives in the Assembly, "and other important Matters tending to the Preservation of their Rights and Liberties." One of the meeting's initiators later explained its genesis. A number of New Yorkers,

> among whom were all those who have to any considerable Effect exerted themselves in giving the People just Ideas of their Rights, and in opposing the Stamp Act as destructive to them, being justly alarmed at the continued Cessation of Business since November 1 ... ; and not seeing the least Appearance of any Remedy, nor any Proposals to that End, they thought it high Time to bestir themselves. ... Since the Discontinuance of Business itself, is a Sort of Admittance of the Legality of the Stamp Act, and has a Tendency to enforce it; and since there is just Reason to apprehend, that the secret Enemies of Liberty, have actually a Design to introduce it by the Necessities to which the People will be reduced by the Cessation of Business. ... Whereas, if the Stamp Act, as being unconstitutional, was entirely disregarded, and Business went on as usual, [as?] if no such Act had ever been made, it is plain it would never take Place here, nor any Penalties be incurred by it, ... for it has no Force but what

we give it, either by submitting to it, or by seeming to fear it, and suspending Business on Account of it.

The plan was to set business going as usual—without stamps.[109]

The plan, and the thought behind it, were not new to New Yorkers. The same thinking had been put into service when John Holt had been pressured into printing the *Post-Boy* on plain, unstamped paper. This was the thought behind a note to the customs officers of November 3 demanding that they do business as usual. And we might speculate that it was opposition to the non-importation policy rather than a suspected funeral celebration for Liberty that drew the seamen to the coffeehouse on October 31.[110] Now the public was to be presented with a series of newspaper articles developing specific aspects of the radical plan.

The first article was first reprinted from a Pennsylvania newspaper on November 25. Some, it said, suggested that all business requiring written instruments subject to duties be stopped. But such conduct was as much an acknowledgment of the Stamp Act's validity as would be the use of stamps. This policy hurt individuals, and they might decide that execution of the act would be less pernicious than obstruction. (Governor Moore said he was content to show "as much indifference as possible, being fully persuaded, that the distress which must attend the suspention of the Act will facilitate the carrying it into execution, more than any attempt I could possibly make in its favour. . . .") Perhaps, therefore, mistaken zeal to avoid the Act's execution would finally result in putting it into effect. And how would the Government respond to a passive policy? They would say that the Americans were successfully intimidated and that their method of fighting the Act would—just as Governor Moore said—ultimately force them to comply with it. Thus the wisest policy would be to proceed with business as usual and not to fear penalties, for Britain would not dare to think of extorting penalties from the whole continent.[111]

On December 19 "Freeman" complained of the state of trade: "Our Business of all kinds is stopped, our Vessels, ready for Sea, blocked up in our Harbours, as if besieged by an Enemy, great Numbers of our poor People and Seamen without Employment and without Support." What could any sensible man think of Americans who, although fully convinced of the Stamp Act's unconstitutionality, still continued to submit to it? Would not Parliament think Americans "a Herd of mean, despicable Wretches" who lacked the courage to defend their rights?[112]

Two days after Christmas "Philolutherus" developed the radical argument at length. He began with the assumption of the Stamp Act's unconstitutionality as his given. But the pleasure which he took in the repeated resolutions to that effect was somewhat abated as he viewed the "almost total stagnation" of business since November first. Perhaps this was best at first, for to expect a people who so venerated Parliament to act directly against its authority might have been too radical a start. Had the boycott policy been merely a temporary expedient to avoid confusion it might have been justifiable. But as a permanent policy, "slavish subjection" to a clearly unconstitutional law was inconsistent conduct. First the Americans forced the stamp distributors to resign; then they contradicted themselves by stopping business, thus tacitly acknowledging the law's authority. After questioning the policy's efficacy "Philolutherus" criticized it as cowardice: "We have been blustering for liberty for some months, but when put to the trial, we shrink back in a most dastardly manner, and all our courage evaporates in smoke." The British must be shown that force—which they would not dare use—would be the only way that the Act could be enforced. But this could be done only by considering the law "absolutely null and void in itself, and behaving ourselves in all things, as though it did not exist."[113]

With these ideas in mind the initiators of the November 26 meeting had drawn up an address to the city's assemblymen to which, they later said, hundreds of New Yorkers were ready to subscribe their names. They expressed the highest respect for Parliament but thought themselves bound "by every sacred Obligation to oppose and repel the Injury, for we act not only for ourselves, but for all succeeding Generations." Parliament had been gradually encroaching on the rights of the colonies, and American acquiescence in this encroachment was construed as an acknowledgment of Parliament's right. This was the way to slavery, and Parliament had saved America from that fate by awakening it with "the most open and violent attack that was ever made upon the Rights of a free People." The Stamp Act—this "most egregious political Blunder"—had roused Americans: " . . . now or never is the Time." The Americans must not miss this, their last opportunity; if they did they would be despised as slaves: " . . . now therefore or never is the Time." Every noble motive called them to a united effort, "and now or never is the time." They concluded by calling on their representatives to match Rhode Island's boldness by sanctioning business as usual without stamps: "Now or never is the time."[114]

The hundreds of people who would doubtless have signed this address were never given the opportunity to do so. When announcements of the meeting were first posted on November 25, they were torn down by unknown persons who were thought to be emissaries of others who wanted to stop the meeting. But the posters were replaced, and, on November 26, about 1,200 people appeared.

Machinations unknown to the bulk of the audience began innocently enough when a few men stood up and suggested that certain gentlemen be named a committee. Without any general assent the gentlemen named agreed to form a committee, provided that it include several other gentlemen, whom they named. The original committee and the expanded version contained the names of some of New York's leading merchants and the liberal triumvirate: Livingston, Smith, and Scott. The names suggested were those of respectable gentlemen "of unexceptionable Character," and the social pressures of the open meeting prevented any protest against them. Thus the Triumvirate, which had nothing to do with initiating the meeting, had made themselves its leaders by skillful maneuvering and were assumed to be the "chief instruments of calling them together." Thus their proposals were assumed to be the meeting's major business, and other proposals were considered "as Things of lesser Moment."[115]

With the liberals in control, the radical address drawn up by the meeting's true initiators was read and generally approved. Immediately after this reading an entirely different set of instructions was read. These asked the city members "by Petitions, Remonstrances, &c. to obtain a Repeal of all unconstitutional and oppressive Acts, particularly the Stamp Act." In the present distresses, they said, it was proper conduct on the part of constituents to express their anxiety "in this Constitutional Way." It protested against taxation without consent, and asked specifically that the city's members in the Assembly act so that

> . . . a full Declaration be made and entered upon the Journals of the House, of the Rights of the People of this Colony, to . . . an exemption from Parliamentary internal Taxations; and that these Claims and the Grievances of the Country be immediately represented to his Majesty and the two Houses of Parliament; and all necessary Relief prayed for, and sollicited by proper Agents, in the most respectful and constitutional Manner.[116]

Just as "it would have been difficult to find an American anywhere who did not believe in the declarations of the Stamp Act Congress—as far as they went," so "The Matter of this Address, so far as it went, was such as none of the Company could disapprove." It was, however—like the declarations of the Stamp Act Congress—"defective in the grand Point, it contained nothing to remove the present Obstructions to Business, and therefore was not the Thing now most wanted." The radicals had attempted to have the New York Assembly in effect repeal Parliament's Stamp Act; the liberals had aimed merely at additional protest. In the as yet hardly democratic politics of New York, the liberal address was adopted; it had been introduced by leading citizens who claimed that it said everything that had to be said. Once again the radicals—led by Isaac Sears—had contested with the liberals—led by the New York Triumvirate. This time superior parliamentary skill had given the victory to the liberals.[117]

The liberal position was still the one which had been proposed by William Livingston in the summer: to oppose arbitrary rule "by every lawful method in our power." The liberal accent was on "lawful," as it had been from the earliest days of opposition to postwar British legislation: in February of 1764 a writer in a New York newspaper had taken pleasure in "the spirit that seems to be raised in the Northern Colonies, to seek Redress of Grievances and the Enjoyment of their natural Rights, by truly rational Methods." Rational methods meant laying their grievances before the throne:

> To oppose and violate the Laws in being, altho' in themselves they should be inconvenient or bad Laws, is seditious and injurious to Government . . . such practices weaken the Bands of Society, corrupt the Morals of a People, and introduce a Spirit of Licentiousness and Disobedience inconsistent with all Law and Government whatsoever. . . .[118]

In October of 1765 "A COLONIST" anticipated November's mob activities and advised his fellow New Yorkers to assert their liberties like "honest freemen." The sort of destruction which would shortly be done to Major James' house was, when seen through this writer's complex of biases, simple robbery: "If such methods are to prevail, its plain all government is at an end . . . ; Let us rather seek redress by serious remonstrances. . . ." Lest his readers think that his timidity implied submission to the Stamp Act, the writer assured them that he was seeking only "proper methods." The method which he suggested was to bring about "a total stagnation of all business."[119]

When the rioting was over and the stamps were lodged in City Hall, the liberal position was reasserted by a peace proclamation whose aim was to prevent further violence. Neglecting to notice that transferring stamps from one place to another was by no means a final solution to the problem, they claimed that the movement of the stamps had "entirely accomplish'd all we wanted"; to take any further steps would only hurt their good cause. When, in the winter, the radicals sought to have the stamps shipped back to England, the liberals called a meeting; they advised those present that they would obtain relief if they behaved "with Temper and Moderation" and gave them one hour to decide whether the Corporation should keep the stamps.[120]

If any professional group clung firmly to the liberal policies it was the same lawyers who were thought to be the leaders of the Stamp Act violence. Sometime in November or December Isaac Sears and William Smith, Jr. engaged in violent argument over the tactics of opposition. Sears was *"ill treated, insulted and bullyed"* at a meeting by Smith, who called him an enemy to government because he urged that business be done without stamps. Throughout the winter the radicals argued against "The strange and alarming Lethargy into which we have fallen . . . with Regard to all Judicial Proceedings." The lawyers would not listen to "the Voice of the People;" the gentlemen of the law seemed to the populace more and more, like the Bishops, "the ready Tools of arbitrary Power." The lawyers spoke as if they were heroes for refusing to do business and revelled in the stagnation of commerce as "a Kind of Jubilee," an opportunity to atone for former extravagances. A committee of twelve asked the lawyers to go back to work, but only three or four lawyers were convinced. The lawyers refused to break the law, and William Livingston saw his income drop more than one-third. The lawyers' conduct became an issue of the 1768 election, and Isaac Sears still remembered the profession's failure of nerve in 1770.[121]

The liberal instructions produced by the November 26 meeting were presented to the City's representatives on the following day. The Assembly, which had been in session for a week, had received a report on the Stamp Act Congress, approved of its declarations and petitions, and appointed a committee to draw up similar ones. The Assembly's resolutions of December 18 were, according to one sympathetic observer, even more moderate than previous declarations. It was the same by now hackneyed form, repeating the same resolutions: they owed allegiance to King George and obedience to all constitutional acts of Parliament. The Stamp Act was unconstitutional, and. . . . And nothing. And they wished that it would go away, but made no suggestion as to how this would be done.[122] Thus the liberals' purposes had been fulfilled; a liberal coup at the November 26 meeting had killed the radical instructions, the liberal instructions had been forwarded to the Assembly, and that body had been pleased to embody the instructions in yet another set of resolutions.

Nullification

Through the winter and on into the spring the radicals did their best to nullify the Stamp Act. There were threats against all sorts of people, high and low: threats against theatre owners[123] and generals, against Army officers and Navy officers,[124] threats against stamp officers and distributors, against Colden, Major James, and Jeffery Amherst, threats to burn houses and to "Barbacue an officer."[125] Adults paraded, children paraded;[126] sermons were preached,[127] and prisoners defied the Stamp Act by breaking out of jail.[128]

Much of this action was taken by a radical organization which had existed in fact since November but which now began to bear a name—the Sons of Liberty. By January 7 they felt strong enough to abandon a secrecy which had long been only nominal; they issued a set of resolutions, including a promise to protect anyone who carried on business as usual. From this time on their meetings were publicly announced in advance, and their membership, led at this time principally by Isaac Sears, was well known.[129]

Nullifying the Stamp Act was a war on many fronts. Back in August James McEvers, New York's first stamp distributor, had found "The Number of his Friends and well Wishers, which was considerable before, . . . greatly increased by [his] Resignation." At the time those responsible for his quitting had remarked that it would be "no more safe than honourable" for anyone else to take the job, and enforcing that promise was one of their many campaigns against the Act. When Peter Delancey arrived late in November, bearing an appointment as stamp distributor, a short conversation sufficed to convince him to resign. Next they set out for Flushing where Zachariah Hood of Maryland had taken refuge. Civil, 'though resolute, explaining; haggling; resignation followed by cheering and an invitation to an entertainment, but "he was in such a Frame of Body and Mind that he should be unhappy in Company." When the party returned to the city, they found that a passenger who had been hiding on a recently arrived ship was a stamp inspector. He too resigned. Spurred on by this orgy of resignations the Sons of Liberty had James McEvers do it all over again. By Christmas the people felt secure enough about the future applicants for the job to propose that the Governor offer the post of stamp distributor to anyone lunatic enough to take it; no one did.[130]

When there were no stamp officers left to attack, there were still the stamps themselves. A British officer contrasted the New Yorkers' great dexterity in putting out housefires with their inability to prevent the burning of stamps. In December the "lower Class" assembled to burn stamps guarded by a corps of guards who had just voted to burn them themselves. Alert municipal authorities were able to turn them aside this time, but there was no intervention in January. On the evening of Tuesday the seventh, just as the Sons of Liberty surfaced, brig *Polly*, Captain Haviland, sailed into the harbor with ten packages

o^c stamps on board. At about midnight the following night a company
of armed men came to the home of mate John Byvanck and told him
that his house would be immediately destroyed by two hundred men
waiting in the shadows if he did not hand over the keys. He did, they set
out for Cruger's Wharf, and, after a search, found the stamps. They
loaded them in a boat and took them up to the boatyard; there they
covered them with tar, made a bonfire, and went home quietly. The
Sons of Liberty, who must have known something about it, were
delighted. Governor Moore was infuriated and issued a proclamation
seeking the capture of the incendiaries. But New Yorkers had caught the
habit, and when a package of stamps removed from a wreck arrived in
the spring, they rushed it down to the coffeehouse and "purified" it
before an audience of a thousand.[131]

In their resolutions of January 7 the Sons of Liberty promised that
anyone who delivered or received any instrument on stamped paper
"shall incur the highest Resentment of this Society, and be branded
with everlasting Infamy." The enforcement of this resolution was
another campaign in the battle against the Stamp Act. At about ten in
the evening of February 13 a message arrived by express from the
Philadelphia Sons of Liberty, notifying their New York counterparts of
the issuance of Mediterranean passes on stamped paper at New York.
The suspect, Lewis Pintard, claimed that a week before he had applied
to Charles Williams, Naval Officer at New York, for a Mediterranean
pass to be sent to Maryland for a vessel which Pintard had ordered
loaded with wheat. Within an hour after the request Williams delivered
the pass—from on board a vessel which had recently arrived from
England. Pintard sent the pass to Philadelphia to be forwarded to
Maryland. He claimed that he was not charged for a stamp and that he
did not know that the bond was stamped until after he had sent it.
Shortly afterwards Pintard repeated the process for a ship he was about
to send to the Mediterranean from New York. Acheson Thompson,
another New York merchant, had also taken and executed a stamped
bond, but he was also not told that it was stamped.[132]

By ten o'clock the following morning perhaps two thousand angry
people had gathered at the coffeehouse. The mob was not satisfied with
the stories it was told, and Allicocke, Lamb, and Sears, who, according
to one observer, were acting as "Counsellors" (rather than instigators)
had a difficult time controlling their resentment. Two men were sent to
the Collector for the thirty stamped bonds he had. He conferred with the
Governor who promised that the stamps would not be used if delivered
to him. The mob disliked the Governor's proposal, and he
accommodated them by handing over the stamps to a committee of
two—attended by a thousand-man entourage. All the bonds were

brought back to the coffeehouse where Lewis Pintard was ordered to kindle a fire in which they were burned to the accompaniment of the cheers of about five thousand people. Then everybody went home.[133]

But the people were not content; in the evening they went to Charles Williams' house where they were well on their way to making it look like Vaux-Hall when Williams promised to beg their pardon—or do anything else they wanted him to do—and the Sons of Liberty managed to stop them. They went to the coffeehouse and after some additional huzzaing were induced to go home in expectation of confessions the next day and in consideration of Mrs. Pintard's advanced pregnancy.[134]

On the following morning two ship carpenters named Tony and Daly—who seemed to be able to create or suppress a mob instantly—gathered some few thousand furious men in the Fields. At about eleven Pintard, Williams, and Thompson appeared, protected by three clergymen. The Sons of Liberty managed to kill the scheme of pillorying them, and the three culprits climbed out of the window of a "pint House" where they sorrowfully begged the people's pardon for what they had done. The mob—always a stickler for legality—demanded sworn confessions before a Justice of the Peace and got them. Then everyone went home, including Colden who later called the proceedings "a most numerous Riot with shamefull Insults on Governmnt. . . ."[135] Shameful or not, the mob had once again proved that it was not out for plunder. Again its leaders had lost control, and again it was only logical political enemies who had to fear the mob's fury.

The Sons of Liberty's ultimate enemy in the fight to nullify the Stamp Act was Admiral Colville, commander of the fleet in American waters. Regardless of what the civil government might allow, Colville was determined that no vessels should get past him without stamped clearances. For his efforts Lord Colville was hanged and burned—in effigy—and his subordinates were publicly threatened for carrying out his orders. With a stupidity worthy of the higher traditions of any branch of the military, the Navy continued blandly to offend the people by impressing seamen throughout the crisis.[136]

All of this had its effect. Governor Moore had arrived full of public statements of cooperation and private intent to do otherwise but could do no better than had Colden. His sense of public relations was superior, but it did him no good.[137] With no stamps being distributed the merchants were more friendly to the radical position than the lawyers, and in a short time vessels with unstamped clearances began to come and go without any regard to the Stamp Act.[138] As time passed, news came of the Act's nullification elsewhere. Captain Blow arrived from Quebec with a stamped let-pass—which confirmed Colonel Montresor in his preference for military government—but New Yorkers learned of the continuation of business without stamps in Virginia, New Jersey, Massachusetts, Rhode Island, New Hampshire, and elsewhere.[139] Finally, in December, fearing the unemployed seamen, the New York Custom House began to issue unstamped clearances.[140]

The radicals had won their battle in principle, but in fact there was little change in the situation of commerce. Civil officials could concede all they wanted to, but the Navy had been fighting a war on American commerce since 1756[141] and was not so ready as the customs officials to throw the law over the side; *Coventry* and *Garland* went to work preventing the sailing of vessels with unstamped clearances.[142] Then winter came—the coldest one, some said, in forty years.[143] The wind blew, and the mercury dropped out of the bottoms of thermometers.[144] *Coventry* and *Garland* were hauled up to the wharves to be unrigged and take their winter berths; they could no longer act as "Enemies to the Trade of this Place."[145] Then, during the third week in January Admiral Colville decided that he, too, would pass the buck: he declared that he would not stop an unstamped vessel until he received orders to that effect from England.[146] Messages crossed back and forth over the Atlantic by way of the "swimming Posts"[147] throughout the winter,[148] and when the spring came and the ice melted, New York's merchant marine found itself free to proceed unstamped, unhindered by the Ships of War.[149] Shortly afterward Archibald Kennedy was superseded, and in June *Coventry* sailed for Philadelphia.[150] But by then sea-going vandals concerned New Yorkers not in the least, for the Stamp Act had been repealed.

In May General Gage watched New York celebrate repeal and wondered. Was it a testimony of gratitude or a victory celebration? The rejoicings, he thought, went somewhat beyond what "Many Moderate People wished to see. . . ."[151] Had the General asked some of what he chose to call "the lower sort" he would have received a shocking answer. The seamen, at least, were celebrating a clear victory. No one could claim that they had not fought hard to get their jobs back. They had played a major role in the Stamp Act riots and perhaps a predominant role in the reopening of trade without stamps. The Governor of Massachusetts had worried about a war of the poor against the rich; customs officials at Philadelphia knew that "People will not sit quiet, and see their Interests suffer, and perhaps Ruin brought upon themselves and Famalies [sic], when they have it in their power to redress themselves. . . ." A customs officer explained the reopening of Philadelphia in this way:

> Nothing is more certain than that so great a Number of
> Seamen, shut up for that Time in a Town destitute of all
> Protection to the Inhabitants . . . would commit some
> terrible Mischief, or rather that they would not suffer
> themselves to be shut up, but would compel the Officers to
> clear Vessels without Stamps—This would undoubtedly have
> been the Consequence of a few days longer Delay. . . .

The same causes operated in New York and seem to have been the
main matter in the minds of New York Customs officers when they
ordered reopening of trade without stamps:

> This step, we thought the more adviseable as we
> understood the Mob (which are daily increasing and gathering
> Strength, from the arrival of Seamen, and none going out, and
> who are the only people that are most dangerous on these
> Occasions, as their whole dependence for a subsistence is upon
> Trade) were soon to have a Meeting.[152]

And if they had caused the reopening of trade without stamps, how
far-fetched would it have been for the seamen to think that they had
played a large part in repeal? Had not the news of their rioting—"the
Madness of the people," Secretary Conway called it—reached the floor
of Parliament?[153] Perhaps they seemed mere plunderers in inaccurate
British newspapers; certainly Parliament might get that impression
from listening to the testimony of extremists like Thomas James, who
had had to leave America to save their lives.[154] Or perhaps the English
thought that the Americans were seeking independence: John Montresor
heard the Sons of Liberty make public declarations to that effect, and he
doubted the loyalty of the people of New York.[155]

In the Stamp Act crisis the sailors had of necessity taken a position
of political radicalism, the only position consistent with their interests.
They had a right to think that they had won a round against the British
government. They had acted, and the result of their actions was success.
Blocked from acting through normal political channels, they had taken
their grievances out of the Assembly and into the streets. Their success
in this new arena—and the resultant opening of a chasm between
themselves and those who preferred to rely on the old politics—was a
first step toward revolution.

Too often we think of the Stamp Act riots as an eccentric
explosion, with people returning to normal after repeal. Eighteenth-
century Americans might have been less sophisticated than the modern
variety, but they could not have been so child-like as to return to the

bosom of Mother England as if nothing had happened. The Stamp Act crisis was a step toward revolution, and henceforth the debate could no longer be carried on in the same terms. Those who contented themselves with declarations of the unconstitutionality of British legislation would be automatically suspect. For that debate was over; "well-defined constitutional principles" had emerged,[156] and Americans had moved on to a new debate in which intelligence would devote itself to the search for means within a context of almost universally accepted ends. And the most promising means seemed to be that of disobedience to bad law, a policy which could be justified only by resort to a law beyond existing law.

In February of 1766 General Gage worried that the people had become "so accustomed to Excess and Riot without Controul" that it might be difficult for them to return to normal after repeal.[157] His worries were more than justified. Ship captains who had cleared without let-passes during the crisis felt no need for a return to legality once the crisis was over, complained Governor Moore; "they ventured to sail without them and from the indulgence then met with in not being seized, they have since the Repeal of the Stamp Act, constantly gone to sea without Let passes."[158] The country people, the tenants of Dutchess and Albany, caught the contagion and turned to violent opposition to the landlords: the Stamp Act crisis was over, but Governor Moore saw "from the Notions which the Common People here had adopted that the Spirit of Licentiousness which had so long prevailed would hardly be subdued without some further attempts on their side to regain their former Power. . . ."[159] The seamen would try again.

Notes

[1.] William Davis (1728–1789), master and part owner of *Edward*, was born in England. He enlisted in the New York militia in 1760. In June of 1766 the Common Council awarded him the freedom of the Corporation after he had delivered a portrait of William Pitt. He died in a fall from Murray's Wharf into the East River on the night of October 7, 1789. New York Port Records, Public Record Office, London, Microfilm C.O. 5/1228 at the Sleepy Hollow Restorations, Tarrytown, New York; *Muster Rolls*, pp. 244–245; *Freemen*, pp. 538–539; "An Inquisition . . . before me Ephraim Prasher Coroner . . . October 20, 1789," Mayor's Court: Pleadings I-106.

2. The *Post-Boy* of October 24 reported Davis' arrival on October 22 and his encounter, six days before, in longitude 66, of a brig bound for Lisbon and, three days later, of another brig bound from Newcastle to Philadelphia. The *Mercury* of November 4 reported the arrival of Captain Johnston at Philadelphia from Newcastle on October 31. Captain Johnston reported that in latitude 39 16' longitude 60 40' he had spoke a ship bound from London to New York which had been out six weeks and had several passengers on board. From this information we may safely conclude that it is Captains Davis and Johnston who crossed paths at sea and that they did so on the northern limits of the Gulf Stream. The difference in arrival dates probably indicates that Johnston was bucking the three-knot current of the Gulf Stream, while Davis' rapid passage could not have taken place if he had not avoided the current. Captain Johnston's ignorance was common among ship-captains both before and after publication of the first chart of the Gulf Stream under Benjamin Franklin's direction in 1769. Rachel L. Carson, *The Sea Around Us* (New York, 1954), p. 107; Carl Van Doren, *Benjamin Franklin* (New York, 1938), pp. 429, 522 (hereafter cited as Van Doren, *Benjamin Franklin*).

3. Two New York prostitutes; see above, p. 57.

4. *Post-Boy*, October 24, 1765.

5. John Watts to General Monckton, November 9, 1765: *Aspinwall Papers*, p. 582.

6. For the number of shippers and the stamps' ballast function see Cadwallader Colden to Secretary Conway, October 26, 1765: *N Y Col Docs*, VII, 768–769. The labeling of the packages of stamps deep in the hold is a problem in algebra; knowns and unknowns are in *ibid.*, David Colden to the Commissioners of the Stamp Office, October 26, 1765: *Colden Letter Books*, II, 50–51; David Colden to Jared Ingersoll, October 28, 1765; *ibid.*, II, 52–53; Cadwallader Colden to the Mayor and Gentlemen of the Corporation, November 5, 1765: *ibid.*, II, 57. The weight of the stamps is another algebra problem: see *Mercury*, November 11, 18, 1765. See also [Cadwallader Colden], *The Conduct of Cadwallader Colden, Esquire, Late Lieutenant-Governor of New York Relating to The Judges Commissions, Appeals to the King, and the Stamp-Duty* (New York 1767), p. 51 (hereafter cited as Colden, *Conduct*); Broadside, January, 1766: New-York Historical Society Broadsides SY 1766–11.

7. *Post-Boy*, October 24, 1765; Dawson, *Sons of Liberty*, p. 79.

8. Journal of Lord Adam Gordon, [October, 1765]: Newton D. Mereness, *Travels in the American Colonies, 1690–1783* (New York, 1916), p. 453; *Post-Boy*, October 24, 1765.

9. *Ibid.*, June 21, 1764.

10. *A Chart of New York Harbour with the Soundings Views of Land Marks and Nautical Directions, for the Use of Pilotage. Composed from Surveys and Observations of Lieutenants John Knight, John Hunter of the Navy &*

Others [with] Nautical Directions to Sail into the Harbour of New-York, &c. ([London,] 1779): Emmet Collection, #11886–7, New York Public Library.

11. Robert R. Livingston to Governor Monckton, November 8, 1765: Chalmers Mss., IV, New York Public Library; *Montresor Journals*, p. 328; Cadwallader Colden to Secretary Conway, October 26, 1765: *N Y Col Docs*, VII, 768. For *Hawke*'s armament see "List of His Majesty's Ships and Vessels in North America," [1767]: *Colden Letters and Papers*, VII, 131.

12. Cadwallader Colden to the Master or Commander of the Ship or Vessell on Board of which the Stamp'd Papers &c. Are for the Province of New York, October 18, 1765: *Colden Letter Books*, II, 47.

13. Cadwallader Colden to Captain Kennedy, September 3, 1765: *ibid.*, II, 29; *Montresor Journals*, p. 328; Cadwallader Colden to Secretary Conway, October 26, 1765: *N Y Col Docs*, VII, 768. For armament information see *Gazette*, October 10, 1763.

14. *Post-Boy*, July 18, 1765, April 27, 1766.

15. Cadwallader Colden to Captain Kennedy, September 3, 1765: *Colden Letter Books*, II, 29; Cadwallader Colden to the Master or Commander of the Ship or Vessell on Board of which the Stamp'd Papers . . . Are . . ., October 18, 1765: *ibid.*, II, 47.

16. Morgans, *Stamp Act Crisis*, pp. 123–125.

17. J. McEvers to Barlow Trecothick: quoted in *ibid.*, p. 152; *Mercury*, September 16, 1765.

18. *Ibid.*, August 29, 1765; *Post-Boy*, November 7, 1765.

19. Cadwallader Colden to Sir William Johnson, August 31, 1765: *Colden Letter Books*, II, 27.

20. "Journal of French Traveller," *American Historical Review*, XXVII, (October, 1921), 82.

21. *Post-Boy*, August 22, 1765; J. McEvers to Cadwallader Colden, [August 30, 1765]: *Colden Letters and Papers*, VII, 56.

22. *Post-Boy*, September 5, 1765; J. McEvers to Cadwallader Colden, [August 30, 1765]: *Colden Letters and Papers*, VII, 56.

23. *Ibid.*

24. Colden is called this in John Watts to Sir Charles Hardy, June 11, 1763: *Watts Letter Book*, p. 147.

25. Abraham Lott to John Wendell, July 8, 1765: Stokes, *Iconography*, IV, 749; Cadwallader Colden to Secretary Conway, September 23, 1765: *N Y Col Docs*, VII, 759.

26. Cadwallader Colden to Sir William Johnson, August 31, 1765: *Colden Letter Books*, II, 27; John Watts to Governor Monckton, June 1, 1765: *Aspinwall Papers*, pp. 573–574; Cadwallader Colden to General Gage, September 2, 1765: *N Y Col Docs*, VII, 758.

[27.] *Ibid.*; Alexander Colden to Cadwallader Colden, [September 2, 1765]: *Colden Letters and Papers*, VII, 72.

[28.] *Ibid.*

[29.] This is a paraphrase of Cadwallader Colden to General Gage, September 2, 1765: *N Y Col Docs*, VII, 758.

[30.] In 1712 and 1741: see Ulrich Bonnell Phillips, *American Negro Slavery: A Survey of the Supply, Employment and Control of Negro Labor as Determined by the Plantation Regime* (New York, 1918), p. 111.

[31.] Colden's fears and the military preparations are in Cadwallader Colden to General Gage, July 8, 1765: *Colden Letter Books*, II, 23; Cadwallader Colden to Sir Jeffery Amherst, [December 26, 1766]: *ibid.*, II, 125–126; General Gage to Cadwallader Colden, July 8, 1765: *Colden Letters and Papers*, VII, 46; Alexander Colden to Cadwallader Colden, [September 2, 1765]: *ibid.*, VII, 72; *Mercury*, August 5, 1765; General Gage to Halifax, August 10, 1765: Carter, *Gage Correspondence*, I, 64; *Montresor Journals*, p. 327; Cadwallader Colden to Secretary Conway, September 23, 1765: *N Y Col Docs*, VII, 758–759. In his letter of December 26, 1766 to Sir Jeffrey Amherst Colden shows a sensitivity to the possible provocative effects of these movements which he did not show at the time of the events; he makes a point of saying that Major James took these steps without his knowledge. This is probably true, except that it would seem that Colden, arriving in the city before noon on the third, would have had some say in the disposition of the troops which arrived that day. In Colden's Account of the State of the Province of New York, December 6, 1765: *N Y Col Docs*, VII, 797 he falsely implies that Gage *initiated* an offer of military assistance. On the question of provocation see also below, p. 82.

[32.] "Journal of French Traveller," *American Historical Review*, XXVII (October, 1921), 82.

[33.] *Ibid.*; Burnaby, *Travels*, p. 76; Alexander Colden to Cadwallader Colden, [September 2, 1765]: *Colden Letters and Papers*, VII, 72; John Montresor to Cadwallader Colden, September 6, 1765: *ibid.*, VII, 73–74; Engineers' Report on Means of Strengthening Fort George, November 2, 1765: *ibid.*, VII, 87–88; Council Session, November 2, 1765: *ibid.*, VII, 65; Cadwallader Colden to Conway, September 23, 1765: *N Y Col Docs*, VII, 759; Cadwallader Colden, Account of the State of the Province of New York, December 6, 1765: *ibid.*, VII, 799; Colden, *Conduct*, p. 54.

[34.] Cadwallader Colden to Sir William Johnson, August 31, 1765: *Colden Letter Books*, II, 27.

[35.] John Montresor to Cadwallader Colden, September 6, 1765: *Colden Letters and Papers*, VII, 72–74.

[36.] *Montresor Journals*, p. 328; Cadwallader Colden to Secretary Conway, September 23, 1765: *N Y Col Docs*, VII, 759.

[37.] "Journal of French Traveller," *American Historical Review*, XXVII (October, 1921), 82.

[38.] Cadwallader Colden to Jared Ingersoll, September 14, 1765: *Colden Letter Books*, II, 32.

[39.] John Watts to General Monckton, September 24, 1765: *Aspinwall Papers*, pp. 576–577.

[40.] *Ibid.*; *Mercury*, November 4, 1765; *Post-Boy*, November 21, 1765.

[41.] Council Sessions, September 7, 9, 1765: *Colden Letters and Papers*, VII, 60–62.

[42.] John Watts to General Monckton, September 24, 1765: *Aspinwall Papers*, pp. 576–577; Sir Henry Moore to Secretary Conway, November 21, 1765: *N Y Col Docs*, VII, 789.

[43.] Alexander Colden to Cadwallader Colden, [November, 1765]: *Colden Letters and Papers*, VII, 93–94.

[44.] Sir William Johnson to Cadwallader Colden, October 1, 9, 1765: J. Sullivan, A. C. Flick, and M. W. Hamilton, eds., *The Papers of Sir William Johnson* (Albany, New York, 1921–53), IV, 853, 857. Hereafter cited as *Johnson Papers*.

[45.] Robert R. Livingston to General Monckton, November 8, 1765: Chalmers Mss., IV, New York Public Library; *Montresor Journals*, p. 336; Burnaby, *Travels*, pp. 74, 76; *Post-Boy*, October 24, 1765, November 19, 1770; Council Session, October 24, 1765: *Colden Letters and Papers*, VII, 63–64; Cadwallader Colden to Secretary Conway, October 26, 1765: *N Y Col Docs*, VII, 768.

[46.] For an account of the Stamp Act Congress see Morgans, *Stamp Act Crisis*, pp. 102–115; for the Declarations see *ibid.*, pp. 106–107.

[47.] James Otis, *The Rights of the British Colonies Asserted and Proved* (Boston, 1764), quoted in *ibid.*, p. 34.

[48.] *Ibid.*, pp. 113, 295.

[49.] *Post-Boy*, December 27, 1765.

[50.] *Ibid.*, November 7, 1765.

[51.] *Ibid.* By January 7 the number of signatures on the merchants' agreement had risen above four hundred: Evert Bancker to , January 7, 176[6]: Stokes, *Iconography*, IV, 974.

[52.] Cadwallader Colden to John Cruger, October 31, 1765: *Colden Letter Books*, II, 53; *Montresor Journals*, p. 336; *Post-Boy*, November 7, 1765; Robert R. Livingston to General Monckton, November 8, 1765: Chalmers Mss., IV, New York Public Library. Livingston tells us of the seamen outside Burns'. From the overlapping of his account with others it is clear that this mob was continuous with the others during the evening. But because of the total absence of numerical evidence we cannot know whether as the evening passed the mob remained one of children and seamen, whether seamen were outnumbered by others, or whether seamen dominated. There is the additional problem of distinguishing seamen from children; John Paul Jones was by no means a prodigy among ship's boys when he first sailed at the age of thirteen: Morison, *John Paul Jones*, p. 11.

53. See above, pp. 34–35.

54. Zachariah Hood to Cadwallader Colden, September 16, 1765: *Colden Letters and Papers*, VII, 77–78; D[avid] Colden to Zachariah Hood, September 16, 1765: *Colden Letter Books*, II, 33.

55. Note signed "Vox Populi," [October 23 (?), 1765]: *N Y Col Docs*, VII, 770.

56. George Bancroft, *History of the United States of America, from the Discovery of the Continent* (New York, 1888), III, 161; Dawson, *Sons of Liberty*, p. 89.

57. Cadwallader Colden to John Cruger, October 31, 1765: *Colden Letter Books*, II, 53; Cadwallader Colden to Archibald Kennedy, November 1, 1765: *ibid.*, II, 53; *Montresor Journals*, pp. 336–337; *Post-Boy*, November 7, 1765; Archibald Kennedy to Cadwallader Colden, November 1, 1765: *Colden Letters and Papers*, VII, 85–86.

58. *Post-Boy*, November 7, 1765; Council Sessions, October 31, November 2, 1765: *Colden Letters and Papers*, VII, 64–65; "New York" to Cadwallader Colden, November 1, 1765: *ibid.*, VII, 84–85.

59. E. Carther to __ , November 2, 1765: *New York during the Revolution*, p. 45; Dawson, *Sons of Liberty*, p. 95n; *Mercury*, November 4, 1765.

60. Robert R. Livingston to General Monckton, November 8, 1765; Chalmers Mss., IV, New York Public Library; E. Carther to __ , November 2, 1765: *New York during the Revolution*, p. 45; *Post-Boy*, November 7, 1765.

61. *Ibid.*; *Mercury*, November 4, 1765; Robert R. Livingston to General Monckton, November 8, 1765: Chalmers Mss., IV, New York Public Library.

62. *Ibid.*; Charles Botta, *History of the War of Independence of the United States of America*, translated by George Alexander Otis (New Haven, 1840), p. 72 (hereafter cited as Botta, *History*); Cadwallader Colden to the Lords of Trade, December 6, 1765: *N Y Col Docs*, VII, 792; *Post-Boy*, November 7, 1765; David Ramsay, *The History of the American Revolution* (London, 1793), I, 65; Dawson, *Sons of Liberty*, p. 94n. The boot in the devil's hand was an unfriendly allusion to Lord Bute. This motif was a common one in colonial protests: e.g. for Boston see *Mercury*, November 4, 1765. As for "The Rebel Drummer": some years before, when he and Daniel Horsmanden were on better terms, Cadwallader Colden had told the Chief Justice of his attempts to raise troops at the then Lord Jedburgh's request, to fight the rebels. He had gone to Kelso with seventy volunteers and had remained there

until Lord Jedburgh advised him to disperse with the Highlanders approaching. Horsmanden had given the story a malicious turn, and it had apparently become part of local gossip. Cadwallader Colden, A Narrative of some Facts Relative to Mr. Colden, Occasioned by a Libell printed in New York, November 4, 1765: *Colden Letter Books*, II, 63–64.

63. *Mercury*, November 4, 1765; *Post-Boy*, November 7, 1765.

64. *Ibid.*; William Smith, Jr. to General Monckton, November 8, 1765: Chalmers Mss., IV, New York Public Library; Cadwallader Colden to Secretary Conway, November 5, 1765: *N Y Col Docs*, VII, 771.

65. Robert R. Livingston to General Monckton, November 8, 1765: Chalmers Mss., IV, New York Public Library: Cadwallader Colden to Lords of Trade, December 6, 1765: *N Y Col Docs*, VII, 792; Cadwallader Colden, Account of the State of the Province of New York, December 6, 1765: *ibid.*, VII, 798; Cadwallader Colden to Secretary Conway, November 5, 1765: *ibid*, VII, 771; *Montresor Journals*, p. 337; *Post-Boy*, November 7, 1765. As for the fort's condition: on November 2 three engineers were sent out to make a survey; they returned with extensive suggestions for changes which had not yet been made and conceded that even with these changes the fort still had several failings: Engineers' Report on Means of Strengthening Fort George, November 2, 1765: *Colden Letters and Papers*, VII, 87–88.

66. Council Session, November 2, 1765: *ibid.*, VII, 64–65; Cadwallader Colden to Lords of Trade, December 6, 1765: *N Y Col Docs*, VII, 792; Cadwallader Colden to Conway, November 5, 1765: *ibid.*, VII, 777; *Mercury*, November 4, 1765; Robert R. Livingston to General Monckton, November 8, 1765: Chalmers Mss., IV, New York Public Library; William Smith, Jr. to General Monckton, November 8, 1765: *ibid.*, IV, New York Public Library; Botta, *History*, I, 72; *Montresor Journals*, p. 337; *Post-Boy*, November 7, 1765. In December Colden ordered an elegant new chariot, which cost him £88:9:0. He claimed losses of £195 3s, but the Assembly never gave him a penny in compensation. Peter Collinson to Cadwallader Colden, March 20, 1766: *Colden Letters and Papers*, VII, 105; Bill for Chariot, May 9, 1766: *ibid.*, VII, 109–110; Cadwallader Colden to Secretary Conway, January 14, June 24, 1766: *N Y Col Docs*, VII, 804–805, 832; Cadwallader Colden to Henry Moore, June 16, 1766: *Colden Letter Books*, II, 109–110.

67. William Smith, Jr. to General Monckton, November 8, 1765: Chalmers Mss., IV, New York Public Library; *Mercury*, November 4, 1765; Thomas James to Cadwallader Colden, [December, 1765?]: *Colden Letters and Papers*, VII, 99. At first Colden thought that James had not given the least cause for the mob's "Savage resentment." Later, when he was trying to shift the blame, he correctly connected the crowd's anger with James' military activities. Cadwallader Colden to Secretary Conway, November 9, 1765: *N Y Col Docs*, VII, 773; Cadwallader Colden to Grenville, October 22, 1768: *Colden Letter Books*, II, 177. James was so proud of himself that he exaggerated the extent of his arrogance. An earlier report says that he had

said that he would cram the stamps down their throats with one hundred men: Robert R. Livingston to General Monckton, November 8, 1765: Chalmers Mss., IV, New York Public Library.

[68.] *Post-Boy*, November 7, 1765; *Mercury*, November 4, 1765; Cadwallader Colden to Lords of Trade, December 6, 1765: *N Y Col Docs*, VII, 792; Robert R. Livingston to General Monckton, November 8, 1765: Chalmers Mss., IV, New York Public Library; William Smith, Jr. to General Monckton, November 8, 1765: *ibid.*, IV, New York Public Library; *Montresor Journals*, pp. 336–337; Thomas James to Cadwallader Colden, November 6, 1765: *Colden Letters and Papers*, VII, 89–90. Major James left for England in the ship that brought the stamps and advised Colden to do the same. When James returned in the spring, the mob again offered to pull his house down for him and, calling him an "authorized beggar," advised the Assembly not to indemnify him. Thomas James to Cadwallader Colden, November 6, 1765: *ibid.*, VII, 90; *Montresor Journals*, pp. 339, 369–370. James estimated his losses variously at £1,500 and £2,000, and the mob assisted him by publishing an account of the destruction. He was luckier than Colden: on December 19, 1766 the Assembly granted him £1745:15:2$\frac{1}{2}$. Robert R. Livingston to General Monckton, November 8, 1765: Chalmers Mss., IV, New York Public Library; Thomas James to Cadwallader Colden, November 6, 1765: *Colden Letters and Papers*, VII, 90; Stokes, *Iconography*, IV, 771.

[69.] *Post-Boy*, November 7, 1765, October 23, 1766; *Montresor Journals*, p. 337.

[70.] William Gordon, *History of the Rise, Progress, and Establishment of the Independence of the United States of America* (London, 1788), I, 185–186 (hereafter cited as Gordon, *History*). Orin Grant Libby, "A Critical Examination of William Gordon's History of the American Revolution," American Historical Association, *Annual Report for 1899* (Washington, 1900), I, 365–388, shows Gordon guilty of extensive plagiarism in his accounts of the *war* and thus condemns the *entire* work. This blanket condemnation based on partial, although thoroughly impressive, attack, is not justified. Gordon is of special value as a source on the Stamp Act riots in New York, for he and Sears were later neighbors in Roxbury, Massachusetts. References to Sears in the Gordon papers indicate that Sears was a contributor to the *History*. Thus Gordon's account may more than likely be considered as Sears' own memories. For this information I am indebted to Robert Jay Christen of Manhattanville College, who is currently at work on a biography of Sears. Botta, *History*, I, 73; James Grahame, *The History of the United States of North America from the Plantation of the British Colonies till their Revolt and Declaration of Independence* (London, 1836), IV, 224 (hereafter cited as Grahame, *History*). After some haggling the stamps had been quietly unloaded from *Edward* and moved into the fort beginning October 23. McEvers had refused to have anything to do with them, and Colden had taken the opportunity—as he had often attempted in the past with other jobs—to try to have his son appointed to the position. Both Jared Ingersoll of Connecticut and William Franklin of New Jersey had found reasons to ask Colden to keep their stamps. Cadwallader Colden's Account Book, October 23, 1765: Stokes, *Iconography*, IV, 751; Council Sessions, October 23, 24, 1765: *Colden Letters and Papers*, VII, 62–64; Jared Ingersoll to Cadwallader Colden, September 9, 14, October 13, 1765: *ibid.*, VII, 74–75, 77, 83–84; William Franklin to Cadwallader Colden, September 25, 1765: *ibid.*, VII, 80; *Post-Boy*, October 24, 1765; David Colden to Commissioners of Stamp Office, October 26, 1765: *Colden Letter Books*, II, 50–51; Cadwallader Colden to Commissioners for Trade and Plantations, April 14, 1764: *ibid.*, I, 321–322; Council Session, February 10, 1762: *Calendar of Council Minutes*, p. 456; "Journal of French Traveller," *American Historical Review*, XXVII (October, 1921), 82.

71. *Post-Boy*, November 7, 1765; Cadwallader Colden to Conway, February 21, 1766: *N Y Col Docs*, VII, 811; Cadwallader Colden to the Lords of Trade, December 6, 1765: *ibid.*, VII, 792; William Smith, Jr. to General Monckton, November 8, 1765: Chalmers Mss., IV, New York Public Library; Robert R. Livington to General Monckton, November 8, 1765: *ibid.*, IV, New York Public Library; Council Session, morning, November 2, 1765: *Colden Letters and Papers*, VII, 65.

72. *Ibid.*; Engineers' Report, November 2, 1765: *ibid.*, VII, 87–88.

73. Robert R. Livingston to General Monckton, November 8, 1765: Chalmers Mss., IV, New York Public Library; William Smith, Jr. to General Monckton, November 8, 1765: *ibid*, IV, New York Public Library.

74. Robert R. Livingston to General Monckton, November 8, 1765: *ibid.*, IV, New York Public Library; Council Session, afternoon, November 2, 1765: *Colden Letters and Papers*, VII, 65–66; Cadwallader Colden to Secretary Conway, October 26, November 9, 1765; *N Y Col Docs*, VII, 768, 774; Cadwallader Colden to Henry Moore, September 23, 1765: *Colden Letter Books*, II, 37; John Watts to General Monckton, September 24, 1765: *Aspinwall Papers*, p. 576. Colden received a dressing-down from Secretary Conway for his conduct; all of Colden's other retreats, he felt, could be explained by necessity rather than want of firmness. But how could he suspend the government when power was fully in his hands? On October 31 he had sworn to do his "utmost that all and every the Clauses contained in [the Stamp Act] be punctually and bona fide observed. . . . So help you God." And yet, a few days later he had promised not to execute the Act. It would take "very strong reasons indeed" to justify this conduct. Colden never produced more than weak reasons. Secretary Conway to Cadwallader Colden, December 15, 1765, February 21, 1766: *N Y Col Docs*, VII, 800–801, 811–812; Council Session, October 31, 1765: *Colden Letters and Papers*, VII, 64.

75. Robert R. Livingston to General Monckton, November 8, 1765: Chalmers Mss., IV, New York Public Library.

76. *Ibid.*; *Mercury*, November 4, 1765.

[77.] *Ibid.*; Robert R. Livingston to General Monckton, November 8, 1765: Chalmers Mss., IV, New York Public Library; Broadside, November 4, 1765: New-York Historical Society Broadsides SY 1765–1; *Post-Boy*, November 7, 1765.

[78.] *Ibid.*; "Benevolus" to Cadwallader Colden, November 3, 1765: *Colden Letters and Papers*, VII, 88; Isaac Q. Leake, *Memoir of the Life and Times of General John Lamb* (Albany, New York, 1850), pp. 13n–14n. (hereafter cited as Leake, *Lamb*); Robert R. Livingston to General Monckton, November 8, 1765: Chalmers Mss., IV, New York Public Library.

[79.] *Ibid.*

[80.] *Ibid.*; William Smith, Jr. to General Monckton, November 8, 1765: *ibid.*, IV, New York Public Library; *Montresor Journals*, pp. 337–338; *Post-Boy*, November 7, 1765. It became a part of local folklore that Colden himself had done the spiking. On November 26 the Clerk of the Assembly received a note demanding that the Assembly "consider what is to be done first drawing of as much money from the Lieutenant Governor's sellery [sic] as will Repare the fort and on spike the guns on the Battery. . . ." The following March a mob of many thousands braved the rain to burn an effigy of Colden sitting on a cannon, working away at it with a chisel. Once again he wore a drum as a badge, and on his chest was written:

"I'm deceived by the devil, and left in the lurch;
And am forc'd to do penance, tho' not in the Church."

Assembly Journal, II, 787; *Post-Boy*, March 13, 1766.

[81.] Robert R. Livingston to General Monckton, November 8, 1765: Chalmers Mss., IV, New York Public Library.

[82.] *Ibid.*; Broadside, November 4, 1765: New-York Historical Society Broadsides SY 1765–1; *Post-Boy*, November 7, 1765. I have assumed that the contents of the broadside were the main business of the meeting. I base this assumption on evidence within the broadside. The meeting between the Governor and the Livingston delegation took place in the morning, which would allow time before the public meeting. The final paragraph of the broadside expresses the satisfaction of the freemen, freeholders, and inhabitants. The parliamentary sensitivities of Livingston et. al. were too strong for them to send out a statement in the name of such a body without actual consultation. The Livingston meeting was the only meeting in town that day. The ambiguous concluding statement should not confuse the reader. There was opposition to Colden in all areas of the political spectrum except the extreme right.

[83.] Robert R. Livingston to General Monckton, November 8, 1765: Chalmers Mss., IV, New York Public Library; Carl Lotus Becker, *The History of Political Parties in the Province of New York*, 1760–1776 (2d ed.; Madison, Wisconsin, 1960), p. 33 (hereafter cited as Becker, *Political Parties*); *Montresor Journals*, p. 338; General Gage to Conway, November 4, 1765: Carter, *Gage Correspondence*, I, 70–71.

[84.] *Ibid.*, Cadwallader Colden to Lords of Trade, December 6, 1765: *N Y Col Docs*, VII, 792; Cadwallader Colden to Secretary Conway, March 28, 1766: *ibid.*, VII, 821–823. By dint of his marriage to Anne, daughter of Councillor John Watts, Kennedy was the owner of several houses—on lower Broadway and near the Battery—and perhaps the largest property-owner in New York. *Ibid.*, VII, 822n.; Cadwallader Colden to the Lords of Trade, December 6, 1765; *ibid.*, VII, 792.

[85.] Cadwallader Colden to Secretary Conway, March 28, 1766: *ibid.*, VII, 821–823; Robert R. Livingston to General Monckton, November 8, 1765: Chalmers Mss., IV, New York Public Library; Cadwallader Colden to Archibald Kennedy, November 2, 1765: *Colden Letter Books*, II, 102; Cadwallader Colden to Lords of Trade, December 6, 1765: *N Y Col Docs*, VII, 792; Archibald Kennedy to Cadwallader Colden, November 2, 1765: *Colden Letters and Papers*, VII, 86. To Colden's great chagrin Kennedy was later superseded in his command for having refused to take the stamps. On March 28, 1766 Colden wrote a letter of explanation to Secretary Conway which he passed on to Kennedy, asking him to make his own copy and reseal it: *Colden Letter Books*, II, 102.

[86.] Robert R. Livingston to General Monckton, November 8, 1765: Chalmers Mss., IV, New York Public Library; *Montresor Journals*, p. 338.

[87.] *Ibid.*; Cadwallader Colden to the Marquis of Granby, November 5, 1765: *Colden Letter Books*, II, 54.

[88.] Cadwallader Colden to Major James, November 6, 1765: *ibid.*, II, 58–59; *Minutes of Common Council*, VI, 438–439; General Gage to Secretary Conway, November 8, 1765: Carter, *Gage Correspondence*, I, 72; Council Session, November 5, 1765: *Colden Letters and Papers*, VII, 67. Robert R. Livingston implies that Colden initiated this plan, asking the Mayor to ask him to deliver the stamps: Robert R. Livingston to General Monckton, November 8, 1765: Chalmers Mss., IV, New York Public Library.

[89.] Council Session, November 5, 1765: *Colden Letters and Papers*, VII, 68; Cadwallader Colden to General Gage, November 5, 1765: *Colden Letter Books*, II, 56.

[90.] General Gage to Conway, November 8, 1765: Carter, *Gage Correspondence*, I, 72; Council Session, November 6, 1765: *Colden Letters and Papers*, VII, 69–70.

[91.] Council Session, November 6, 1765: *Calendar of Council Minutes*, p. 469.

[92.] Robert R. Livingston to General Monckton, November 8, 1765: Chalmers Mss., IV, New York Public Library; *Post-Boy*, November 7, 1765; *Montresor Journals*, pp. 338–339.

[93.] *Ibid.*, p. 339; Thomas James to Cadwallader Colden, November 5, 6, 1765: *Colden Letters and Papers*, VII, 89–90.

[94.] *Post-Boy*, November 14, 1765; *Gazette*, November 25, 1765; Henry Moore to Secretary Conway, November 21, 1765: *N Y Col Docs*, VII, 789; John Watts to General Monckton, November 22, 1765: *Aspinwall Papers*, p. 585; *Montresor Journals*, p. 340. The Sons of Liberty gave Moore a bonfire in the Fields, and he was warmly received by people of all political inclinations. This recalled to William Johnson the reply of his friend Richard Shuckburgh when asked if he knew the name of a newly-appointed governor: "No faith (says he) nor do I give myself any concern about it, as I shall hear him called Names enough before he is here long." The story was not without its consolations for Colden, to whom Johnson sent it, January 9, 1766: *Johnson Papers*, V, 7. For the bonfire see *Post-Boy*, November 21, 1765.

[95.] John Watts to General Monckton, November 22, 1765: *Aspinwall Papers*, p. 585; Robert R. Livingston to General Monckton, November 8, 1765: Chalmers Mss., IV, New York Public Library; Cadwallader Colden to Thomas James, December 11, 1765: *Colden Letter Books*, II, 65.

[96.] Cadwallader Colden to Thomas James, November 6, 1765: *ibid.*, II, 59; Cadwallader Colden to Sir William Johnson, August 31, 1765: *ibid.*, II, 27; Cadwallader Colden to Secretary Conway, September 23, 1765, March 28, 1766, February 21, 1766: *N Y Col Docs*, VII, 759, 823, 812.

[97.] William Johnson to Lords of Trade, November 22, 1765: *ibid.*, VII, 790; Henry Moore to Lord Dartmouth, November 21, 1765: *ibid.*, VII, 789; General Gage to Secretary Conway, December 21, 1765, January 16, 1766: Carter, *Gage Correspondence*, I, 78–79, 81; Cadwallader Colden to Sir Jeffrey Amherst, October 10, 1765: *Colden Letter Books*, II, 44; Henry Moore to _ , December 30, 1765: Emmet Collection, #2610, New York Public Library; *Montresor Journals*, p. 339; Sir William Johnson to Cadwallader Colden, October 11, 1765: *Johnson Papers*, IV, 857. Many modern historians have taken this view: Arthur M. Schlesinger:

> In New York . . . the lawyers seemed to be at the bottom of the tumults, aided beyond a doubt by the merchants and printers . . . these classes . . . felt impelled to take a leading part in instigating popular demonstrations against the measure.

(Arthur M. Schlesinger, *Colonial Merchants and the American Revolution, 1763–1776* [New York, 1918], pp. 73, 66.

The Morgans seem to share this view of the Stamp Act riots in New York, focusing on the role of the lawyers in general and specifically William Livingston, John Morin Scott, and William Smith, Jr. Of the Colonies in general the Morgans suggest that "merchants, lawyers, and plantation owners directed the show from behind the scenes. . . ." "Actually the lower classes probably had little to lose directly by the Stamp Act." "How then," the Morgans ask, "did the Sons of Liberty rouse these people to fury, and more important, how did they control that fury once they had aroused it?" *Stamp Act Crisis*, pp. 184, 181, 187.

98. Cadwallader Colden to Lords Commissioners for Trade and Plantations, April 7, 1762: *Colden Letter Books*, I, 187; Thomas Jones, *History of New York during the Revolutionary War* (New York, 1879), I, 2; Sabine, *Smith Memoirs*, p. 3; Cadwallader Colden to Secretary Conway, September 23, 1765: *N Y Col Docs*, VII, 759; "Sentinel XXI," *Post-Boy*, July 18, 1765; Milton Martin Klein, "The American Whig: William Livingston of New York" (unpublished Ph.D. dissertation, Dept. of History, Columbia University, 1954), p. 561 (hereafter cited as Klein, "Livingston"); Dawson, *Sons of Liberty*, p. 105. Colden also labeled as "inflammatory" another article which invited readers to "besiege the throne with petitions and humble remonstrances, and not doubt of a favorable issue. . . ." Cadwallader Colden to Secretary Conway, October 12, 1765: *N Y Col Docs*, VII, 767; [Woodbridge, New Jersey] *Constitutional Courant*, September 21, 1765.

99. John Watts to General Monckton, September 22, 1765: *Watts Letter Book*, p. 291; Cadwallader Colden to Lord Egremont, September 14, 1763: *Colden Letter Books*, I, 231; Cadwallader Colden to Lords Commissioners for Trade and Plantations: *ibid.*, II, 14; Cadwallader Colden, Account of the State of the Province of New York, December 6, 1765: *N Y Col Docs*, VII, 796. On writs of error see Dillon, *New York Triumvirate*, pp. 68–81.

100. John Watts to John Erving, June 14, 1762: *Watts Letter Book*, p. 62; for the relations between lawyers and seamen, see above, p. 53.

101. General Gage to Conway, December 21, 1765: *Gage Correspondence*, I, 79; *Post-Boy*, November 7, 1765; Bridenbaugh, *Cities in Revolt*, pp. 86–87; E. B. O'Callaghan, ed., *The Documentary History of the State of New York* (Albany, 1850–51), I, 493, 513; Paul A. Chadbourne and Walter Burritt Neale, eds., *The Public Service of the State of New York. Historical, Statistical, Descriptive and Biographical. Illustrated with Views and Portraits* (Boston, 1887), I, 411; Edwards, *New York as Eighteenth Century Municipality*, p. 62; Robert R. Livingston to General Monckton, November 8, 1765: Chalmers Mss., IV, New York Public Library.

102. Cadwallader Colden to Conway, November 5, 1765: *N Y Col Docs*, VII, 771; Alexander Colden to Cadwallader Colden, [November, 1765]: *Colden Letters and Papers*, VII, 94.

103. *Post-Boy*, November 7, 1765.

104. *Mercury*, November 4, 1765.

105. General Gage to Secretary Conway, November 4, 1765: Carter, *Gage Correspondence*, I, 71; Robert R. Livingston to General Monckton, November 8, 1765: Chalmers Mss., IV, New York Public Library. Sears is named in Botta, *History*, I, 73; Gordon, *History*, I, 185–186; Grahame, *History*, IV, 224. As shortly after the riots as November 27, and frequently thereafter, *Montresor Journals* call Sears a "ringleader": pp. 340, 361, 362. Thomas, *Willett*, p. 23 has Willett and Sears leading the riot November 1 but gives no source. Diverse information on New York's privateers may be

found in Fish, *New York Privateers, passim*. Names of Sons of Liberty taken from signatures on correspondence in Lamb Papers, New-York Historical Society. For more on Tolmie, see above, p. 29.

[106.] *Montresor Journals*, p. 339; *Post-Boy*, June 7, 1764; Stokes, *Iconography*, IV, 749; John Watts to General Monckton, November 22, 1765: *Aspinwall Papers*, p. 585; Becker, *Political Parties*, p. 30n. For postwar trade and unemployment see above, p. 26ff.

[107.] Klein, "Livingston," p. 53; Governor Bernard to Lords of Trade, September 7, 1765: quoted in Morgans, *Stamp Act Crisis*; Bridenbaugh, *Cities in Revolt*, p. 322; Benjamin Rush to Ebenezer Hazard, November 8, 1765: L. H. Butterfield, ed., *Letters of Benjamin Rush* (Princeton, 1951), I, 18. Here I disagree with Morgans, *Stamp Act Crisis*; see above, note 97.

[108.] *Assembly Journal*, II, 783; *Post-Boy*, December 6, 1764, August 1 ("Sentinel"), September 26, 1765. Trade continued uninterrupted in Rhode Island, and the Providence Sons of Liberty were later able to twit their New York colleagues: "It is to be lamented that in some of the Colonies, who hold the same Sentiments with us a Suspension of public Business hath found place. . . ." Lamb Papers, 1762–73 folder, #21, New-York Historical Society.

[109.] *Post-Boy*, November 28, 1765.

[110.] Robert R. Livingston to General Monckton, November 8, 1765: Chalmers Mss., IV, New York Public Library. For the seamen at the coffeehouse see above, p. 78.

[111.] Governor Moore to Lord Dartmouth, December 27, 1765: *N Y Col Docs*, VII, 802; *Gazette*, November 25, 1765; *Post-Boy*, December 5, 1765.

[112.] *Ibid.*, December 19, 1765.

[113.] *Ibid.*, December 27, 1765.

[114.] *Ibid.*, November 28, 1765.

[115.] *Ibid.*; for the Triumvirate's leadership see Klein, "Livingston," p. 565.

[116.] *Post-Boy*, November 28, 1765.

[117.] *Ibid*; Morgans, *Stamp Act Crisis*, p. 107; *Montresor Journals*, p. 340. For the pressures operating in an open meeting, see the secret ballot controversy, *Post-Boy*, January 8, 1770.

[118.] "Sentinel XXI," *ibid.*, July 18, 1765; *ibid.*, November 2, 1764.

[119.] *Ibid.*, October 10, 1765.

[120.] "To the Freeholders and Inhabitants of New York City," November 6, 1765: *Colden Letters and Papers*, VII, 91; Broadside, January, 1766: New-York Historical Society Broadsides SY-1766-11.

[121.] *Journal*, May 10, 1770; *Post-Boy*, December 27, 1765, January 30, 1766, October 10, 1765, February 20, 1766; "Freeman," *Journal*, April 19, 1770; Milton M. Klein, "The Rise of the New York Bar: The Legal Career of

William Livingston," *William and Mary Quarterly*, third series, XV (July, 1958), 354; Broadside, February, 1768: "New York Broadsides, 1762–1779," *Bulletin of the New York Public Library*, III (1899), 23.

122. *Post-Boy*, November 28, 1765; *Assembly Journal*, II, 781–783, 807–808; Peter Hasenclever to Sir William Johnson, December 23, 1765: (burned in 1911 Albany fire; summarized in) *Johnson Papers*, IV, 885 and quoted in Becker, *Political Parties*, p. 40n.

123. *Montresor Journals*, p. 357; *Gazette*, May 12, 1766.

124. *Montresor Journals*, p. 346 mentions for the first time friction because captains of ships of war allowed their men to take jobs in the shipyards. This becomes a major issue: see below, p. 125ff.

125. *Ibid.*, p. 365.

126. *Ibid.*, pp. 348–349.

127. *Ibid.*, p. 350.

128. *Post-Boy*, December 26, 1765.

129. *Ibid.*, January 9, 16, 1766.

130. *Ibid.*, August 29, November 28, December 5, 1765; *Montresor Journals*, pp. 340, 343. As to Delancey's appointment, one can only suppose that the Treasury had acted with unaccustomed speed. After McEvers' resignation, David Colden, the Lieutenant-Governor's son, had applied for the office, but it had apparently been given to Delancey. I have been unable to discover the details of the appointment and must be content with this indefinite account which follows Becker, *Political Parties*, p. 42n.

131. *Montresor Journals*, pp. 343, 345, 358; General Gage to Conway, December 21, 1765: Carter, *Gage Correspondence*, I, 78; *Mercury*, January 9, April 7, 1766; Henry Moore to Lord Dartmouth, January 16, 1766: *N Y Col Docs*, VII, 807; *Post-Boy*, January 13, 1766.

132. *Ibid.*, January 9, February 20, 1766; *Montresor Journals*, p. 349.

133. *Ibid.*; *Post-Boy*, February 20, 1766; John Holt to Deborah Franklin, February 15, 1766: quoted in Morgans, *Stamp Act Crisis*, p. 195.

134. *Ibid.*, pp. 195–196; *Montresor Journals*, p. 349.

135. *Ibid.*, p. 350; John Holt to Deborah Franklin, February 15, 1766: quoted in Morgans, *Stamp Act Crisis*, pp. 195–196; Cadwallader Colden to Secretary Conway, February 21, 1766: *N Y Col Docs*, VII, 813; *Post-Boy*, February 20, 1766.

136. *Ibid.*, December 19, 1765, April 24, 1766; *Montresor Journals*, pp. 342–344, 354, 367.

137. *Post-Boy*, November 21, 1765; Council Session, November 21, 1765: *Calendar of Council Minutes*, p. 470; Alexander Colden to Cadwallader Colden, [November (?), 1765]: *Colden Letters and Papers*, VII, 93–94; Henry Moore to Lord Dartmouth, November 21, 1765: *N Y Col Docs*, VII,

789. Colden was extremely displeased with Moore's attempt to present at least the appearance of flexibility: Cadwallader Colden to Sir Jeffrey Amherst, June 24, 1766: *Colden Letter Books*, II, 112.

138. *Journal*, April 19, 1770; Collector and Comptroller of New York to Commissioners of Customs, December 20, 1765: quoted in Morgans, *Stamp Act Crisis*, p. 168.

139. *Montresor Journals*, p. 342; *Post-Boy*, December 12, 19, 1765, January 9, February 27, 1766; Providence, Rhode Island Sons of Liberty to New York Sons of Liberty: Lamb Papers, 1762–73, #21, New-York Historical Society.

140. General Gage to Secretary Conway, December 21, 1765: Carter, *Gage Correspondence*, I, 78; Collector and Comptroller of New York to Commissioners of Customs, December 4, 1765: quoted in Morgans, *Stamp Act Crisis*, p. 162.

141. Dickerson, *Navigation Acts*, pp. 168–170.

142. *Montresor Journals*, pp. 341–342.

143. *Post-Boy*, January 31, 1765.

144. *Ibid.*

145. *Ibid.*, January 2, 1766; *Montresor Journals*, p. 344; *Mercury*, January 6, 1766.

146. *Post-Boy*, January 23, 1766.

147. John Watts to Isaac Barre, February 28, 1762: *Watts Letter Book*, p. 25.

148. Lords of Admiralty to Secretary Conway, March 31, 1766: Redington, *Calendar of Home Office Papers*, II, 32.

149. *Montresor Journals*, p. 360.

150. *Ibid.*, pp. 352, 375.

151. General Gage to Secretary Conway, May 28, 1766: Carter, *Gage Correspondence*, I, 92.

152. Governor Bernard to Lords of Trade, September 7, 1765: quoted in Morgans, *Stamp Act Crisis*, pp. 130–131; Collector Abel James and Comptroller Henry Drinker to Commissioners of Customs, December 1, 1765: quoted in *ibid.*, p. 161; Charles Stewart to Commissioners of Customs, December 8, 1765: quoted in *ibid.*, p. 162; Collector and Comptroller of New York to Commissioners of Customs, December 4, 1765: quoted in *ibid.*, p. 162.

153. *Montresor Journals*, p. 348; Secretary Conway to Governors in America, March 31, 1766: *N Y Col Docs*, VII, 824.

154. *Ibid.*; *Post-Boy*, December 19, 1765; Thomas James to Cadwallader Colden, [December (?), 1765]: *Colden Letters and Papers*, VII, 98–100.

155. *Montresor Journals*, pp. 351, 361.

156. *Ibid.*, p. 295.

157. General Gage to Secretary Conway, February 22, 1766: Carter, *Gage Correspondence*, I, 84.

158. Governor Moore to the Lords of Trade, January 14, 1767: *N Y Col Docs*, VII, 891.

159. Governor Moore to the Duke of Richmond, August 23, 1766: *ibid.*, VII, 867. For a recent view of the upstate tenants see Staughton Lynd, "Who Should Rule at Home? Dutchess County, New York, in the American Revolution," *William and Mary Quarterly*, third series, XVIII (July, 1961), 330–359.

V. Jack Tar in the Streets: Before the Mast of Liberty, 1766–1770

New Yorkers *wanted* to celebrate. In the Spring of 1766 they knew that "that Hydra the Stamp Act was giving its last Gasp" and expected every vessel—be it skiff, packet or pilot boat—to bring the news that the time had come to dance on the coffin.[1] Crowds assembled in the Merchant's Coffeehouse at night to await word, and reports of no repeal sent the cryer and newsmongers into the streets shouting, "Bloody news for America. . . ."[2]

At four in the afternoon on the twenty-fourth of March, only a day after the latest disappointment, good news came through. A special express sent by the Philadelphia Sons of Liberty to their brothers in New York brought word that a brig had arrived from Cork, that the captain had a Cork newspaper, that the Cork newspaper contained a paragraph reprinted from a Dublin paper, that the paragraph was an excerpt from a letter sent by an M.P. in London to a friend in Ireland on the twenty-eighth of January—that the Stamp Act had been repealed. Battalions of six-year-olds pledged "their Lives and Fortunes" to liberty and raced through the streets shouting, "The Tamp-Act is pealed." But what was adequate information for six-year-olds was not, on second thought, good enough for their elders. In fact the report could say little more than that debate on repeal had begun in Parliament; the editor of the *Post-Boy* advised his readers to be patient, and the Sons of Liberty told their White Plains counterparts to " . . . pay no regard to common reports untill we have an Acct. of the repeal properly Authenticated."[3]

One false alarm taught New Yorkers little caution; they wanted a celebration. A month later, on April 25, the pilot boat's skiff raced up from the Hook with news of repeal brought by *Duke of Cumberland*, Captain Goodrich, from Falmouth. The report was good enough for anxious New Yorkers: the coffeehouse crowd took up a collection for the messenger; the streets were illuminated, muskets fired, and fire-crackers set off. Captain Isaac Sears issued orders for the ministers to ring their bells at three in the morning—and so they did, every last bell in town, producing what was, to one alien and sensitive ear, "a most hideous Din." At eight the captain of the packet arrived with the mail; even before he came ashore the Sons of Liberty demanded confirmation of the news of repeal. "Yes," shouted Captain Goodrich, "*Totally*." The bearer of good news was rewarded with a chair-ride to the post-office, accompanied all the way by cheering and shouts of joy. There, to the sound of the still-ringing bells, the mail was opened. Clearly the Stamp Act was breathing its last; just as clearly it was too early for a celebration, for the repeal had gone through two not three readings in the Commons. At about ten the bells were unwillingly silenced, and, equally unwillingly, the celebrants went home, all the more dissatisfied for having been "so premature in their rejoicings. . . ."[4]

On the afternoon of the twentieth of May definite news of repeal arrived. Hundreds of children ran through the streets with play effigies, cheering in competition with the din of the church bells. The celebration continued until late at night, and the bells began again at dawn. The Rector at Trinity Church added to his planned sermon a "congratulatory Discourse on the joyful Occasion." Shops were shut, and the people followed the Sons of Liberty to the Fields where a ship mast—New York's first Liberty Pole—had been set up. There a twenty-one gun "Royal Salute" was fired for "General" Allicocke at one o'clock. Then the Sons of Liberty set out for an elegant entertainment at Howards', where they dined, accompanied by a band, and drank twenty-eight toasts, each echoed by a blast of the cannon. At night the city was illuminated—except at the military and naval officers' residences—and two great bonfires were set, one for the Sons of Liberty and one for the Corporation. The night ended in drunkenness, with tossing of fire-crackers and firing of muskets and pistols. The Sons of Liberty went to the fort and there—drunk as they were—went in to congratulate the Governor.[5]

The British Army in New York

On the Common stands the mast of a ship. At its base is nailed a placard; it reads "George 3rd, Pitt—and Liberty." New York is celebrating the repeal of the Stamp Act, and the Sons of Liberty have just erected the city's first Liberty Pole.[6]

The Sons of Liberty remove their homespun clothes. Their hearts are still homespun; daily they go to the Liberty Pole.[7]

The fourth of June. The King's birthday. The people assemble at the Liberty Pole. A St. George flag is raised. At the base, again, "George, Pitt, and Liberty;" "Pitt" stands out. Two oxen are roasted; twenty-five barrels of strong beer, a hogshead of rum. Toasts, each echoed by twenty-five cannon in the Fields, these echoed in turn by the guns of *Garland* and *Coventry*. Cheering, the band playing "God Save the King." In the evening a bonfire. It is the last time the people of New York will pay for a bonfire for the King of England.[8]

June: "intollerably hot & very little air;" winds from the south and southeast, sometimes from the northwest but still "extremely hot." July, August: heavy, mizzling; ninety degrees in the daytime, still intense at midnight.

"Close, sultry, disagreeable. . . ." Sunday, August 10. The heat is excessive. At night the soldiers of the Twenty-Eighth Regiment swelter in their barracks. They hate the weather, they hate the town, they hate the people: some of them leave the barracks, push through the heavy air to the Fields and cut down the Liberty Pole.[9]

At about three o'clock Monday afternoon a crowd of 2,000 to 3,000, led by Captain Isaac Sears, assembled on the Common to demand an explanation for the destruction of the old Liberty Pole and to erect a new one. A drummer passed, and angry words were exchanged. "Do you resent it?" someone heard the drummer shout. "I do resent it," replied mariner John Berrien. The drummer drew a weapon, and the mob attacked him and the corporal who came to his aid. Some wanted the drummer taken to the Mayor, some wanted him let go; in the end he and the corporal were chased to the gate of the barracks. Soon two or three dozen men of the Twenty-Eighth, led by Major Arthur Brown, emerged to be assaulted by "the most scurrilous and abusive language"—Brown was called a "rascal"—and a volley of brickbats. Those soldiers who had not already drawn their bayonets did so, and they charged into the crowd, cutting and slashing as they went. Sears and Berrien suffered light wounds, and the mob was driven clear to Chapel Street. Finally some officers nearby gained control of the situation and forced the angry soldiers back to their barracks. In the presence of the city officials the mob surrounded the barracks and issued taunts provocative enough to frighten the better sort who, although present throughout, were, in the words of one British officer, "(for a wonder) not immediately at the bottom of this." The people were all for forcing the soldiers out of the city immediately, but they seem to have been pacified by vague assurances that if the soldiers were found to be aggressors they would be punished.[10]

The uniform of the British Army was not an unfamiliar sight to New Yorkers. Troops had first come to the city in large numbers during

the French and Indian War. Under the special conditions of wartime the
presence of the Army had been good for the economy of New York. But
even whiie fighting for a common cause, certain frictions had arisen
between Provincials and Regulars, leaving antagonisms which would
explode in later years. The victory of a combined army of New Yorkers
and British regulars over the Spanish at Havana in 1762 had "entirely
broke the heart of the stoutest little Army in the world," and almost a
year afterwards New York's military force was still "rather weak, the
woefull Havanna having undone us." While New Yorkers were
convinced that the battle could never have been won without their men,
they bitterly recalled the "Hyde Park Generals" who had treated the New
Yorkers with contempt because they were not "high dressed" and
because their clothes were soiled from hard labor—because they had
been "too long away from St. James' to be fashionable."[11]

British troops left New York, nonetheless, as allies. When they
returned, in the summer of 1765, they did so as enemies. They came as
members of a new military establishment, and the unfriendly purpose of
that establishment seemed to be made clear when they responded to
Cadwallader Colden's plea for troops to implement the Stamp Act. An
administration which was viewing with increasing sympathy the idea of
military strength—perhaps even of a military government[12]—as a
means of carrying out policy demonstrated this new sympathy in
November at Fort George.[13]

An angry populace, as we have seen,[14] responded violently: their
attack on the fort and on Major James' house initiated a new phase of
civilian-military relations. While the major effort of the counterattack
was aimed at nullifying the Stamp Act, and thus at the Navy,[15] New
Yorkers did not slight the Army—nor did it slight them. Soldiers
stabbed Sons of Liberty;[16] officers were threatened and beaten,[17] effigies
were paraded and burned,[18] and even the commander-in-chief learned that
he must huzza when the Sons of Liberty huzza.[19] And, increasingly,
soldiers and common seamen found themselves at odds.

A full understanding of these antagonisms and of the seamen's
leading role in them demands a review of the economic situation. The
end of the French and Indian War, it will be recalled, left great numbers
of former privateers unemployed. New trade regulations exacerbated the
post-war trade depression. Ships did not sail, and thus seamen could not
find work.[20]

So they came ashore to look for work. They went to the shipyards,
to the rope-walk, they went wherever they thought work could be
found. Too frequently they were disappointed. Many others were
unemployed, and the labor supply was swollen by the continuing
arrival of new immigrants and by discharged soldiers. The latter, instead

of clearing uncultivated lands as had been expected, "for the most part crowded into the Towns" where their activities so disrupted the pattern of British mercantilism that General Gage once suggested "that no Soldier who has any Trade should receive his Discharge in America. . . ."[21]

But the most annoying competition for jobs ashore came from men who already had employment: British soldiers and sailors. Longstanding practice in the British Army allowed men to take civilian employment when they were free of military duties. Complaints about it were nearly as old as the system itself; as early as 1717 merchants and owners of ships trading from Poole to Newfoundland wrote the Board of Trade:

> To prevent any oppression to poor labouring fishermen by any military or publick officer, *pray that* no millitary person under any pretence wtsoever do intermeddle with the fishery or fishermen inhabitants or others, nor keep any fishing boat by himself or company *etc.*, nor let any soldier out to hier, nor any soldier be imployed in catching, cureing or makeing fish, nor shall use any manner of merchandise or trade, nor have any suttling house, without the lines of the fortifications, nor shall any officer or soldier have any house without the lines of the fortifications, nor take up any gardens for private use to themselves that have served or may serve for fishing room, according to the judgment of the fishing Admirals.[22]

In New York the same problem underlies many of the antagonisms of the 'sixties. Time and again hungry seamen on the brink of employment found themselves turned away, their places taken by off-duty soldiers. The colonial employer's preference for the soldier was easily explained: the soldier would do for 18d or 2s what would normally cost the employer 4s. Thus soldiers consistently undercut seamen: the result was a generally lowered level of wages, fewer jobs, and, for the seamen, a frustration economic in its root, daily intensified by the omnipresence of what seemed an arrogant army of occupation.[23]

The destruction of the Liberty Pole in August of 1766 strengthened old antagonisms and brought new ones to the surface; henceforth anti-military incidents would occur with increasing regularity. It began to dawn on New Yorkers that they were living "as in a Military or conquer'd Town," their streets patrolled by ostentatiously armed soldiers, their ears assaulted by the din of drums and bugles, their nights troubled by new fears. Governor Moore was not precisely correct when he reported home that New Yorkers had no "particular objection" to either of the regiments in the City—the people did have very particular objections against the conduct of the Twenty-Eighth and the Forty-Sixth—but he felt the pulse properly when he wrote that "The great objection here is that of having any Troops at all. . . ." Why, New Yorkers asked, are we saddled with a great number of armed men with no visible occasion for their presence? What, they wondered, are they here for?[24]

Supplying the Army

A new Liberty Pole was erected, and the Sons of Liberty swore that they would see justice done. The evidence was assembled against the soldiers for their conduct on August 11, and two writs were served on Major Brown, each for £5,000 damages. Some friends offered to pay his bail, but the Major raised his own "bail"—"2 orderly Grenadiers, with fixed business who always attend him."[25]

If nothing could be achieved in the courts, the Sons of Liberty were always willing to return to the streets. Daily the soldiers assembled in the heat for their exercise; the people heckled and insulted them and gave serious thought to charging through the square of artillery-men with fixed bayonets which protected the exercising soldiers from their angry audience.[26]

The soldiers continued their field days, and the Sons of Liberty sought new strategies. They demanded that the drummers stop beating retreat and tattoo through the streets. If they could not silence the soldiers, perhaps they could disarm them: they demanded that the soldiers not be allowed to carry their side arms when off duty. If the soldiers could not be silenced or disarmed, perhaps they could be starved: the Sons of Liberty proposed that innholders, market people, indeed people in general, refuse to sell provisions to the military and exile them from their homes. Finally a petition was circulated demanding that the garrison get out of town.[27]

So it went, all through the summer. The hot months ended in heightened antagonism with the destruction of the second Liberty Pole on the night of September 23. The game of destruction and reconstruction was to become part of the routine of the cold war between the city's population and the military. A new pole went up September 24; it was destroyed the following spring. The next pole lasted until January of 1770, and its replacement was cut down in October of 1776. Meanwhile, each destruction saw New York lifted to a new plateau of scorn for the British troops.[28]

An old enmity was renewed on a Saturday night in November of 1766 at an inn on the Common. A group of seamen found themselves sharing the bar with some soldiers of the Forty-Sixth Regiment. Neither group liked the other; they had words, came to blows and one of the seamen suffered a possibly mortal beating. It was little satisfaction to the seamen that the "Transgressors" were apprehended and jailed.[29] Seamen were competing with soldiers for jobs, and the flare-up on the Common was a pale reflection of what was to come.

Bar fights between soldiers and the civilian population were by no means unusual in the 1760's. Less than a month before, a party of soldiers had picked up their bayonets and made the rounds of the houses in the Fields where they were noisy and abusive, frightening the inhabitants; this visit was said to be a mission of revenge for some ill treatment which the soldiers had received the night before. New Yorkers complained about the soldiers' whores and their bastards and passed laws against selling strong liquors to privates; the bars would remain a major locus for antagonisms between soldiers and civilians.[30]

On March 18, 1767 New Yorkers celebrated the first anniversary of the repeal of the Stamp Act. During the night a few soldiers motivated, it seemed to the inhabitants, by "a malevolent Disposition," destroyed the third Liberty Pole. The horizontal mast was discovered in the morning and was immediately replaced. The new one was larger and more substantial, a large part of it secured with iron. That night the soldiers tried unsuccessfully to undermine it. On the night of Saturday the twenty-first the Pole proved itself impervious even to an explosion of gunpowder placed in a hole bored within it. On Sunday night a newly assembled watch was able to talk a small party of soldiers out of trouble; the soldiers had their coats turned and were armed with bayonets and sticks, but they had no guns, and inquiries as to who they were and what their business was were sufficient to drive them away. On Monday night the Pole defenders were gathered in Bardin's Tavern, a favorite meeting place, at six in the evening when a party of soldiers marched by and emptied their muskets; two fired at the house, one ball passing through and the other lodging in a timber. Finally, after five days harassment the soldiers made a final feeble attempt on the pole Tuesday afternoon. An officer spotted them headed in that direction with a ladder and ordered them back; finally the Governor, General, and city authorities took action to prevent further assaults on New York's shaky symbol of liberty.[31]

During the reign of the fourth Liberty Pole events moved rapidly toward the great explosion of January 1770. The poor multiplied, and soldiers continued to take their jobs. When General Gage hired some vessels to transport two regiments from St. Augustine to Boston the owners suddenly backed down, responding to pressures of unknown origin; they would not assist in the military occupation of Boston.[32]

Tempers flared in 1769 when " . . . the audacious, domineering and inhuman Maj. Pullaine . . . ordered a Guard to protect a sordid Miscreant, that transgressed the laudable Non-Importation Agreement of the Merchants. . . ."[33] Governor Moore described the deterioration of relations between troops and populace:

> . . . the Inhabitants of the Town, by withdrawing themselves from those opportunities of intercourse with the Military, which were calculate[d] to promote society and a good understanding between them, have already began to behave towards them with a coldness & distance too visible not to be remark'd.[34]

Increasingly alienated from the military which was so much a part of their daily lives, New Yorkers naturally began to think of the burden of supporting these unfriendly parasites and sought, once again, to make the conflicts of the street heard in the Assembly Hall.

New Yorkers paid for the privilege of having an occupying army. They paid for such items as barracks, firewood, candles, beds, bedding, molasses, and beer.[35] They had paid for the imperial military establishment, directly or indirectly, for many years. During the French and Indian War they gave in generous amounts, if unwillingly, in response to the King's requisitions. "The Load of Warr, . . . tho' very glorious, has been very expensive too," commented a merchant; the colonies' contributions, he thought, were "as heavy as they can well bear." Cadwallader Colden had difficulties with his Assembly: he accused them of "backwardness" in meeting requisitions, and they invariably replied that the burden was not fairly apportioned among the colonies. But they paid, announcing that they would "rather go beyond what can justly be expected from us, than suffer the least shadow of an Imputation to be laid on our Zeal for his Majesty's Service. . . ." Pleased with their willingness to go beyond what could justly be expected of them, Colden asked them to do just that and was privately pleased when they partially complied.[36]

With the war over the "Enjoyment of solid Tranquillity" was unhappily interrupted by Pontiac's Indians. Once again New York felt that it was being asked to pay more than a fair share, and once again it did so, this time receiving the King's praise for its action, standing out as it did "amidst the general Backwardness."[37]

With the return to peace on all fronts the controversy over New York's contribution to the military took on a new form. In May of 1765 the King signed a bill requiring the colonies to provide British troops stationed in America with "fire, candles, vinegar and salt, bedding, utensils for dressing victuals, and small beer, cyder, or rum."[38] In December of 1765, despite a desire on the part of certain members to please the recently arrived Governor Moore, New York's Assembly refused to comply; the legislators smelled a tax disguised as an old-fashioned requisition.[39] With troops marching to New York in June of 1766 a new call for money brought another negative response from the Assembly.[40] The Governor conferred with the General and sent a second message to the Assembly, this time demanding a "categorical answer." They replied with a set of resolutions which were, to Governor Moore, "as evasive as they were unexpected": they provided barracks, firewood, candles, bedding, and utensils, but refused to include salt, vinegar, and cider or beer on the grounds that these items did not have to be furnished for His Majesty's troops in England.[41]

The Government in England was displeased with New York's evasion. Moore was instructed to hold up all legislation until the Assembly made proper provision for the troops, but once again in December the Assembly refused. During the winter Parliament passed a restraining act, suspending New York's legislative privileges until the Assembly chose to follow the letter of the Mutiny Act. But before news of the restraining act arrived the Assembly had a change of heart. In June of 1767 it passed a bill providing the £3,000 needed but without mentioning the items to be furnished nor the act under which they were required. Although he had earlier supposed that such a device would be the only workable scheme,[42] Moore now resolved not to sign the bill in this form. But then he reconsidered, thinking of the officers who were about to leave and would have to do so without any remuneration for the money they had already spent;[43] he signed the bill. In November the Assembly's action was interpreted as meeting the requirements of the restraining act, and the body passed several new laws, including an additional £1,500 appropriation for the Army.

A newly elected Assembly met in November of 1768. Under pressure of a steadily worsening economic situation the Sons of Liberty again took to the streets. They marched through the town and burned effigies and presented their representatives with a set of instructions. The Assembly responded by refusing to take action on appropriations for the troops. This inaction, when combined with certain of the Assembly's other actions, was considered adequate cause for dissolving the body and calling for new elections.

The new Assembly was almost identical with the old one, but hoping to obtain permission for the colony to print paper money they compromised and granted £1,800 for provisioning troops. The bill was sent off for the King's inspection, but no reply had been received when the Assembly reconvened in November, and since the grant was contingent upon a paper currency, there seemed little prospect of the provision bill going through. The Assembly sat on its hands for almost a month, and finally Colden—back in the saddle but riding for a fall— gave in. He violated his instructions, assenting on December 15 to a provision bill and another providing for the emission of £120,000 in bills of credit. General Gage was given £2,000 to be spent for beds, blankets, firewood, candles, repairs, lodgings, utensils, molasses and the establishment of a spruce brewery for the soldiers.[44]

The Sons of Liberty took immediate action. On Saturday, December 16, a broadside addressed "To the Betrayed Inhabitants of the City and Colony of New-York" appeared. "A Son of Liberty" declared that the legislators had betrayed their trust by voting money for the troops. Such a grant was an implicit acknowledgment of "the Authority that enacted the Revenue-Acts, and their being obligatory on us." Worse yet, the money would go to the support of troops whose job was "not to protect, but to enslave us." The author advised that the people meet in the Fields the following Monday, express their disapproval of the provision bill, and go in a body to the City's Assemblymen insisting that they oppose the bill; if they did not succeed, a committee of correspondence should be set up to bring New York's situation to the attention of the other American assemblies and of friends in England. On the following day "Legion" also urged a meeting, and early Monday morning another handbill appeared, reminding the people to meet at noon and also reminding them that they must choose between "UNION, ACTIVITY and FREEDOM" and "DIVISION, SUPINENESS and SLAVERY."[45]

By noon more than 1,400 people had gathered in the Fields. John Lamb, the Son of Liberty who was appointed chairman, began by asking, "Do you approve of the vote?" "No!" "Are you for giving money to the troops, on any consideration whatsoever?" "No!" "Will you appoint a committee to communicate the whole of this transaction to your members?" "Yes." A ten-man committee, including Captains Isaac Sears and Alexander McDougall, was appointed. They received a decent reception but were told, even in the face of the evidence of the mass meeting, that the majority of the people favored support of the troops; the city members would not budge.[46]

But the Assembly did not entirely ignore the petitions of their constituents. On December 19 the body declared "Legion" and the December 16 broadside false, seditious and infamous libel and offered a reward for the apprehension of the authors. On December 20—while sea-captains Sears, McDougall, and Berrien were supporting Lamb's action of the previous day—McDougall was brought before the Assembly to answer for libel. McDougall was identified as the author and Berrien was implicated. McDougall, whose trial and imprisonment constitute one of the *causes celebres* in the history of colonial civil liberties, threw the mantle of Wilkes over himself, identifying himself in every possible way with the author of the *North Briton*. The American Wilkes, like the English one, had worked to democratize elections: shortly before his imprisonment he had led a movement to replace *viva voce* voting by the secret ballot.[47]

The prominence of maritime people as leaders in 1769–70 is not difficult to explain. Men like McDougall and Sears had had their debut in politics in connection with the Stamp Act. Now together with Berrien they were reasserting their leadership. It is not simply coincidence that, just as these men were reappearing in politics, steps were being taken to organize the New York Marine Society.[48] Seamen of all ranks were out of work, and they blamed the English for their condition. The Marine Society was an attempt to better that condition through voluntary association; the Battle of Golden Hill was an attempt to achieve the same end by different means.

The Battle of Golden Hill

At about eight in the evening of January 13 a party of nearly forty soldiers of the Sixteenth Regiment set out for the Fields. Having left guards on all the major streets they began to saw away at the Liberty Pole's supporting braces. Some passersby in the Fields observed the soldiers at their labors and rushed into Montagnie's, a tavern with a long history as a hang-out for the Sons of Liberty and consequently as a target for British insults and bullets. The tavern's alerted inmates sent two scouts out into the dark; they returned with confirmation: the soldiers were indeed attacking the Liberty Pole; now they were boring a hole in it. While the people inside Montagnie's sought a plan, outside, Captain White was passing by. A soldier spotted the mariner, drew his bayonet and threatened to run him through if he let anyone know of the strange doings on the Common. White, unarmed and prudent, managed to talk the soldier out of harming him and into letting him go.[49]

At this point the crowd emerged from Montagnie's. Across Broadway and some distance away on the Common stood the Liberty Pole, a hole bored into it, the hole filled with powder and plugged up; the soldiers intended to split the Pole by setting off the explosive charge. To alert the rest of the town, the people in front of Montagnie's shouted fire. As if to oblige them, the soldiers lit the fuse. The fuse failed. The people hissed. The soldiers rightly took this as an insult and, drawing their swords and bayonets, left the Liberty Pole and advanced on Montagnie's. The people retreated, leaving no opposition to the soldiers who proceeded to break every one of the seventy or eighty window panes in the house. Then they went in, cornered Montagnie with their swords, threatening to kill him if he should stir. People poured out of windows, egress having been simplified by the British softening-up operation. The soldiers now turned from Montagnie to a waiter, whom they beat; one soldier made a thrust with a bayonet, and the intended victim escaped with a slight wound on the forehead only because he had been skillful enough to parry the thrust with his hand. Then they broke some lamps and bowls and hurried off into the dark, fearing that they would be recognized. (Three of them, including a colonel, had been recognized.) By this time word had finally gotten to the officer commanding at the nearby upper barracks. He ordered a sentinel to the Pole, but this faithful guard disappeared shortly. The people inspected the Pole; seeing that the British assault had hardly scratched the tough iron braces and that no further danger was anticipated that night, they all went home.[50]

Although three soldiers were disciplined for their part in Saturday night's events, that did not deter their fellows from similar conduct again on Sunday and on Monday. On Monday they again placed sentinels in various parts of the Fields and set up a system of signals to warn of the approach of any townspeople. An alderman spotted the men in the Fields when he knew they should be in their barracks and reported to their officer. Once again the soldiers had tried, and once again they had been frustrated.[51]

On Tuesday a broadside signed "Brutus" presented the grievances of the poor and unemployed, those who were forced to compete with British soldiers for work:

> Whoever seriously considers the impoverished State of this City, especially of many of the poor Inhabitants of it, must be greatly surprised at the conduct of such as employ the Soldiers, when there are a Number of the former that want Employment to support their distressed Families.

After all, was it not clear to "Every Man of Sense" that the Army's job was not to protect, but to enslave New York? And despite this, the Assembly had given vast sums, sums better given to the poor.

These supplies, Brutus went on, were paid for by a tax on the colony, one-third of which was paid by New York City. Added to this were the double burdens of the duties on sugar and other goods; they hurt trade and thus put men—seamen especially, he might have said— out of work and make them public charges:

This might, in a great measure, be prevented, with
Comfort to their distressed Families, and a Saving to the
Community, if the Employers of Labourers would attend to it
with that Care and Benevolence that a Citizen owes to his
Neighbour, by employing him. Is it not enough that you pay
Taxes for Billeting Money to support the Soldiers, and a Poor
Tax, to maintain many of their Whores and Bastards in the
Work House, without giving them the Employment of the
Poor, who you must support if you don't employ them, which
adds greatly to swell your Poor Tax?

Brutus hoped that his fellow citizens would consider the situation
and refuse to countenance a set of liberty's enemies; to do so would be
to earn "the just Reproaches of the Poor." Had not experience shown
soft treatment only made soldiers insolent and ungrateful? Did not the
"atrocious Wickedness" of Saturday night prove this? Indeed it had, and
no friend to liberty should employ another soldier. In addition all such
friends to liberty should find means to avoid "a literal Compliance"
with the Billetting Act; a meeting would be held at noon on
Wednesday.

The friends of whores and progenitors of bastards read Brutus with
close attention, and he gave them the courage and the skill finally to
achieve what they had been attempting for almost three years. At about
eight in the evening of the day Brutus hit the streets (Tuesday, January
16) three soldiers were hard at work around the Liberty Pole. Together
with them were several others, in their cloaks, lying behind a split
canoe nearby. Guarding this group were armed men in a nearby house
owned by the Corporation and used as a temporary barracks for "a
Number of Disorderly Soldiers." Shortly an explosion was heard;
finally the Pole was split. The soldiers retreated, and the noise brought
a mob of citizens. They milled about the Fields, looking at the
smoking Pole and growing angrier by the minute. Some of the angriest
went into Montagnie's and drew up a set of resolutions for the next
day's meeting: they called for non-employment of soldiers and demanded
that soldiers not be allowed to carry arms in the streets at night. By ten
o'clock the citizens had gone home. In doing so they underestimated the
vindictiveness of the soldiers who bided their time until the night grew
still, and then, at one in the morning, crept back, cut down the Pole,
sawed it in pieces, and, in a final burst of rancor, deposited the pieces in
front of Montagnie's. Only then did they wipe their hands off and say
"let us go to our Barracks."[52]

At noon the next day between two and three thousand people met at
the spot where the Liberty Pole had stood eleven hours before. The

vacuum infuriated them, and they could hardly be restrained from violence as a speaker attempted to get their attention.[53] He spoke of the Liberty Pole and of what it meant—it was "a Memorial of Freedom." He urged them to drop all party differences and unite in support of their common liberties: then he read the resolutions conceived the night before:

> RESOLVE[D], That we will not employ any Soldier, on any Terms whatsoever; but that we will treat them with all the Abhorrence and Contempt which the Enemies of our happy Constitution, deserve. And whereas many of them have repeatedly travelled the Streets of this City, in the Night, with Arms, with which they have attempted to take the Lives of many of the Citizens, and notwithstanding made their escape, and thereby eluded the Laws, and passed with Impunity: THEREFORE, that the Inhabitants may not for the future be insulted, and put in Peril of their Lives,
>
> RESOLVED, that if any Soldier shall be found in the Night having Arms, (except Centinels and Orderly Serjeants) or out of the Barracks after the Roll is called, such as are found even without Arms, and behave in an insulting Manner, shall be treated as Enemies to the Peace of this City. . . .[54]

Those present signed the resolutions.[55] The policy which had had a premature birth in August of 1766[56] had now become universally accepted strategy: the soldiers were taking bread out of New Yorkers' mouths, and no good New Yorker would henceforth be permitted to hire the King's troops.

But the day's business was not yet complete. Throughout the meeting the crowd had looked with angry eyes at the house facing the Common which had been used as a guard house by the soldiers the night before. Many people felt that they had tolerated the insults of the house's inhabitants long enough; it especially irritated them to have the enemy's arrogance safely sheltered so close to their favorite meeting place. A committee was chosen and directed, "with loud Acclamations," to demand that the Corporation have the house destroyed. As if intent upon demonstrating the justice of the crowd's grievance, a number of soldiers drew their cutlasses and bayonets and invited the people to pull the house down then and there. The challenge was accepted, and only the intervention of magistrates and officers postponed further bloodshed.

While this extralegal body was assembled on the Common, the seamen were carrying extralegality a step further. From house to house, from dock to dock, and from vessel to vessel, armed—according to an unfriendly observer—with great clubs, a gang of seamen made their violent way; whenever they found soldiers at work—in a house, in vessels, in stores—they forced them out and drove them away. Not content with taking vengeance on the men who snatched their jobs, they also promised vengeance to those men who had so little patriotism as to hire Redcoats who would work for lower wages than would starving American seamen.[57]

On Friday January 19 the soldiers struck back. In a widely distributed broadside signed by the Sixteenth Regiment of Foot they gave vent to all the frustrations which had arisen out of their duty in New York, a duty which displeased them in a place that disgusted them:

God and a Soldier all Men doth adore
In Time of War, and not before:
When the War is over, and all things righted,
God is forgotten, and the Soldier slighted.

Whereas, they began, "an uncommon and riotous disturbance prevails throughout this city," caused by those who *call* themselves Sons of Liberty, but would better be called enemies of society; "whereas the army now quartered in New York" (hateful place—do they think we *wanted* to come here?) "are represented in a heinous light" for having tried to destroy the Liberty Pole, a thing which has finally been done without (they lied) "the assistance of the army, we have reason to laugh at them, and beg the public to observe, how chagrin'd those pretended S__s of L__y look as they pass thro' the streets, especially as these great heroes thought their freedom depended on a piece of wood" (a piece of wood: "a Memorial of Freedom.") Those "shining" Sons of Liberty have no right to cast aspersions on the Army:

> . . . we are proud to see those elevated genius's reduced to the low degree of having their place of general rendezvous, made (a Gallows Green) a vulgar phrase for a common place of execution, for murder[er]s, robbers, traitors and r__s, to the latter of which we compare those famous L__ B_s, who have nothing to boast of but the flippancy of tongue, altho' in defiance of the laws and good Government of our most gracious sovereign, they openly and r__y assemble in multitudes, to stir up the minds of his Majesty's good subjects to sedition. . . .

(A gallows green, or a memorial to freedom?)

> Brutus lies. Ever since we arrived in this town we have protected them night and day. We have suffered "the rays of the

scorching sun and the severe cold of snowy nights." It would
be fifty times worse if there were a war, "which we sincerely
pray for, in hopes those S_s of L__ may feel the affects
of it, with famine and destruction pouring on their heads"
(would that there were a war; would that we could kill them
and be done with it.)

"'Tis well known . . . that the soldiers of the sixteenth
always gained the esteem and good will of the inhabitants, in
whatever quarter they lay, and was never counted neither
insolent or ungrateful, except in this City." (This City, this
country, was something different; they did not understand it.)

But the means of making your famous city, which you so
much boast of, an impoverished one, is your acting in
violation to the laws of the British government; but take heed,
lest you repent too late,—for if you boast so mightily of your
famous exploits, as you have heretofore done (witness the late
stamp-act) we may allow you to be all ALEXANDERS, and
lie under your feet, to be trodden upon with contempt and
disdain. . . .

But be assured that we will not so tamely submit: "we will stand in
defence of the rights and privileges due to a soldier" (you are not the
only ones who have rights and privileges). And so will our officers, and
every "honest heart" support our wives and children—"not whores and
bastards, as has been so maliciously, falsly [sic], and audaciously
inserted in their impertinent libel, . . . for which, may the shame they
mean to brand our names with, stick on theirs."

(Audacity indeed! And yet one cannot help but feel pity for men
sent by ignorance to play the role of tyrants, men too ignorant and
uncomprehending themselves to understand just how audacious they
were. But this is the way to make a great empire into a small one.)

On Friday, January 19, these broadsides were posted in various
places; one was even thrown in the Mayor's doorway. One group of six
or seven soldiers proceeded up the Fly towards the market, pasting the
broadsides up as they went. They were spotted by Captain Isaac Sears
and by Walter Quackenbos, another Son of Liberty. Sears grabbed by
the collar the soldier who was hanging the paper. "What business," he
asked the soldier, did he have "to put up Libels against the Inhabitants?"
While Sears began to drag his man away to the Mayor, Quackenbos
seized the one who was holding the papers. A soldier to Sears' right
drew his bayonet. Sears threw a ram's horn at his attacker, hitting him

in the head. Then all the soldiers except the two captains ran off to alert their barracks-mates.

Confronted with Sears, Quackenbos and the two soldiers, the Mayor sent for an alderman for advice. As a small crowd gathered in front of the Mayor's, about twenty soldiers, armed with cutlasses and bayonets, approached from the lower barracks at the Battery.[58] Peter Remsen warned them that they were looking for trouble and would find it, but one or two of their leaders were drunk and in no mood to take advice from New Yorkers. The crowd parted quietly, clearing a path for the soldiers to go through. But Captain Richardson[59] led a small group to the door to prevent what looked like an attempt to rescue the two soldiers within. The soldiers came up on the other side of the street, stopped to take a look at the crowd and at Richardson's small force; then they drew their swords and bayonets, faced the door and demanded that their fellows be freed. A few tried to rush the door, but Richardson fended them off and tried to talk them into returning to their barracks. Even the soldiers within urged their drunk comrades to leave the situation to the Mayor. At the sight of arms, the crowd had scattered; some ran to some nearby sleighs and pulled some rungs out.

At this point the Mayor and an alderman came out and ordered the soldiers to their barracks. The soldiers paused sullenly and then started up the Fly. The people accompanied them, trying, with remarkable patience, to convince them to sheathe their swords. When the soldiers, still brandishing their swords, arrived at Golden Hill[60] they turned instead of proceeding south toward their barracks. By the time they reached the summit they were joined by reinforcements. Now they were courageous, and surliness replaced sullenness. They turned and faced the crowd, and one of them, whose silk stockings and neat buckskin breeches marked him as an ill-disguised officer, shouted, "Soldiers, draw your Bayonets, and cut your Way through them." Some of the vinegar of their broadside revived, the soldiers started cutting and slashing their way through the crowd, some shouting, "where are your Sons of Liberty now?" Except for six or seven people who had clubs and sticks, the rest were "naked." Those with sticks stood their ground, allowing the unarmed to get away until the front line broke when one man lost his stick; then the soldiers poured through and into a main street.

Francis Field, a Quaker, was standing inoffensively in a doorway when the soldiers rushed by. One of them took a swipe with his cutlass; Field came out of it with a severe wound on the right cheek, his life saved only by the corner of the doorway, which broke the stroke.[61]

Moving down the street, one party slashed at a teawater man
pushing his cart, then at a fisherman. They attacked everyone within
reach.

A boy who had gone out to borrow sugar from a neighbor was
pursued into a house and cut on the head with a cutlass; the woman
who opened the door for him was lunged at with a bayonet.[62]

Two soldiers attacked Captain Richardson with swords and were
about to cut him and the puny stick with which he defended himself to
bits when someone thrust a halbert into his hands and he sent them
running.

From his house John Targe heard a cry of murder. He reached the
street just in time to be chased back by three soldiers; he too managed
to grab a halbert. Since they could not reach him with their arms they
began to toss firewood at his legs.

A twenty-year old chairmaker's apprentice named Michael Smith
was at work in his shop on Broad Street when word came of the
struggle on the Hill. A small man, he nonetheless reached for a chair
leg and charged up the Hill. There he beat a grenadier into surrender and
took his musket, belts, bayonet, and cartridge box as souvenirs.[63]

On top of the Hill some seamen were struggling with those
soldiers who were still there. One seaman tried to defend himself and
was cut in the head and finger. Another was run through the body with
a bayonet; he died shortly, the day's only fatality.[64]

More and more townspeople rushed to the scene of the conflict.
Many of them used their sticks well. Their goal was not so much to
harm but rather to disarm their opponents, and they were making real
progress toward the latter goal, gradually surrounding the troops and
forcing them back to the top of the Hill. Then another party of soldiers
appeared behind the civilians. They shouted up to their fellows to cut
their way down; they would meet half-way. At the same time another
group of soldiers came down the Fly; now the British could mount a
two-pronged attack through their enemies' rear and join the group on
the summit. But before this scheme could be carried through some
officers and magistrates came and dispersed the soldiers, ordering them
back to their barracks. This time they obliged—all of them except the
few who emerged in the evening to cut one lamp-lighter in the head and
knock the other off his ladder.[65]

It is clear from the casualty lists that seamen were deeply involved
in the action of January 19. One seaman had been killed and others had
been wounded; they had been led by Captains Sears and Richardson. But
Saturday was to be the seamen's day as they sought revenge for the
death of a fellow Jack Tar.

Saturday began with the soldiers taking the initiative; a woman leaving the market with a bundle of fish was stabbed. The bayonet ran through her cape and clothes.[66]

At about noon the battle began at the head of Chapel Street between the soldiers and the seamen. No one was quite certain how it had begun, and the soldiers and seamen had conflicting versions. According to the seamen it all began when a soldier drew his bayonet against them; the seamen seized him and handed him over to a constable for delivery to a magistrate; some soldiers saw this and ran to the barracks, returning with reinforcements to beat the seamen. In the soldiers' version the seamen had caused the violence: they had thrown stones at the soldiers, forcing one of them to take shelter in the New Presbyterian Meetinghouse. The onus of initiation seems to fall on the seamen when one considers the subsequent role of the Meetinghouse along with the testimony of a third witness who claimed that he had seen "Sailors with Clubs [out] to revenge the Death of their Brother. . . ."[67] Sticks or stones regardless, it seems clear that the seamen were in a vengeful mood—with good reason—and that Friday's activities merely whetted their appetite for more of the same on Saturday.

Meanwhile the Mayor and Aldermen were holding an inquiry into Friday's events in the New Gaol. As they looked out they saw a body of soldiers running toward the Meetinghouse. It is not clear whether they were running to protect their companions who had taken shelter nearby or simply taking flight from the seamen's barrage; another witness reports that the seamen fought with courage and put the soldiers to flight in a direction which would have taken them past the Meetinghouse.[68] At any rate the Mayor and Aldermen went into the street followed by some prominent citizens who had been together with them inside.[69] The citizens promised to take no action unless ordered to do so by the magistrates; it was up to the City officials to see if the soldiers would be more attentive to their orders than they had been the day before. The Mayor and Aldermen led the way until they arrived at the north side of the Meeting, where they stood between fifteen soldiers, their bayonets drawn, lined up on both sides of the street.

But the soldiers were not interested in Mayors or Aldermen. The seamen, one of them drunk, stood at the northwest corner of the Meeting Yard. The Aldermen had all they could do to keep the drunk from attacking the soldiers; he was ready to take on the whole British Army. The soldiers attacked the seamen "with great Rage." One seaman was thrust through the body; another, who had arrived at the battle late, had his head cut.[70]

The Mayor ordered the soldiers back to their barracks. Once again the soldiers refused. The Aldermen told a messenger to go to the barracks in Whitehall Street to tell the officers what their men were doing. The soldiers intercepted the messenger with drawn bayonets, and he was unable to carry out his mission. The Mayor decided that he would undertake the mission, but *his* way was blocked by citizens who feared that if he left the place the soldiers would kill everyone.

Into this stalemate entered a group of Liberty Boys who had been playing ball at the corner of Broadway and John Street. The soldiers fled. Meanwhile, as rumors of a slaughter spread, a great crowd gathered at the New Gaol. While the crowd was buzzing with diverse accounts of the violence, twenty soldiers appeared from the lower barracks. Although they could easily have reached their destination by crossing the Fields, the soldiers made a point of marching right through the crowd. The crowd wisely parted. One of the soldiers, frustrated by this passive opposition, grabbed a stick—or perhaps it was a cane, or a sword—from one of the bystanders. The battle recommenced, with cutting and slashing on both sides. This time it lasted two minutes. One citizen was wounded in the face and had two of his teeth broken by the stroke of a bayonet; a soldier sustained a bad cut on the shoulder. The soldiers found themselves outnumbered and retreated to the barracks, pursued clear to the gates by the mob.[71]

So ended the two days of battle. Much blood had been spilled on both sides. In an effort to prevent more of the same Mayor Hicks issued a none-too-reassuring notice that the General had ordered that no soldiers were to leave the barracks when off duty except under command of a non-commissioned officer. The officer was to be answerable for the "orderly Behaviour" of his men. Thus, the Mayor advised his constituents, they need not be troubled by the sight of soldiers marching about the streets; they could be there only under these orders.[72]

And what of the Liberty Pole? New Yorkers would not allow themselves to be without one for long. A temporary Pole was erected in the Fields, but some unknown persons made easy work of it, and the Sons of Liberty set about erecting a permanent Pole. Isaac Sears, Alexander McDougall and three others applied to the Mayor for permission to erect a new one where the old one stood or near St. Paul's Church; they would then present the Pole, as a gift, to the Corporation. To the committee's astonishment, the Corporation refused, 9–6. The problem was solved when Isaac Sears bought a forty by one hundred foot strip near the Pole's original location. The new Pole was erected, with great ceremony, on the morning of Tuesday,

February 6. This time it was strong enough to stand until October 28, 1776.[73]

Whenever seamen took to the streets—be it against impressment, against the Stamp Act or against the cessation of trade without stamps—they expressed a grievance which they held, to a greater or lesser degree, in common with the rest of the population; the events of 1766–70 culminating in the Battle of Golden Hill are no exception to this pattern.[74] In January of 1770 seamen and the unemployed ashore patrolled the streets armed with clubs, "entering Houses and Vessels, and forcibly turning out and driving away, all the Soldiers whom they found at work in either, denouncing Vengeance against any Inhabitants, who should presume to employ them again. . . ."[75]

Once again the official explanation for the riots rested heavily on a puppet theory: "The Persons who appear on these occasions are of inferior Rank," reported Cadwallader Colden to the Earl of Hillsborough, "but it is not doubted they are directed by some Persons of distinction in this Place."[76] Once again the mob had adequate reason to act on its own, without prodding by some offstage devil. And again their actions were directed—not instigated—to an extraordinary degree by men connected with the sea. Captain Isaac Sears plays a prominent role in every act of political violence between 1765 and 1770, and his leadership is confirmed by those who opposed him.[77] Along with him were other sea captains such as Alexander McDougall, John Berrien, Richardson.

These people—the seamen, the population in general, the sea captains who led them—were moved by various grievances: the arrogance of the troops, the destruction of the Liberty Pole, competition with the soldiers for work. An unfriendly observer who mistakenly saw mere political opportunism in the slogans of the 'sixties and 'seventies nonetheless saw correctly the unity of the grievances:

> . . . may it not from what has happened, be justly suspected, that the frequent Notices to meet at *Liberty* Poll [sic], the violent Rage and Resentment which *some* People have endeavoured generally to excite against Soldiers, pretended to proceed from a Love of Liberty, and a Regard to the *Interests* of the Poor; do all tend to the same End, although the Pretences have been so very different.—May not,—No Money to the Troops,—whoraw for Ballotting,—employ no Soldiers,—all mean the same Thing?—Liberty is the Pretext. . . .[78]

The issue of competition for work most adequately explains the special antagonism between New York's unemployed seamen and the British troops. The Boston Massacre, six weeks after the Battle of Golden Hill, was rooted in the same problem.[79] In New York "A Merchant" who sided with the soldiers presented this issue in cynical form:

> But what can be more just and reasonable, than that a Preference should be given to some of our own poor People, who will do at least half as much Work for Four Shillings a Day, as a Soldier would do for Eighteen Pence or Two Shillings?—Or if a Man has Charity to bestow, what Right has he, or how dare he give it to a Soldier, to buy a Loaf of Bread for his starving *Whores* and *Bastards*, when he can bestow it so much better on the poor Inhabitants, too proud and lazy to work, who want it to purchase Rum for themselves, and Tea, Butter, Sugar, and fat Turkeys for their poor Wives, and honestly begotten Children?[80]

The seamen were neither lazy nor proud, but they were poor. They looked for work and found British troops had taken their jobs; they looked for the Liberty Pole and found that it had been cut down by the same men; they looked to the Assembly and found it voting money for the troops; they went to the houses in the Fields and found that even the whores had deserted them for the same Redcoats. They were bound to make their reply, and they did so, in the traditional way, in the streets, in January of 1770.

Notes

[1.] New York Sons of Liberty to Sons of Liberty at Fairfield, Connecticut, March 17, 1766: Lamb Papers, 1762–63, #20, New-York Historical Society. The bill to repeal the Stamp Act passed the House March 4, the Lords March 17, and received the King's signature March 18.

[2.] *Montresor Journals*, p. 355; *Post-Boy*, March 27, 1766.

[3.] *Montresor Journals*, p. 355; *Post-Boy*, March 27, 1766; New York Sons of Liberty to Sons of Liberty at White Plains [New York], April 3, 1766: Lamb Papers, 1762–63, #31, New-York Historical Society.

4. *Montresor Journals*, p. 362; *Post-Boy*, April 26, 28, 1766; *Gazette*, April 28, 1766.

5. *Montresor Journals*, p. 368; *Post-Boy*, May 22, 1766; *Mercury*, May 26, 1766; Stokes, *Iconography*, IV, 765.

6. *Montresor Journals*, pp. 368, 382. Stokes, *Iconography*, IV, 765 calls the Pole a "Flag Staff" and a "pine post" while *Post-Boy*, August 14, 1766 calls it a "Mast or Flag Staff." Stokes suggests that an old vessel may have been dismantled for the occasion.

7. *Montresor Journals*, pp. 369, 382.

8. *Ibid.*, pp. 370–371; *Minutes of Common Council*, VII, 23; Leake, *Lamb*, p. 28; Stokes, *Iconography*, IV, 766.

9. *Post-Boy*, August 14, 1766. For weather in the summer of 1766 see *Montresor Journals*, pp. 370–382.

10. *Ibid.*, pp. 382–383; *Post-Boy*, August 14, 21, 1766; General Gage to Richmond, August 26, 1766; Carter, *Gage Correspondence*, I, 103–104. As the *Post-Boy* assessed the evidence, the soldiers had clearly been the agressors. Montresor disagreed, as did Major Brown; the latter tossed away a stack of depositions with the statement, "I will prove every Word of it to be false." Isaac Sears, John and Cornelius Berrien, Philip Will, Joseph Dwight, and John and Alexander McGinnis replied with additional depositions further contradicting the Major's position. For Berrien see also *Freemen*, p. 229; Catherine Lawrence v. John Berrien, Notice, January 7, 1770, March 7, 1771, December 6, 1771; Chancery Minute Book, IV (April 5, 1770–January 9, 1776), 25–26, 46–48, Office of County Clerk, Hall of Records, New York City; The King v. John Berrien, Recognizance, April 6, 1775, New York Supreme Court: Pleadings K-855.

11. John Watts to Moses Franks, October 27, 1763: *Watts Letter Book*, pp. 92–93; John Watts to Captain Carter, June 25, 1763; *ibid.*, p. 148.

12. *Montresor Journals*, pp. 342, 346.

13. See above, p. 75ff.

14. See above, p. 77ff.

15. See above, p. 28.

16. *Montresor Journals*, p. 341.

17. *Ibid.*, pp. 355–357, 365, 369.

18. *Ibid.*, p. 353.

19. *Ibid.*, p. 352.

20. See above, pp. 51–52.

21. General Gage to Shelburne, January 23, 1768: Carter, *Gage Correspondence*, I, 160–161.

22. *Calendar of State Papers, Colonial Series, America and West Indies* (London 1860–1953), XXIV, 2; see also Morris, *Government and Labor*, p. 190n. Under Washington, men in the Continental Army were permitted to work at their trades between retreat and tattoo: Charles Knowles Bolton, *The Private Soldier under Washington* (New York, 1902), pp. 156–157. Bolton notes that sailors on British men-of-war still carried on private work as late as 1899; *ibid.*, p. 157n.

23. *Montresor Journals*, p. 346; Broadside, "The Times," February 1770: New-York Historical Society Broadsides 1770–21; *Journal*, January 18, 1770; *Post-Boy*, February 5, 1770.

24. *Ibid.*, August 14, 1766; Governor Moore to the Duke of Richmond, August 23, 1766: *N Y Col Docs*, VII, 867–868.

25. *Montresor Journals*, pp. 383–384; *Post-Boy*, August 21, 1766.

26. *Montresor Journals*, p. 383.

27. *Ibid.*, pp. 383–384; General Gage to the Duke of Richmond, August 26, 1766: Carter, *Gage Correspondence*, I, 104.

28. *Post-Boy*, September 25, 1766. For a summary of New York's Liberty Poles see Stokes, *Iconography*, IV, 806.

29. *Post-Boy*, November 20, 1766.

30. *Ibid.*, October 23, 1766, February 5, 1770; Bridenbaugh, *Cities in Revolt*, p. 358; *Minutes of Common Council*, VII, 195.

31. *Journal*, March 26, 1767; Stokes, *Iconography*, IV, 774. On Bardin's and its successor, Montagnie's, see *ibid.*, IV, 647, 774.

32. General Gage to Hillsborough, September 26, October 10, 1768: Carter, *Gage Correspondence*, I, 198, 200–201. In the spring of 1766 a similar situation had arisen: the Army needed vessels to transfer powder and arms from the shore to the safety of the men-of-war. One merchant vessel had been hired, but the owners withdrew. "Other vessels were sought, though lying at the wharves by scores, out of employ, notwithstanding refused." The Commander-in-Chief sought unsuccessfully to impress vessels and finally had to make do with wood boats. *Montresor Journals*, p. 356.

33. Broadside, "To the Betrayed Inhabitants of New-York," December 16, 1769: New-York Historical Society Broadsides SY 1769-4.

34. Governor Moore to Lord Hillsborough, August 19, 1768: *N Y Col Docs*, VIII, 99.

35. See below, pp. 129–130.

36. John Watts to Colonel Isaac Barre, February 28, 1762: *Watts Letter Book*, p. 26; John Watts to John Mackintosh, April 22, 1763: *ibid.*, p. 137; John Watts to Sir William Baker, May 13, 1763: *ibid.*, p. 142; *Assembly Journal*, I, 690–691, 700; Cadwallader Colden to Jeffrey Amherst, March 13, 1762: *Colden Letter Books*, I, 171–172.

37. *Assembly Journal*, II, 720; Thomas Gage to Cadwallader Colden, January 19, 1764: *Colden Letters and Papers*, VI, 279; Lord Halifax to Cadwallader Colden, May 12, 1764: *ibid.*, VII, 309; John Watts to Colonel Isaac Barre, January 21, 176[4]: *Watts Letter Book*, p. 218.

38. 5 Geo III, c. 33: *Annual Register for 1765* (London, 1766), p. 87; Becker, *Political Parties*, p. 54. Except where otherwise noted, the following account of the events of 1765–68 is based on *ibid.*, pp. 54–58, 64.

39. *Assembly Journal*, II, 788–789, 803; *Post-Boy*, February 26, 1770.

40. *Ibid.*; *Montresor Journals*, p. 373.

41. Governor Moore to Secretary Conway, June 20, 1766: *N Y Col Docs*, VII, 831.

42. *Ibid.*, VII, 832.

43. Governor Moore to Lord Shelburne, August 21, 1767: *ibid.*, VII, 948–949.

44. *Journal of the Votes and Proceedings of the General Assembly of the Colony of New York, from 1766 to 1776, Inclusive* (Albany, New York, 1820), I, 38 (hereafter cited as *Assembly Journals*, 1766–76); Cadwallader Colden to Hillsborough, December 16, 1769, April 25, 1770: *N Y Col Docs*, VIII, 193, 212; Cadwallader Colden to the Lords of Trade, January 6, 1770: *ibid.*, VIII, 198; Copy of an Agreement between General Gage and Cadwallader Colden, January 15, 1770: *Colden Letter Books*, II, 204–206; Becker, *Political Parties*, p. 77.

45. Broadside, "To the Betrayed Inhabitants of New York," December 16, 1769: New-York Historical Society Broadsides 1769–4; Broadside, "Union, Activity and Freedom," December 18, 1769: *ibid.*, SP 1769-5; Gordon, *History*, I, 301; Wilbur C. Abbott, *New York in the American Revolution* (New York, 1929), 203; Becker, *Political Parties*, p. 80. There is some disagreement about the date of "Legion" in the secondary sources. It is clear that it follows the handbill of the sixteenth and precedes the meeting of the eighteenth; thus I date it the seventeenth.

46. *Mercury*, December 25, 1769; *Post-Boy*, January 1, 1770; Gordon, *History*, p. 301.

47. *Assembly Journal*, 1766–76, I, 42–43; Sabine, *Smith Memoirs*, p. 74; *Post-Boy*, January 1, 1770, February 12, 1770. On McDougall's troubles, see Dillon, *New York Triumvirate*, pp. 106–123.

48. See above, pp. 56–57.

49. The most extensive account of the events of January 13–20 appears in *Post-Boy*, February 5, 1770. This is the basic source used for the following account and is the source for all statements not otherwise identified. See also *ibid.*, January 15, 1770. The only record I have of a White who would be called "Captain" is of Henry White, a slave trader, originally of Dunbar,

Scotland, who made out a will November 19, 1769: *Wills*, VII, 377; *Post-Boy*, May 24, 1764.

50. *Post-Boy*, January 15, 1770.

51. *Journal*, January 18, 1770.

52. *Minutes of Common Council*, VII, 200–201; *Post-Boy*, January 22, 1770.

53. *Journal*, January 18, 1770.

54. *Post-Boy*, January 22, 1770.

55. *Ibid.*; *Journal*, January 18, 1770.

56. See above, pp. 126–127.

57. Broadside, "The Times," February, 1770: New-York Historical Society Broadsides 1770–21.

58. Stokes, *Iconography*, IV, 803.

59. Possibly John Richardson: *Wills*, VIII, 135.

60. Golden Hill was a hill on John Street between Cliff Street and Burling Slip. In the spring of 1774 the Common Council moved to level the hill, but homeowners managed to kill the proposal: *Minutes of Common Council*, VIII, 16–24, 26, 28.

61. William J. Davis, "The Old Bridewell," in Henry B. Dawson, *Reminiscences of the Park and its Vicinity* (New York, 1855), p. 61. Hereafter cited as Davis, "Old Bridewell," in Dawson, *Reminiscences of Park*.

62. *Ibid.*

63. Dawson, *Sons of Liberty*, p. 116.

64. Letter from New York, January 22, 1770: *ibid.*, p. 117n.

65. *Ibid.*

66. *Ibid.*

67. *Ibid.*, p. 118n.

68. *Ibid.*

69. These citizens may be the ones referred to by Colden in later accounts of the rioting. According to the Lieutenant-Governor a considerable number of leading citizens met together and sent forty-two representatives to the Mayor to assure him of their assistance in keeping the peace. Colden attributed the fact that there was so little bloodshed to the magistrates, the Mayor, those citizens, the officers, and, of course, himself. Cadwallader Colden to Lord Hillsborough, February 21, 1770, April 25, 1770: *Colden Letter Books*, II, 210–212, 217–218.

70. Davis, "Old Bridewell," in Dawson, *Reminiscences of Park*, p. 61.

71. *Ibid.*

72. Broadside, "To the Inhabitants of the City," January 22, 1770: New-York Historical Society Broadsides SY 1770-2.

73. *Mercury*, February 5, 12, 1770; Stokes, *Iconography*, IV, 805–806, plate 40.

74. Leake, *Lamb*, p. 57; Davis, "Old Bridewell," in Dawson, *Reminiscences of Park*, p. 62.

75. Broadside, "The Times," February, 1770: New-York Historical Society Broadsides 1770–21.

76. Cadwallader Colden to Lord Hillsborough, February 21, 1770: *Colden Letter Books*, II, 211.

77. Sabine, *Smith Memoirs*, p. 73; Broadside, "The Procession," March 15, 1770: New-York Historical Society Broadsides SP 1770-13.

78. Broadside, "The Times," February, 1770: *ibid.*, 1770-21.

79. For such an interpretation see Morris, *Government and Labor*, pp. 190–192. Colden saw similarities between the events in Boston and those in New York, but once again he attributed the similarities to manipulation rather than seeing them as genuine responses to genuine grievances. Cadwallader Colden to Hillsborough, April 25, 1770: *Colden Letter Books*, II, 247.

80. Broadside, "The Times," February, 1770: New-York Historical Society Broadsides 1770-21.

Epilogue: Jack Tar and the American Revolution

"I took the command . . . in the midst of a hurricane," Lord North told a naval friend, "and have almost reached a port of security; when I cast an anchor to my satisfaction there, the Admiral may give the rudder to whom he pleases, and my best wishes for a prosperous voyage shall certainly attend the new captain." Throughout the 'seventies the hurricane raged on; Lord North stuck to the helm and never managed to sail "the political vessel into a quiet harbor."[1]

The beginning of the new decade brought no slackening in the storms which had battered New York in the 'sixties. Hundred of poor overflowed the workhouse,[2] and the prisoners in the City Jail remained dependent on the bounty of others for food and fuel.[3] The founding of a society for employing the industrious poor and promoting manufactures made little difference.[4] Seamen met in the Fields, looking desperately for any way "for procuring employment and support for themselves and families."[5] The storm which had cast them up on the beach had been stirred up by the British Parliament, "a mercenary, indolent, stupid crew of lieutenants and midshipmen"[6] sailing a vessel captained by Lord North.

The Admiralty continued to compete with the parliamentary vessel in giving offense to American seamen. In England the press was as hot as ever, not the least bit cooled by the mounting debate over its efficiency as a means of manning the Navy or by qualms over its morality, legality, and constitutionality.[7] The repeal of the Sixth of Anne in 1775 finally settled the issue for America, but continued impressment incidents in the early years of the decade—one, right in New York Bay—had left their scar. Why, Americans asked, could not the Navy protect American trade rather than devoting itself to the harassment of loyal subjects?[8]

In New York seamen continued to counterfeit, steal, assault, and murder; they stole from ships and from captains; they rioted.[9] But their dissatisfactions were now being expressed in channels more readily identifiable as political. In 1770 the Sons of Liberty split into two factions; in March when the organization planned its customary dinner at Montagnie's to celebrate the anniversary of the repeal of the Stamp Act, it was discovered that a group of more conservative merchants, calling themselves "The Friends of Liberty and Trade," had usurped the location. The "Friends" opposed what they labelled "lawlessness" and favored an end of non-importation; the radicals, led by Captains Sears and McDougall, favored a harder line. The merchants were content with the repeal of the Townshend duties, but those who remained Sons of Liberty were not.[10] The more radical stand seemed to have been justified when in 1773 New York was confronted with the Tea Act. Although there is no clear evidence of seamen's participation in the meetings opposing the act, they must have been there. That they had good reasons for opposition is made clear in the following broadside, addressed by "Tom Bowline . . . From my Moorings, in Ratline-Lane, Dec. 20, 1773" to "his worthy Messmates, the renowned Sons of Neptune, belonging to the Port of New-York":

> My dear Boys,
>
> As the Time is approaching, in which the Ship with the East-India Company's Tea, may be expected to arrive, and be moored in our Harbour, to put the finishing Stroke to our Liberties, and ruin the Trade of our Country, by establishing a Monopoly; which will in Time (should it be effected) deprive Numbers of our worthy Merchants of their Sheet-Anchor, and oblige them to quit their Moorings, and steer into the Country to take a Trick at the Plough; and will (as sure as the Devil's in London) drive many of us to the cruel Alternative of seeking Employment in a foreign Country, to prevent starving in our own;—and as much depends upon our Steadiness and Activity, in regard to weathering this Storm; I must therefore strongly recommend the Necessity of keeping a good Look-out; and that we do, one and all, hold ourselves in Readiness, and heartily join our Merchants and other worthy Citizens, in preventing the pestilential Commodity, from being parbuckled on Shore, I am,
>
> My Hearts of Oak,
> Your Friend and Messmate. . . .[11]

Again the seaman's prosperity had been linked to the success of trade; and once again Parliament's attack on American trade was construed by the common seaman as a not very indirect attack on his own livelihood. In defence of their long-run interests seamen increasingly saw the necessity of sacrificing short-run employment. They were faithful to the various non-importation agreements and furnished some of the coercive power which helped to make them effective. In February of 1775 Captain Watson imported certain goods in ship *James* contrary to the Association. He could find no one to unload his vessel except a band of "banditti" who were easily dispersed by the inhabitants. When the Captain saw that his only hope was in flight, his seamen refused to help him escape, and he had to head for the Bay with a crew of volunteers temporarily recruited from among the city's "ministerial tools."[12]

If seamen's loyalty to the American cause and to their own interests made jobs scarce in February of 1775, the situation was much changed by the summer and more so by the fall. With the coming of armed conflict there was a decrease in the number of berths available in the merchant service but a compensatory growth of provincial navies. By the summer time British ships were being attacked along the full length of the coastline, mostly on local initiative. On October 30 what was to become the United States Navy was born when Congress appointed a Naval Committee and authorized the arming of ships for the defense of the United Colonies. In the following spring a full-scale offensive against British maritime commerce was authorized.[13] Thus there was plenty of work for American seamen. Would they take it?

Certainly there were great risks involved in joining the new Navy. Added to the usual dangers of naval life was the real possibility that the American seaman might find himself hanged as a pirate. Since the English so treated men not sailing under an established flag, mariners pressured the Continental Congress into producing the Grand Union Flag in December of 1775. But the British continued to treat captured American sailors as rebels and pirates until 1780, indicting them for treason, committing them to jail, and refusing to exchange them for their own sailors who had been captured by the Americans.[14]

American seamen remained Americans during the Revolution. Their names appear only rarely in lists of those who became Loyalists.[15] This is not to say that there was no Loyalism among New York's seamen. Alpheus Avery lived all his life in Westchester County until he went to sea between the ages of seventeen and eighteen. Some six years later, in 1774, he found himself an unpopular person when he and his father refused to take part in the election of representatives to a patriot body. Fearful of personal abuse, Avery sailed to England as a second mate and went through the War as master and mate of trading vessels and transports in the government service. Richard Jenkins came to New York from his native London in 1763 and served as a mate in the merchant service until December of 1776 when he joined the British army in New Jersey and so "preserved the Character of a Loyal Man and . . . a zealous Loyalist."

Both of these men were possessed of personal wealth extraordinary among common seamen: in 1775 Jenkins married Elizabeth Popplesdorf, the widow of a baker, and received with her a house with a bake shop and other buildings worth £810 sterling; Avery sought £2,365 sterling from the Loyalist Commissioners for various properties including one hundred acres which his father had given him in 1770 but which the father had continued to manage, leaving his son free to follow his chosen profession. Partially counterbalancing these apparent ingredients in an economic interpretation of Loyalism among seamen is the presence of some runaway American servants in the British Navy. As with slaves, so much dissatisfaction with their status and the prospect of freedom from indentures drew many from the lower ranks into enemy vessels.[16]

Generally the British experienced great difficulty in recruiting seamen in New York. The Admiralty showed real understanding of the ways of seamen in choosing men such as Brooklyn innholder John Hills to furnish seamen.[17] But the innholder's contacts were worth little alongside the seamen's recalcitrance. A 1779 report from Governor Tryon to Vice-Admiral Arbuthnot indicating great success in recruiting privateers among "Converts from the Rebels, and other persecuted Loyalists"[18] is qualified by a report from a later governor to Lord George Germain that " . . . all the Sailors who were dead to the calls of generosity were with the assistance of the inhabitants pressed into the Service."[19] The Navy was forced by the seamen's patriotism to resort to its old ways and with little success, for, as the Governor noted, " . . . by pressing we force sailors to fly & man rebel ships of war."[20]

(The American Navy had its difficulties recruiting in New York too, but these problems do not indicate any defection from the American cause. American seamen could be patriots, but richer patriots, if they went privateering, as many did; both Navies had trouble with the competition offered by privateering, but both American *and* British sailors deserted to American privateers.[21] Writing from on board sloop *Providence* in New York harbor in May of 1776, John Paul Jones noted another problem also reminiscent of the difficulties experienced in the French and Indian War:[22]

> I shall now apply to Shipping men, if any can be
> Obtained but it appears that the Seamen almost to a man had
> entered into the Army before the Fleet was set on Foot, and I
> am well informed that there are four or five thousand Seamen
> now in the Land Service.[23]

Again this tells us of recruiting problems but hardly furnishes evidence
of Loyalism among New York's seamen.)

Testimony to the patriotism of American seamen in the early
phases of the war comes from French agent Pierre Augustin Caron de
Beaumarchais, who was making it his business to find out what was
going on in America:

> All those persons who were engaged in the fisheries,
> which the English have destroyed, have become soldiers, and
> feel that they have to avenge the ruin of their families and the
> liberty of their country; all those persons who took part in
> maritime commerce, which the English have brought to an
> end, have joined the fishermen to make war on their common
> persecutors; all the persons who worked in the harbors have
> increased the army of furious men, whose actions are all
> animated by a spirit of vengeance and hatred.[24]

Many years later, at the Constitutional Convention, Benjamin
Franklin, who had had constant experience with American seamen
during the Revolution,[25] gave evidence that the phenomenon which
Beaumarchais had observed had endured throughout the War:

> The revolutionary war is a glorious Testimony in favor of
> Plebeian Virtue—our military and naval men are sensible of
> this Truth. I myself know that our Seamen who were
> Prisoners in England refused all the allurements that were made
> use of, to draw them from their allegiance to their Country—
> threatened with ignominious Halters, they still refused. This
> was not the case with the English Seamen, who, on being
> made Prisoners entered into the American Service and pointed
> out where other Prisoners could be made. . . .[26]

Why did New York's seamen—along with the masters who
employed them[27]—display such plebeian virtue and refuse to fight for
England? Generally it was because they were such good Englishmen. At
an early stage in the revolutionary crisis a London newspaper recalled
that when Charles I had sent a warship and seven armed merchantmen to
assist the French king at the siege of Rochelle, "the honest tars actuated

with a true British spirit and love of religion, all mutinied, rather than serve against the Rochellers, who were contending for their liberty and religion." If British seamen had refused to fight against foreigners "in the cause of oppression and injustice," how much more strongly, a New Yorker asked, would they be prevented

> by every principle of justice, love to their country, honour and humanity, from embracing their hands in the blood of their countrymen, and acting as instruments in the hands of tyrants, to destroy that constitution, which is the most valuable inheritance, and the glory of an Englishman, and entailing slavery upon themselves, their country, and posterity?[28]

The British seaman's heart was known to tradition to be constructed of "*solid English oak*"[29] and had been so described in David Garrick's popular song, "Hearts of Oak."[30] American versions of the song multiplied[31] along with English adaptations, culminating in a version published in 1775:

> Come listen my cocks, to a brother and friend,
> One and all to my song, gallant sailors attend,
> Sons of Freedom ourselves, let's be just as we're brave,
> Nor America's freedom attempt to enslave. . . .
>
> To the ground may disputes with our Colonies fall,
> And George long in splendor reign King of us all;
> And may those who would set the two lands by the ears,
> Be put in the bilboes, and brought to the jears.
>
> Firm as oak are our hearts, where true
> glory depends,
> Steady, boys, steady,
> We'll always be ready
> To fight all our foes, not to murder our friends.[32]

American sailors—and their English brothers—responded to such exhortations because they were so well bred to the English tradition, so sensitive to invasions of their rights. They had been the victims of many such invasions. Their unhappy experience with impressment had brought Locke alive, teaching them first-hand the dangers of tyranny. More generally, the arrogance of the British Navy in its execution of unjust laws had further irritated them. And the unjust laws had made the simple pursuit of one's livelihood a difficult matter indeed. So they responded with anger, converting old means of expression to the expression of new sentiments. Some were misled by their violence, but

the seamen themselves had a very clear idea of what they wanted—
justice. As they sailed from town to town, these most mobile of
Americans carried their grievances with them and communicated by
their dissatisfied presence the desire for justice. By 1776 many other
Americans felt the same desire; the seamen's situation had forced them
to feel it a little sooner and a little more intensely.

Notes

1. *Post-Boy*, November 11, 1771.

2. *Ibid.*, February 11, 1771.

3. *Journal*, February 6, 1772.

4. *Ibid.*, November 16, 1775.

5. *Ibid.*, October 5, 1775.

6. The words appear in a Swedish author's parody of English politics
originally published in London and reprinted in *Post-Boy*, October 23,
1766.

7. *Ibid.*, November 19, November 26, December 10, December 17, December
31, 1770, January 14, February 11, February 18, March 25, 1771; *Journal*,
May 26, 1774.

8. *Ibid.*, June 3, July 8, 1773; *Post-Boy*, July 27, 1772; Willard, *Letters on
American Revolution*, p. 65; Clark, "Impressment," *Andrews Essays*, pp.
223–224.

9. The King v. Jacob Abrahams, Indictment for Grand Larceny, filed January
Term, 1775, New York Supreme Court: Pleadings K-15; The King v.
Nicholas Bassong, Indictment for Passing a Counterfeit Quarter of a Dollar,
filed April 25, 1775, New York Supreme Court: Pleadings K-12; The King v.
Nathaniel Cooley, Indictment for Assault, filed October 25, 1773, New
York Supreme Court: Pleadings K-27; The King v. Samuel Doren,
Indictment for Robbery, filed January 23, 1772, New York Supreme Court:
Pleadings K-529, K-851; The King v. Thomas Farinscomb, Indictment for
Receiving Stolen Goods, filed January 19, 1770, New York Supreme Court:
Pleadings K-266; The King v. John Forster, Indictment for Petty Larceny,
filed October 23, 1772: Pleadings K-495; The King v. William Hill and
Isaac Garrard, Indictment for Grand Larceny, filed October 24, 1775, New
York Supreme Court: Pleadings K-5; The King v. John Kendal and Thomas
Clark, Jr., Indictment for a riot, filed April 24, 1771, New York Supreme

Court: Pleadings K-384; The King v. John Kendal, Indictment for Assault and Battery, filed April Term, 1775, New York Supreme Court: Pleadings K-868; The King v. James McLaughlin, Samuel Dobbins, Thomas McLaughlin, John Dobbins, Indictment for a Riot, filed October Term, 1774, New York Supreme Court: Pleadings K-316; The King v. William McMon, Patrick Larkin, William Clubb, Richard Smith, Indictment for a Riot, filed January 17, 1771, New York Supreme Court: Pleadings K-346; The King v. Robert Mitchner, Indictment for Assault and Battery, filed April Term, 1773, New York Supreme Court: Pleadings K-379; The King v. William Pollitt, Examination, taken June 14, 1775, New York Supreme Court: Pleadings K-42.

[10.] Becker, *Political Parties*, pp. 86–87; White, *Beekmans*, pp. 433–434.

[11.] Broadside, December 20, 1773: New-York Historical Society Broadsides SY 1773-21.

[12.] *Journal*, February 16, 1775.

[13.] *Ibid.*, October 5, 1775; Morison, *John Paul Jones*, pp. 34, 36–37; William Bell Clark, "American Naval Policy: 1775–1776," *American Neptune*, I (January, 1941), 26; Billias, *Glover*, p. 73.

[14.] Hugh F. Rankin, "The Naval Flag of the American Revolution," *William and Mary Quarterly*, third series, XI (July, 1954), 340–341; Morison, *John Paul Jones*, pp. 135, 166.

[15.] This statement, following Dickerson's (*Navigation Acts*, p. 219) is based on my own examination of the Loyalist Transcripts and of Lorenzo Sabine, *Biographical Sketches of Loyalists of the American Revolution with an Historical Essay* (Boston, 1864).

[16.] Jenkins: Loyalist Transcripts, XVIII, 11–15; Avery: *ibid.*, XLIII, 495, 499–504; servants: *Journal*, August 10, 1775; Negroes: Quarles, *Negro in the Revolution*, pp. 152–156.

[17.] Loyalist Transcripts, XVII, 477.

[18.] Governor Tryon to Vice-Admiral Arbuthnot, June 29, 1779: *N Y Col Docs*, VIII, 772. This is the sole source for Alexander Clarence Flick's statement that "A large part of the 6000 seamen in the metropolis [New York] were loyalists": *Loyalism in New York during the American Revolution* (New York, 1901), p. 107.

[19.] Governor James Robertson to Lord George Germain, November 8, 1781: *N Y Col Docs*, VIII, 814.

[20.] Governor James Robertson to Lord George Germain, May 6, 1781: *ibid.*, VIII, 811.

[21.] Governor James Robertson to Lord George Germain, June 29, 1779: *ibid.*, VIII, 772.

[22.] See above, p. 23.

[23.] Morison, *John Paul Jones*, p. 55.

[24.] Louis Leonard De Lomenie, *Beaumarchais and His Times*, trans. by Henry S. Edwards, (London, 1856), 262ff.: quoted in Henry Steele Commager and Richard B. Morris, eds., *The Spirit of 'Seventy-Six: The Story of the American Revolution as Told by Participants* (New York, 1958), I, 246.

[25.] See Van Doren, *Benjamin Franklin*, pp. 616–618.

[26.] Rufus King's notes, August 7, 1787: Charles C. Tansill, ed., *Documents Illustrative of the Formation of the Union of the American States* (Washington, 1927), p. 875.

[27.] In 1775 the members of the Marine Society formed an artillery company: Morris, *Government and Labor*, p. 189n.

[28.] *Journal*, May 26, 1774.

[29.] *Post-Boy*, December 10, 1767.

[30.] Davidson, *Propaganda*, p. 189.

[31.] See above, p. 36.

[32.] *Journal*, June 8, 1775.

Bibliographical Note

Maritime history, as it has been written, has had as little to do with the common seaman as business history has had to do with the laborer. The term "seaman" has more often meant Sir Francis Drake than Jack Tar, and even the W.P.A. Writer's Program thoroughly neglected the seaman in *A Maritime History of New York* (Garden City, New York, 1941).[1] The focus has been on trade, exploration, the great navigators, but rarely on the men who sailed the ships. The romance of the sea has also drawn a great number of amateurs, and although there is much of use in journals such as *The American Neptune: A Quarterly Journal of Maritime History* (21 vols.; Salem, Massachusetts, 1941–61), with "only four out of the forty members of the *Neptune*'s board . . . engaged in university teaching of American history,"[2] the magazine's definition of maritime history is too genteel, dwelling too often on such matters as ship design and construction, yachting history, reminiscences, and model-building.

If maritime history, amateur and professional, has largely ignored the seaman, this is only part of a larger pattern in the writing of American history: neglect of the lower classes. We live, it is said, in an affluent, mobile society, we are all middle class, and it has always been so, more or less: thus the biases with which we view the contemporary scene have been reflected in our view of the past, and the existence of a lower class has been denied, or, when its actions forced some recognition, it has been contended that it acted as the tool of more prominent citizens. Richard Walsh, in his good account of *Charleston's Sons of Liberty: A Study of the Artisans, 1763–1789* (Columbia, South Carolina, 1959) notes that historians have said "much about the planters, more about the merchants, and a great deal about battles," but very little about those forgotten men, the artisans, who have been treated merely as followers of the planters" (pp. x-xi). With the change of a few words the same statement would hold true of seamen in colonial New York. I hope I have dispelled this picture; at very least, I believe I have demonstrated that the seamen did exist, which they hardly did in previous historiography despite their frequent and prominent appearances in the primary sources.

Although the seamen have been largely ignored by scholars, even in such works as Samuel McKee, Jr., *Labor in Colonial New York, 1664–1776* (New York, 1935) and Marcus Wilson Jernegan, *Laboring and Dependent Classes in Colonial America, 1607–1783* (Chicago, 1931), a few books have proven constantly useful to me. Much of the original inspiration for this dissertation came from the several accounts of violence involving seamen in Carl Bridenbaugh, *Cities in Revolt: Urban Life in America, 1743–1776* (New York, 1935); I wondered why the seamen were so violent, and I was unwilling to attribute it to manipulation from above or to irrationality. Having played some role in the original conception, *Cities in Revolt* continued during my research to furnish a great deal of information about the subject of its sub-title. Similar inspiration came from Edmund S. Morgan and Helen M. Morgan, *The Stamp Act Crisis: Prologue to Revolution* (Chapel Hill, 1953); several references to seamen suggested to me that they had played an important role in the Crisis, a role worthy of further exploration. During that exploration I came to disagree with the Morgans on some points: most centrally, I feel that during the Crisis the significant area for leadership was in action rather than in continued assertion of right. But I continue to see the central themes of the Stamp Act Crisis through the Morgans' eyes. Richard B. Morris, *Government and Labor in Early America* (New York, 1947), Chapter V ("Maritime Labor Relations") explained many complex matters and furnished invaluable leads in connection with wages, impressment, and other subjects. J. R. Hutchinson, *The Press-Gang, Afloat and Ashore* (New York, 1914) is an exciting and delightfully written book which, although rooted in English sources, told more about all aspects of the seaman's life than any other single work; it was especially helpful, of course, in connection with impressment. Although details about merchant seamen were peripheral to his central concern, Samuel Eliot Morison's usual thoroughness made two of his books useful as reference works: *The Maritime History of Massachusetts, 1783–1860* (Boston, 1921) and *John Paul Jones: A Sailor's Biography* (Boston, 1959). I disagree with Morison about the source of merchant mariners (see above, Chapter I) but am otherwise deeply indebted to these books for information about the sea, ships, and seamen and for furnishing, in *John Paul Jones*, a model of writing about these subjects.

The sources for a study of seamen in New York are, inevitably, all the sources for a study of New York in the pre-Revolutionary period, and most of the sources listed below contributed some information about seamen. Jack Tar generally did not leave written accounts of his doings, and they must be ferreted out of the accounts of others. The closest one comes to first-person reports is in court records; here otherwise anonymous men are forced to present their names and situations to the historian. Nowhere, indeed, do the anonymous—prostitutes, seamen, slaves—live so fully as in court records; here they speak, generally in the ritualistic forms of the law, but nonetheless informatively. Here we learn not only of crimes but of impressment, of the seamen's family lives, their wages, their friends, their enemies. And sometimes, if only rarely, the seamen speak to us directly in the first person.

The records of most value to this study were those of the Mayor's Court of New York City and the Supreme Court of Judicature of the Province of New York. These records exist, in great disorder, in the custody of the County Clerk in the Hall of Records in lower Manhattan. They consist of minute books, pleadings, and miscellaneous file papers. A brief introduction to this maze may be found in Evarts B. Greene and Richard B. Morris, *A Guide to the Principal Sources for Early American History (1600–1800) in the City of New York* (2d ed. rev.; New York, 1953), pp. 208–210; information about the courts is in Richard B. Morris, ed., *Select Cases of the Mayor's Court of New York City, 1674–1784* (Washington, 1935), Paul M. Hamlin and Charles E. Baker, eds., *Supreme Court of Judicature of the Province of New York, 1691–1704* (New-York Historical Society, *Collections*, 1945 [New York, 1952]), and Julius Goebel, Jr. and T. Raymond Naughton, *Law Enforcement in Colonial New York: A Study in Criminal Procedure (1664–1776)* (New York, 1944).

The items used in the Hall of Records were parchments pertaining to cases in various courts and arranged in no particular order; file papers from different courts, somewhat more usefully arranged under the names of litigants; Minute Books of the Mayor's Court dated 1757–1765, 1764–1765, 1765–1768; a Chancery Minute Book dated 1770–1776; the following Minute Books of the Supreme Court of Judicature: October 19, 1762–April 28, 1764, July 31, 1764–August 2, 1766, July 31, 1764–October 28, 1767, October 21, 1766–January 21, 1769, April 18, 1769–May 2, 1772, April 21, 1772–January 17, 1776; also, in the Criminal Courts Building, Minute Book of the General Quarter Sessions of the Peace, November 4, 1760–February 6, 1772.

Although little of the work done by genealogists was useful to this study, many of their techniques and much of their approach to the sources was helpful. A card file was kept in which were entered the names and any known facts about every New York seaman found. As it now stands, the file contains slightly more than two thousand separate entries. As the file grew, names began to repeat themselves: a man who served in the militia during the French and Indian War would appear in court some years thereafter or perhaps make out a will. Thus the skeletons of biographies of otherwise anonymous people began to emerge. Records of seamen were taken wherever found, but some sources were searched purely for seamen. Many good leads were found in Rosalie Fellows Bailey, *Guide to Genealogical and Biographical Sources for New York City (Manhattan), 1783–1898* (New York, 1954), John H. Moriarty, "Directory Information Material (Printed) for New York City Residents, 1626–1786," *Bulletin of the New York Public Library*, XLVI (October, 1942), 807–864, and *New York Genealogical and Biographical Record* (90 vols.; New York, 1870–1959).

Most useful among these sources were *Muster Rolls of New York Provincial Troops, 1755–1764* (New-York Historical Society, *Collections*, 1891 [New York, 1892]). These lists, aside from furnishing the names of a great number of seamen, were especially useful in connection with the ages of seamen and their countries of birth. Much use was made of *Abstracts of Wills on File in the Surrogate's Office, City of New York* (New-York Historical Society, Collections, 1892–1901 [New York, 1893–1902]); these give diverse information about seamen and, by listing beneficiaries, tell a great deal about the seaman's relations with his family and with the rest of society. *The Burghers of New Amsterdam and the Freemen of New York, 1675–1866* (New-York Historical Society, *Collections*, 1885 [New York, 1886] provided many names, but its usefulness was limited as many of the "mariners" listed here were not common seamen. Viola Root Cameron, ed., "Emigrants from Scotland to America, 1774–1775, Copied from a Loose Bundle of Treasury Papers in the Public Record Office, London, England" (typewritten; New York Public Library, 1930) is rich reading, for each person listed gives a brief summary of his reasons for emigration; unfortunately the list includes few seamen and few who came to New York. Although *Indentures of Apprentices: October 21, 1718, to August 7, 1727* (New-York Historical Society, *Collections*, 1909 [New York, 1910]) deals with an earlier period and thus did not produce names useful to this study, it was the best source on master-apprentice relations.

There were few seamen but much information about those few in American Loyalists: Transcripts of the Manuscript Books and Papers of the Commission of Enquiry into the Losses and Services of the American Loyalists held under Acts of Parliament of 23, 25, 26, 28 and 29 George III. preserved amongst the Audit Office Records in the Public

Record Office of England 1783–1790 (New York Public Library), I-VIII, XLI-XLVIII. The latter volumes deal with New York; the former are the especially useful claims for temporary support, and their value as a source for the study of the lower class was suggested by Catherine S. Crary's excellent "The Humble Immigrant and the American Dream: Some Case Histories, 1746–1776," *Mississippi Valley Historical Review*, XLVI (June, 1959), 46–66. Another and less useful source on Loyalism among seamen was Lorenzo Sabine, *Biographical Sketches of Loyalists of the American Revolution with an Historical Essay* (Boston, 1864). Alexander Clarence Flick, *Loyalism in New York during the American Revolution* (New York, 1901), p. 107 makes a statement about the prevalence of Loyalism among seamen with which I disagree.

Information of a diversity too great to enumerate here came from newspapers. The following newspapers were examined for the period from 1756 until the end of 1775:

The New-York Gazette (William Weyman), 1759–1767.

The New-York Gazette; or Weekly Post-Boy (James and Samuel Parker, William Weyman, John Holt, Samuel Inslee, Anthony Car), 1747–1773.

The New-York Journal; or, the General Advertiser (John Holt), 1766–1776.

The New-York Mercury (Hugh Gaine), 1752–783.

The files of *The Mariner's Mirror* (47 vols.; London, 1911–61) are rich with information, both primary and secondary; the magazine is similar to *The American Neptune* but more oriented towards matters of solidly historical interest. Many secondary works were of more narrow usefulness than the works of Bridenbaugh, the Morgans, Morris, Hutchinson, and Morison mentioned above but nonetheless quite useful in special fields. Benjamin Quarles, *The Negro in the American Revolution* (Chapel Hill, 1961) deals in detail with the Negroes' service during the war but contains much information on the Negro as merchant seaman. The brief section on "Invasion of Seamen's Rights" in Oliver M. Dickerson, *The Navigation Acts and the American Revolution* (Philadelphia, 1951), pp. 218–219 suggested another seamen's grievance against England. Carl Ubbelohde, *The Vice Admiralty Courts and the American Revolution* (Chapel Hill, 1960) had some value as a guide to the sources but was less useful than Morris' *Government and Labor* on seamen and the law. Allyn B. Forbes, "Greenwich Hospital Money," *New England Quarterly*, III (July, 1930),

519–526 was useful on that topic. Kenneth Scott, *Counterfeiting in Colonial New York* (New York, 1953) is largely an uncritical compendium of sources but contains some useful material on seaman counterfeiters. Some insight into the role which the sea played in the life of a New England youth may be found in Max Farrand, ed., *Benjamin Franklin's Memoirs: Parallel Text Edition: Comprising the Texts of Franklin's Original Manuscript, the French Translation by Louis Guillaume le Veillard, the French Translation Published by Buisson, and the version edited by William Temple Franklin his Grandson* (Berkeley and Los Angeles, 1949). Information on privateering may be found in Howard M. Chapin, *Privateer Ships and Sailors: The First Century of American Colonial Privateering, 1625–1725* (Toulon, France, 1926) and in Stuyvesant Fish, "Log of Cruises of New York Privateer Duke of Cumberland, Capt. James Lilley, 1758–1760," New-York Historical Society, *Quarterly Bulletin*, XXXIX (July, 1945), 161–171 and the same author's *The New York Privateers, 1756–1763: King George's Private Ships of War which Cruised against the King's Enemies* (New York, 1945); the latter is chatty and uncritical but contains useful listings of captains and vessels.

Hutchinson's *Press-Gang*, cited above, was most useful on that subject. Two mariner's biographies contained some information on impressment: George Athan Billias, *General John Glover and his Marblehead Mariners* (New York, 1960) and Howard Thomas, *Marinus Willett* (Prospect, New York, 1954). Useful accounts of impressment and of legal action connected with impressment appear in Lawrence S. Mayo, ed., *The History of the Colony and Province of Massachusetts-Bay by Thomas Hutchinson* (Cambridge, 1936), II, 167n., [George Gregerson Wolkins], "The Seizure of John Hancock's Sloop 'Liberty'," Massachusetts Historical Society, *Proceedings*, LV (October 1921 - June 1922), 239–284, "Testimony Taken in Case of Michael Corbet," *ibid.*, XLIV (October 1910–June 1911), 429–452, Margaret Wheeler Willard, ed., *Letters on the American Revolution, 1774–1776* (Boston, 1925), and Bernhard Knollenberg, *Origin of the American Revolution: 1759–1766* (2d ed. rev.; New York, 1961), Dora Mae Clark, "The Impressment of Seamen in the American Colonies" in *Essays in Colonial History Presented to Charles McLean Andrews by his Students* (New Haven, 1931), pp. 198–224 is an excellent account of the legal questions surrounding impressment, although it loses something by the detachment with which it approaches so patently tyrannical an institution (see above, Chapter II, note 13). Benjamin Franklin takes a hard-headed and, at the same time, more feeling view of impressment in his Remarks on Judge Foster's Argument in Favor of Impressing Seamen, Jared Sparks, ed., *The Works of Benjamin*

Franklin (10 vols.; Boston, 1837–44), II, 331–339. Elizabeth Cometti, "Impressment during the American Revolution" in Vera Largent, ed., *The Walter Clinton Jackson Essays in the Social Sciences* (Chapel Hill, 1942), pp. 97–109 deals more with the impressment of equipment than of men but furnishes some basis for comparison with the English practice before the Revolution. R. Pares, "The Manning of the Navy in the West Indies, 1702–63" in Royal Historical Society, *Transactions*, fourth series, XX (1937), 31–60 was more useful to this study than its title suggests, for its implications are by no means limited to the West Indies. James Fulton Zimmerman, *Impressment of American Seamen* (New York, 1925) all but denies that impressment existed before the Revolution and is wrong about what little it does say about this period (see above, Chapter II, note 176).

Faced with sparse sources, the historian will be forced to discover, as I have, that non-historians have much to contribute. The seaman's special position vis-a-vis the rest of society has changed little with time, and some modern studies explore this situation with fruitful results for those interested in the earlier period: Elmo Paul Hohman, *Seamen Ashore: A Study of the United Seamen's Service and of Merchant Seamen in Port* (New Haven, 1952) and the same author's "Seamen" in *Encyclopedia of the Social Sciences* (New York, 1934), XIII, 611–616 contain a thorough exploration of the seaman's special psychology. Robert Straus, *Medical Care for Seamen: The Origin of Public Medical Service in the United States* (New Haven, 1950) supplements Hohman's writings. James C. Healey, *Foc's'le and Glory-Hole: A Study of the Merchant Seaman and his Occupation* (New York, 1936) is paternalistic and romantic in its view of the seaman; the same spirit dominates *American Seamen: A Review* (5 vols.; New York, 1941–45). Charles Napier Robinson and John Leyland, *The British Tar in Fact and Fiction: The Poetry, Pathos, and Humour of the Sailor's Life* (London, 1909) and Harold Francis Watson, *The Sailor in English Fiction and Drama, 1550–1800* (New York, 1931) tell us something of how the seaman has been viewed by the society around him. I have made use of the insight into the seaman's psychology displayed in Ishmael's opening words in Herman Melville, *Moby Dick or the Whale* (New York, 1952). For a very readable account of the physical environment in which the seaman works see Rachel L. Carson, *The Sea Around Us* (New York, 1954).

The events which I have described take place within the context of the political life of New York. The best single source on that life functioned here as bibliography and checklist: I.N.P. Stokes, *The Iconography of Manhattan Island, 1498–1909* (6 vols.; New York, 1895–1928), IV contains a detailed day-by-day compilation of primary accounts, thorough and well indexed, furnishing many leads and filling many gaps in connection with seamen, New York politics, and non-political areas of the city's life. A listing of the government documents found most useful follows. With the exception of the *Minutes of the Common Council* and the *Colonial Laws* none furnished very much about seamen, but most were essential for an understanding of the politics of the time.

Calendar of Council Minutes, 1668–1783 (New York State Library, *Bulletin* 58 [March, 1902]).

The Colonial Laws of New York from the Year 1664 to the Revolution including the Charters to the Duke of York, The Commissions and Instructions to Colonial Governors, the Duke's Laws, The Laws of the Dongan and Leisler Assemblies, The Charters of Albany and New York and the Acts of the Colonial Legislatures from 1691 to 1775 (5 vols.; Albany, 1894).

Journal of the Legislative Council of the Colony of New-York. Began 8th Day of December, 1743; and Ended the 3d of April, 1775 (Albany, 1861).

Journal of the Votes and Proceedings of the General Assembly of the Colony of New-York. Began the 8th Day of November 1743; and Ended the 23d of December, 1765 (2 vols.; New York, 1764–66).

Journal of the Votes and Proceedings of the General Assembly of the Colony of New York, from 1766 to 1776, inclusive (Albany, 1820).

Minutes of the Common Council of the City of New York, 1675–1776 (8 vols., New York, 1905).

Edmund B. O'Callaghan, ed., *Calendar of New York Colonial Commissions, 1680–1770* (New York, 1944).

On the British side, scattered items were found in the following:

The Annual Register (London, 1758–)

Calendar of State Papers, Colonial Series, America and West Indies (42 vols.; London, 1860–1953).

Journal of the Commissioners for Trade and Plantations (14 vols.; London, 1920–38).

James Munro, ed., *Acts of the Privy Council of England, Colonial Series* (6 vols., Hereford, 1908–12).

Danby Pickering, ed., *The Statutes at Large from 1225 to 1867* (London, 1762–1807).

James Redington, ed., *Calendar of Home Office Papers of the Reign of George III* (2 vols.; London, 1878–79).

The meat on the skeleton of official records is found in the correspondence and papers of men involved in government. Much of the correspondence of the men at the center of New York's government appears in Edmund Bailey O'Callaghan, ed., *Documents Relative to the Colonial History of the State of New York* (15 vols.; Albany, 1865–87) and in the same editor's *Documentary History of the State of New York* (4 vols., Albany, 1849–51). The unfortunate man most centrally involved in the government of New York during the 'sixties and 'seventies was Cadwallader Colden, the Lieutenant-Governor who acted as Governor during the long absences of the appointed governors; his correspondence is in *The Colden Letter Books, 1760–1775* (New-York Historical Society, Collections, 1876–77 [New York, 1877–78]) and in *The Letters and Papers of Cadwallader Colden, 1711–1775 (ibid., Collections, 1917–23, 1934–35* [New York, 1918–37]). The observations of a man long a member of the Governor's Council are in William H. W. Sabine, ed., *Historical Memoirs from 16 March 1763 to 9 July 1776 of William Smith* (New York, 1956). Reports to authorities at home and their replies are in Clarence Edwin Carter, ed., *The Correspondence of General Thomas Gage with the Secretaries of State, 1763–1775* (2 vols.; New Haven, 1931) and in Gertrude Selwyn Kimball, ed., *Correspondence of William Pitt* (2 vols.; New York, 1906). A New York journalist, viewing government from the outside, adds to our understanding of pre-Revolutionary politics in Paul Leicester Ford, ed., *The Journals of Hugh Gaine, Printer* (2 vols.; New York, 1902).

Some sources were more narrowly useful than those listed above, including those which had special reference to the Stamp Act Crisis. Scattered manuscript sources were found in Volume IV of the Chalmers Manuscripts at the New York Public Library and in the Emmet Collection at the same institution (see John S. Kennedy, *Calendar of the Emmet Collection of Manuscripts Relating to American History* [New York, 1959]). The John Lamb Papers at the New-York Historical Society are the best single source on the Sons of Liberty. The Lieutenant-Governor justifies his conduct in [Cadwallader Colden], *The Conduct of Cadwallader Colden, Late Lieutenant-Governor of New York Relating to the Judges Commissions, Appeals to the King, and the Stamp-Duty* (New York, 1767). Detailed and alien observations of the New Yorkers' activities by a British Army officer are in *The Montresor*

Journals (New-York Historical Society, *Collections*, 1881 [New York, 1882]). *Letter Book of John Watts, Merchant and Councillor of New York: January 1, 1762-December 22, 1765* (*ibid.*, *Collections*, 1928 [New York, 1928]) is an indispensable source on the immediate post-war period and on the Stamp Act troubles. Scattered useful items were found in *The Aspinwall Papers* (Massachusetts Historical Society, *Collections*, fourth series, X [Boston, 1871]); *New York City during the American Revolution, Being a Collection of Original Papers (Now First Published) from the Manuscripts in the Possession of the Mercantile Library Association of New York City* (New York, 1861); and J. Sullivan, A. C. Flick, and M. W. Hamilton, eds., *The Papers of Sir William Johnson* (12 vols.; New York, 1921–57).

Two groups of broadsides are essential sources for the political history of the period. The New-York Historical Society's extensive collection is supplemented by "New York Broadsides, 1762–1779," *Bulletin of the New York Public Library*, III (1899), 23–33.

Wherever possible an attempt has been made to put events in their precise physical setting. Several travellers' accounts were useful here: Andrew Burnaby, *Travels through the Middle Settlements in North America. In the Years 1759 and 1760. With Observations upon the State of the Colonies* (Ithaca, New York, 1960); "Journal of a French Traveller in the Colonies, 1765," *American Historical Review*, XXVII (October, 1921), 70–89; Newton D. Mereness, ed., *Travels in the American Colonies, 1690–1783* (New York, 1916). Extremely useful in understanding events in New York harbor was *A Chart of New York Harbour with the Soundings Views of Land Marks and Nautical Directions, for the Use of Pilotage. Composed from Surveys and Observations of Lieutenants John Knight, John Hunter of the Navy & Others [with] Nautical Directions to Sail into the Harbour of New York &c.* ([London], 1779). A useful nineteenth-century account is William J. Davis, "The Old Bridewell," in Henry B. Dawson, *Reminiscences of the Park and its Vicinity* (New York, 1855), pp. 58–64.

Information about New York's trade drawn from other sources was supplemented by the microfilms of the Public Record Office's New York Port Records at the Sleepy Hollow Restorations, Tarrytown, New York; William S. Sachs, "The Business Outlook in the Northern Colonies, 1750–75" (unpublished Ph.D. dissertation, Dept. of History, Columbia Unversity, 1957); David Macpherson, *Annals of Commerce, Manufactures, Fisheries and Navigation, with brief Notices of the Arts and Sciences Connected with them* (London, 1805). Information about New York's population is in Evarts B. Greene and Virginia D. Harrington, *American Population before the Federal Census of 1790* (New York, 1932). The details of public welfare measures and of the mechanics of city government are in David M. Schneider, *The History of Public Welfare in New York State* (2 vols., Chicago, 1938–41) and in George William Edwards, *New York as an Eighteenth Century Municipality, 1731–1776* (New York, 1917); the latter is a poorly written but extremely useful catalogue of facts.

Many histories of the United States and of New York were searched and found to be without value. Among those found useful was Henry B. Dawson's brief study of *The Sons of Liberty in New York* (New York, 1859). Although marred by some New York chauvinism, this work of the first of the great New York historians has stood up extraordinarily well over the century since its publication. Rooted in thorough research in then-unpublished sources, *The Sons of Liberty* is actually a brief political history of pre-Revolutionary New York. In seeing that the Sons of Liberty were opposed both by the English government and by New York's conservatives, Dawson anticipated by fifty years Carl Lotus Becker's thesis that the Revolution was not only a war for home rule but also a struggle over who should rule at home: *The History of Political Parties in the Province of New York, 1760–1776* (2d ed.; Madison, Wisconsin, 1960). The continuing historiographical debate about Becker's book obscures the fact that it is a fine history of New York politics; as such, it furnished indispensable background for this study. The Dawson-Becker thesis is continued in Herbert M. Morais, "The Sons of Liberty in New York," in Richard B. Morris, ed., *The Era of the American Revolution: Studies Inscribed to Evarts Boutell Greene* (New York, 1939) and confirmed, more recently, in Staughton Lynd, "Who Should Rule at Home? Dutchess County, New York, in the American Revolution," *William and Mary Quarterly*, third series, XVIII (July, 1961), 330–359. Despite the challenge of such works as Robert E. Brown, *Middle-Class Democracy and the Revolution in Massachusetts, 1691–1780* (Ithaca, New York, 1955) this writer remains convinced that the Revolution included a struggle over who should rule at home—*in New York*, at least. There seems no reason why the Revolution should not have been one thing in Massachusetts and another in New York. Only further research will tell which of these two polar cases is more nearly typical. As for New York, I align myself with the Becker thesis, thinking only that it is more fruitful to see the essential conflict as one between radicals and liberals rather than between radicals and conservatives.

Among the general histories, a few had value in connection with the Stamp Act Crisis: Charles Botta, *History of the War of Independence of the United States of America*, translated by George Alexander Otis (New Haven, 1840); William Gordon, *History of the Rise, Progress, and Establishment of the Independence of the United*

States of America (4 vols.; London, 1788) (for authenticity, see above, Chapter IV, note 70); James Grahame, *The History of the United States of North America from the Plantation of the British Colonies till their Revolt and Declaration of Independence* (4 vols.; London, 1836); and the Loyalist Thomas Jones, *History of New York during the Revolutionary War* (2 vols.; New York, 1879). Diverse items were found in the New-York Historical Society's *Quarterly Bulletin* (42 vols.; New York, 1917–58) and in *New York History* (40 vols.; New York, 1920–59).

A few biographies of New Yorkers were valuable. Dorothy Rita Dillon, *The New York Triumvirate: A Study of the Legal and Political Careers of William Livingston, John Morin Scott, William Smith, Jr.* (New York, 1949) is adequate in what it sets out to do and is the only recently published political history of New York. Dillon's work on Livingston is superseded by Milton Martin Klein, "The American Whig: William Livingston of New York" (unpublished Ph.D. dissertation, Dept. of History, Columbia University, 1954) and the same author's "The Rise of the New York Bar: The Legal Career of William Livingston," *William and Mary Quarterly*, third series, XV (July, 1958), 334–358. Philip L. White, *The Beekmans of New York in Politics and Commerce, 1647–1877* (New York, 1956) is an excellent introduction to the mechanics of New York's trade but contains next to nothing about seamen. Isaac Q. Leake, *Memoir of the Life and Times of General John Lamb* (Albany, 1850) is useful primarily because, in the style of its day, it consists largely of Lamb's letters joined together by commentary. To complete the biographies, R. W. Postgate, *That Devil Wilkes* (New York, 1929) should be mentioned; as any good biography of John Wilkes must inevitably be, this book is also a brief history of eighteenth-century English radicalism.

Notes

1. For a review which criticizes this neglect, see *American Seamen*, II (Winter-Spring, 1942), 1.

2. *American Neptune*, X (October, 1950), 239.

3. See prospectus in *ibid.*, XII (January, 1952), 5–6.

Selected Other Work by the Author

Early America

Postscript to reprinting of "Jack Tar in the Streets: Merchant Seamen in the Politics of Revolutionary America," Michael McGiffert, ed., *In Search of Early America: The William and Mary Quarterly, 1943–1993* (Williamsburg, 1993).

"A Short Life of Andrew Sherburne, a Pensioner of the Navy of the Revolution," in Stella Cieslak et al., eds. *The Colonel's Hat: A History of the Township of Augusta* (Mohawk Valley, N.Y.: Mohawk Valley Printing Co., [1977]), 129–131.

Review of Alfred F. Young, ed., *The American Revolution: Explorations in the History of American Radicalism,* in *American Historical Review,* LXXXII (June 1977), 737–739.

"Bailyn Besieged in his Bunker," *Radical History Review,* IV, no 1 (Winter 1977), 72–83.

"The White Oaks, Jack Tar, and the Concept of the 'Inarticulate'" [with John K. Alexander], *William and Mary Quarterly,* 3rd Ser., XXIX (January 1972), 109–134.

"The American Revolution Bicentennial and the Papers of Great White Men: A Preliminary Critique of Current Documentary Publication Programs and Some Alternative Proposals," *AHA Newsletter,* IX (November 1971), 7–21.

"Radical Plot in Boston (1770): A Study in the Use of Evidence," *Harvard Law Review,* LXXXIV (December 1970), 485–504.

"Listening to the 'Inarticulate': William Widger's Dream and the Loyalties of American Revolutionary Seamen in British Prisons," *Journal of Social History,* III (Fall 1969), 1–29.

"Response to Aileen Kraditor," *American Historical Review*, LXXIV (June 1969), 1766–1768.

"Jack Tar in the Streets: Merchant Seamen in the Politics of Revolutionary America," *William and Mary Quarterly*, 3rd Ser., XXV (July 1968), 371–407; also published as "The Radicalism of the Inarticulate: Merchant Seamen in the Politics of Revolutionary America," in Alfred F. Young, ed., *Dissent: Explorations in the History of American Radicalism* (Dekalb: Northern Illinois University Press, 1968), 37–82. Widely reprinted including: Michael McGiffert, ed., *In Search of Early America* (Williamsburg, 1993) [a volume containing the Institute of Early American History and Culture's selection of the eleven "most significant" articles in early American history published in the *William and Mary Quarterly*, 1943–1993] and Bobbs-Merrill Reprint Series in American History (1972).

"What Made Our Revolution?" *The New Republic*, May 25, 1968.

"The American Revolution Seen from the Bottom Up," in Barton J. Bernstein, ed., *Towards a New A Past: Dissenting Essays in American History* (New York: Pantheon Books, 1968; Vintage paperback, 1969; London: Chatto & Windus, 1970), 3–45.

Review of Leonard W. Labaree et al., eds., *The Papers of Benjamin Franklin*, X, in *American Historical Review*, LXXIII (December, 1967).

Review of Claude-Anne Lopez, *Mon Cher Papa: Franklin and the Ladies of Paris*, in *William and Mary Quarterly*, 3rd Ser., XXIV (July, 1967).

"Jack Tar: The Common Seaman" in "The Making of The American Revolution," Edmund S. Morgan, ed. (Part VI of *From Subject to Citizen*, a junior high school course under the general editorship of elting E. Morison, Jerome S. Bruner, Morton G. White; Cambridge, Mass.; Educational Services, Inc., 1966; Education Development Center, 1970). Reprinted in *From Subject to Citizen* (Chicago: Denoyer-Geppert, 1973).

"New York's Petitions and Resolves of December 1765: Liberals vs. Radicals," *New-York Historical Society Quarterly*, XLIX (October 1965), 313–326.

Editor and Reader, *Benjamin Franklin: Autobiography* (New York: Folkways Records, 1961).

Editor, *Benjamin Franklin: Autobiography and Other Writings* (New York: New American Library, 1961) fifteen printings.

Past and Present, Historiography, and the Historical Profession

"American History Seen Through a (No Longer) Red Lens: Present-Mindedness, *Konyunkturschina,* and the Divorce of Truth from Power," *Novaya i Noveishaya Istoria [New and Contemporary History]* (Moscow, January–February, 1992).

"Radicals, Marxists and Gentlemen : A Memoir of Twenty years Ago," *Radical Historians Newsletter,* no. 59, November, 1989.

"Statement on Proposed Constitutional Changes" [with Eric Foner and Kathryn Kish Sklar], *Organization of American Historians Newsletter,* V, no. 2 (January, 1978).

"Bicentennial Schlock," *The New Republic,* November 6, 1976.

"A Statement in Support of the [Yale-Aptheker] Resolution," *Organization of American Historians Newsletter,* IV, no. 1 (July, 1976).

"The Bicentennial of the American Revolution," *Radical History Review,* III, no. 3 (Spring, 1976).

"If Howard Cosell Can Teach at Yale, Why Can't Herbert Aptheker?" *Newsletter of the Radical Historians Caucus,* no. 22 (May, 1976), 1–9.

On Active Service in War and Peace: Politics and Ideology in the American Historical Profession (Toronto: New Hogtown Press, 1975).

"The Papers of a Few Great Black Men and the Few Great White Women," *Maryland Historian,* VI (Spring, 1975), 60–66.

"History, Complete with Historian," *New York Times Book Review,* November 19, 1972.

"'What's Your Evidence?': Radical Scholarship as Scientific Method and Anti-Authoritarianism, not 'Relevance,'" *New University Conference Papers,* no. 2 (1970).

"A College Course on Women's Liberation" *American Institute for Marxist Studies Newsletter,* VI, nos. 2–3 (March–April, May–June, 1969). Revised and expanded from "A College Course on Women's Liberation" *New University Conference Newsletter,* II, no. 1 (January, 1969).

"No Work for [Staughton] Lynd," *New University Conference Newsletter,* May 24, 1968.

"Who Will Write a Left History of Art While We are all Putting our Balls on the Line?" (Boston: New England Free Press, 1968). Reprinted in *Journal of American History,* LXXVI (September, 1989).

"New Left Elitism," *Radical America,* I (September–October, 1967), 43–53.

"Some remarks on the Lemisch Case," *University of Chicago Maroon,* May 19, 1967.

"Towards a Democratic History," Radical Education Project, *Occasional Paper,* February, 1967.

"Who Won the Civil War, Anyway?" *The Nation,* April 8, 1961.

Contemporary Debates about Culture and Politics

"Angry White Men on the Left," *New Politics,* VI, 2 (Winter, 1997) [revised version of:] "Angry White Men on the Left; and No Exit: The Death of Utopia at the 1996 Socialist Scholars Conference," *Radical Historians Newsletter,* no. 74, June, 1996.

"The First Amendment is Under Attack in Cyberspace," *The Chronicle of Higher Education,* January 20, 1995.

Jesse Lemisch and Naomi Weisstein, "Cornucopia Isn't Consumerism: How We Learned to Love our White Rabbit Hats," *Against the Current,* January–February, 1992.

"Social Conservatism on the Left: The Abandonment of Radicalism and the Collapse of the Jewish Left Into Faith and Family," *Tikkun,* IV, 3 (May–June, 1989).

"The Politics of Left Culture," *The Nation,* December 20 1986.

"Pop Front Culture: I Dreamed I Saw MTV Last Night," *The Nation,* October 18, 1986.

Naomi Weisstein, Virginia Blaisdell, Jesse Lemisch, *The Godfathers: Freudians, Marxists, and the Scientific and Political Protection Societies* (New Haven: Belladonna Publishing, 1976).

Naomi Weisstein and Jesse Lemisch, "Boogeyman's Background," *Harper's,* January, 1975.

Jesse Lemisch, "'If You Gotta Ask, Man, You'll Never Know'," *Independent Socialist,* September, 1969.

Health Care Issues

Testimony on Chronic Fatigue Syndrome before Antiviral Drugs Advisory Committee of US Food and Drug Administration, Rockville, Maryland, February 18, 1993.

"Do They Want My Wife to Die?" Op-Ed, *New York Times,* April 15, 1992.

Exhibitions

"Bicentennial Schlock: the Iconography of America's Birthday," SUNY at Buffalo, October, 1976. 1199 Gallery, New York City, August–September, 1977 (2nd edition, revised). Collection on deposit, Yale University Library.

Index